An anonymous text from the Tradition says that in life, each person can take one of two attitudes; to build or to plant. The builders may take years over their tasks, but one day, they finish what they are doing. Then they find they're hemmed in by their own walls.

Then there are those who plant. They endure storms and all the many vicissitudes of the seasons, and they rarely rest. But, unlike a building, a garden never stops growing and while it requires the gardener's constant attention, it also allows life for the gardener to be a great adventure.

Paulo Coelho (2008: 4)

If you want to be adventurous then be yourself and go for the things you really want to do – just take it step by step.

Sasha, aged 8

The Adventurous School

The Adventurous School

Vision, community and curriculum for primary education in the twenty-first century

Jane Reed, Kathy Maskell, David Allinson, Rosemary Bailey, Fernanda Bates, Siân Davies and Catherine Gallimore

Institute of Education, University of London

First published in 2012 by the Institute of Education,
University of London, 20 Bedford Way, London WC1H 0AL

www.ioe.ac.uk/publications

© Jane Reed, Kathy Maskell/Limeside Primary School, David
Allinson, Rosemary Bailey, Fernanda Bates, Siân Davies and
Catherine Gallimore 2012

British Library Cataloguing in Publication Data:
A catalogue record for this publication is available from the
British Library

ISBN 978 0 85473 916 5

The opinions expressed in this publication are those of the
authors and do not necessarily reflect the views of the Institute
of Education, University of London.

Typeset by Quadrant Infotech (India) Pvt Ltd
Printed by CPI Group (UK) Ltd, Croydon, CR0 4YY

Contents

Tables and figures

Tables

Figures

Dedication and Acknowledgements

The Adventurous School is dedicated to the pupils of Malorees, Limeside and St Vigor and St John schools. It is also for all the known and unknown pioneers of English Primary Education and to the memory of three in particular, James Heald, Chris Thew and Patrick Whitaker each of who sadly passed away while we were working on the book. Their work and inspiration, however, has significantly influenced the thinking in these pages.

Deep gratitude is also owed to the staff, governors and parents of the three schools whose stories are written in these pages. While the authors in each school are leaders in their own right, they are indebted to colleagues at every level who have demonstrated outstanding leadership themselves. This book is a testament to all of their work – they know from the inside out what it takes to become an Adventurous School, and if it were not for their inspiration, inventiveness, commitment and hard work this book could not have been written.

Grateful thanks are also due to Jim Collins and his publishing team at the Institute of Education for all their interest in the writing of this book and for their support and guidance during its publication process. The Authors would also like to thank the many colleagues, academics, practitioners and local authority advisers who have been our teachers and inspiration on this journey.

Foreword: Enjoying the learning adventure

A revolutionary transition is ahead of us, and our children have a vital role to play in it; so there is much that we need to teach them about their future. Given the nature of the 21st century, our young people need to be shown the long-term views.

James Martin (2006: Preface and p.4)

The Adventurous School is an adventurous read. The reader goes on a journey of exploration, always exciting, sometimes not quite sure where next, sometimes seeking a way out of a forest we have been lost in before, sometimes a frolic downhill, and always with the tools to find the way towards the goal of real education.

Making learning better for children is the prime job of the school and most schools are constantly seeking to develop the professional work they do. They like to enjoy the learning adventure as much as their pupils but their adventure takes place on another level. In this book the adults learn as much from and with the children as they do from each other. Not many books manage to combine the practical work of helping children to learn with the complexity of the world of research and the philosophy of how education might be. This one does!

It is a book full of analogy that makes concepts easy to grasp and assimilate. We meet icebergs, see stars, climb mountains and steps, fly, and …; all as ways to explain some profound principles. The book is laden with those quotes that can be put around school as watchwords for the learning community. The historical development of the system and the research on progress are presented in ways that link directly with the matter under discussion so that they illuminate and provoke thought rather than being potholes to avoid.

What binds it all together is the brilliant reference to the practice of schools that have taken a journey to adventure. There are real-life, easy-to-picture classroom examples where the conversation with teachers and partners, the voice of the community, and the excitement of the child can almost be heard through the text. The schools in different settings tell the story of their adventure and the reader will hear themselves saying, 'We could do that.'

The central message in the book is that our primary schools can successfully take charge of renewing their vision, their relationship with their community and their curriculum. The social and environmental challenges we face globally mean that education has an important and adventurous task to undertake during the coming decades. As the authors say, we need to enable our children to take hold of their lives in real contexts that give them a sense of themselves as community builders who can contribute in ways that ensure we have a planet worth living on.

The diagrams chart a course, the stories make it appetising, the analogies make it accessible, the research gives it depth. What more could we need? Enjoy the read and enjoy the adventure in your own school!

Mick Waters
Professor of Education, University of Wolverhampton

About the authors

Jane Reed has been a teacher, teacher educator, senior local authority inspector and academic. She worked at the Institute of Education, University of London, from 1994, culminating in a period as head of its International Network for School Improvement from 2005–10; she is currently a visiting fellow at the Institute. Jane is now a freelance lecturer, consultant and coach. Interested in creativity and innovation in school improvement for over thirty years, her main expertise is in connecting pedagogy, professional learning, school leadership and change. Having co-led the Sustainable Schools Leadership research programme for the National College for School Leadership (NCSL), she is also committed to ensuring school improvement asks environmental questions as well as social ones.

Kathy Maskell is deputy head at Limeside Primary School in Oldham, where she has worked for the last 10 years, following a secondment as a literacy consultant. She has a particular interest in developing pupil responsibility and agency for effective learning. She has co-led teacher enquiry communities investigating effective learning and curriculum design to reflect the present and future needs of individual schools, their children and their communities. This has led to a growing commitment to the importance of a school's role in promoting community learning.

David Allinson has worked in education for 25 years. He has been a classroom teacher, local authority adviser and a part-time lecturer in higher education. David has recently been appointed as the head teacher of St Vigor and St John Primary School in Somerset, where he had previously been an advanced skills teacher and deputy head. He has been involved with research into children's creativity for some time, particularly focusing on the ways in which children become powerful determiners and co-creators of their learning pathways. David is interested in how the school curriculum enables curiosity, enquiry and adventure in learning, for both children and staff.

Rosemary Bailey, through teaching, lecturing and advising in most sectors of education, has a first-hand understanding of learning at all ages and stages of young people's development. For 12 years Rosemary has been head teacher of a Somerset primary school, becoming a National Leader of Education in 2007. She is also a School Improvement Partner. She is passionate about the importance of multi-agency working, having led the development of an outstanding nursery and two Children's Centres. Her particular interest is in the vision and values of our education system and the consequences for every pupil.

Fernanda Bates moved from Argentina to the UK in 2001, completing a BA (Hons) in Linguistics and Languages at Birkbeck College in 2006. She has been working in different departments and projects at the Institute of Education, University of London, since 2003, including the Research Assessment Exercise of 2008. She recently completed an MA in Education and International Development; her dissertation was entitled 'Universities and community engagement'. She has been involved as the lead researcher throughout the Adventurous School project, which has helped develop her research skills and given her the opportunity to learn about innovative school improvement implementation in UK schools.

Siân Davies has had extensive experience of teaching in London. Her initial induction was in the heart of Soho, where she spent 13 very enriching years. In 1996 she returned to lead Malorees Infant School in Brent, which she had been fortunate enough to attend as a pupil in her formative years. Siân has always been enthused by the role creativity has in developing young children's engagement and ownership of their learning. She has enjoyed co-leading an action research project with the Brent School Improvement Service and collaborating with senior leaders to facilitate change and innovation in their own schools.

Catherine Gallimore has taught in the London boroughs of Camden and Brent for a total of 20 years, mainly as a class teacher in KS1 and now as deputy head of Malorees Infant School. Catherine has always been interested in experimenting with new ways of promoting children's wholehearted engagement with their learning. She has a particular interest in the development of a creative curriculum with opportunities for all children to discover that they can excel. She really enjoys sharing ideas and leading professional learning with colleagues in and beyond the school, and encouraging practitioners to be adventurous in their teaching.

Adventure!

An unusual and exciting experience.
A daring enterprise/undertaking.
A hazardous activity.
A risk-taking activity.

Oxford English Dictionary

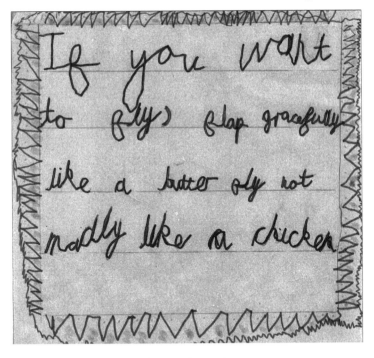

'On an adventure if you don't have a map you can walk around and explore or ask someone else.'

'On an adventure you go to places you don't usually go to and do things you don't usually do.'

'You can't give up on an adventure – you have to keep going or you won't get good at it.'

'To be a good adventurer you need good ideas,
a friend and you need not to be scared.'

'An adventure is a place you want to go to and
explore and find interesting things like crystals and
dinosaur bones and then bring them home.'

'On an adventure you need to know how
to keep safe. You can use a map.'

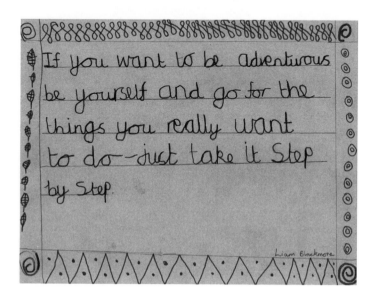

If you want to be adventurous
be yourself and go for the
things you really want
to do – just take it step
by step.

Liam Blackmore

'On an adventure you can get attacked by animals with sharp claws.'

'On an adventure you could do swinging on the trees across a
swamp. You can see loads of wild animals. You can see actually
for yourself which way you're going without following the signs.'

'Poppy is adventurous because she even walks when it's raining.'

'a person who explores different things'

'Adventurous people go somewhere where they've never been.'

'They are brave and they do scary things.'

'The climbing wall was a very big adventure for me because I
am scared of heights. I was able to reach the top because of the
support from the instructors and my classmates. I was able to face
my fears. It has helped me in the classroom to face new things.'

Introduction

If you want to build a ship don't drum up the people to gather wood, divide the work and give orders. Instead teach them to yearn for the vast and endless sea.

(St Exupery, 1950)

The Adventurous School describes a five-year enquiry into learning and change in three English primary schools. The book describes the improvement processes at work in these schools, the professional and pedagogical practice that is resulting together with insights into the leadership of the changes. What has inspired and motivated colleagues from these schools? How have they engaged with and served their children and community and at the same time kept a grip on external demands and accountability? Is there any new school improvement, pedagogical or leadership knowledge to offer to the wider field? If so, what can it contribute to the existing stories of schools that work from an adventurous perspective?

The Adventurous School investigates how the foundations of learning for life are being laid in these three schools and why this might be an important focus at this moment in time. It is an investigation that has children at its heart and is written at a time of both danger and possibility for our planet home. The book makes connections between the importance of learning, becoming a learner and the social and environmental challenges of the early twenty-first century. The intention is to share what has been discovered in this project with others who may be on a similar journey. The account seeks to honour the unnoticed, quiet experiments that professional educators engage in daily to re-inspire the wellsprings of public schooling. It is a celebration of their pioneering spirit. As Senge *et al.* (2010: 364) acknowledge: 'New social movements do not come from those in the centres of power'.

Understanding the nature of adventure

When we asked friends and relatives as well as each other what exactly *adventure* means, it was often about stepping out, venturing or questing.

Sometimes there was a particular destination in mind. There may be a definite route to travel, but what was certain was that on the adventure events would occur, circumstances would arise and obstacles would be in the path that would introduce us to the unknown. Skills and resources would be challenged; the purpose of the journey might change.

The notion of adventure also conjured up excitement and seizing of opportunities to take us out of our comfort zone. An adventure is an invitation not to be afraid of new experiences; to enjoy an encounter with something challenging that will expand our sense of who we are and the view of the world we have had. Adventure can describe awareness of where we are on the one hand and where we would like to be on the other. As Margaret Wheatley in *A Simpler Way* writes: 'We ourselves engage in change only as we discover that we might be more of who we are by becoming something different' (Wheatley and Kellner-Rogers, 1999: 50).

An adventure then is often an experience that compels and challenges us to go beyond what we have known on the path so far. It may well, as Wheatley suggests, give us a different sense of who we are. It often takes place in wild or uninhabited places but could just as well happen in the middle of a busy city. It involves meeting or crossing a threshold that means we have changed, grown or see life differently. An adventure might be a response to a prompt to go on a journey because we need to learn something new or traverse or create a new path.

'They live in places you wouldn't expect to find them,' says Anil. He is contributing to a Year 2 conversation that draws on learning the children have been doing about habitats to predict where they will find the minibeasts. Ben's 'Naturalists Notebook' is full of carefully drawn large-scale pictures of all the creepy crawlies he and his classmates have been finding out about since Easter. Nathan has drawn a ladybird on the cover of his notebook; he wants to find out what they eat.

A wiggly line of children in twos and threes follows their teacher out of the classroom and across the tarmac in the direction of the wild garden. They find it in a secluded corner of the urban school grounds at Malorees Infant School. Quietly everyone goes through the gate into a magical, burgeoning, wild space. There aren't many rules for this lesson. Only, 'identify as many minibeasts as you can,' and 'do so respectfully, without damage or loss of life'.

'It's enormous!' shouts Robert as he carefully fishes out a very long white worm from under a stone. Over the next 15 minutes centipedes, millipedes, woodlice, slugs, snails, ants and ladybirds are all found, noted and photographed as children scramble through brambles, turn over logs and examine leaves to find them. Children are excitedly drawing, predicting and recording what they find. They stand with careful precision on the stones in the pond in order to find water snails for their nets.

'You get to smell the earth and see them!' exclaims Priya. 'I feel just like an explorer!' says Alex. Billy is suddenly down on the ground, moving on the path and improvising a spider. 'Spiders get new legs like we get new teeth,' he explains, 'lose a leg get another, lose a leg get another'.

'It's like being on an adventure,' volunteers Kai, 'but we haven't had to go that far.'

The aim and background of the book

The central enquiry in *The Adventurous School* has been a search for how approaches to adventurous learning could contribute towards a renewed paradigm for state primary education in the twenty-first century. The three schools tell the story of growth and change in each of their settings, a story of a gradual shift in perspective as they have developed an expanding view of what they are aiming to achieve. It is a positive story of how they have built on their accomplishments during a time of central direction and surveillance in order to keep moving forward.

An adventurous school as an idea has been an intriguing one to understand. We have let it evolve as a concept as well as interrogating it with as much precision as possible. It has become a number of related things for the contributors: an emerging reality, a creative process, three organisations in flow and flux, an aspiration and a journey. Above all it is alive; a living organisational form that constantly moves and changes and has its own energy and momentum. Having achieved conventional success and reputation the schools have been able to let go of overconcern for regulation outcomes and consequently have found themselves in a larger field of endeavour and concern. They are well aware that they haven't completed their journey or yet become as adventurous as they might like to be; that destination is always just up ahead. They know too that the adventure is also about enjoyment, and learning from the experience no matter how successful. While being alert to arriving at a particular end point, they are not fixated on it. At first sight the aims of an adventurous school are not very different to the predominant goals of all schools. Pressures for accountability and results, however, can easily distort healthy, purposeful, empowering learning. These schools do not let that happen because everyone's achievement is important and learning and well-being in equal measure are the keys to success.

The background to the book originated in one of the main projects that were set up at the International Network for School Improvement (INSI, formerly ISEIC) at the Institute of Education, University of London (IOE), between 1997 and 2010. The purpose was to give more of a pedagogical, classroom emphasis to school improvement and leadership practice. Strategies were tried and tested over an extended period with the broad intention of enabling young people to take part and lead in the world of the twenty-first century. The work took place in partnership with primary school leaders who were finding ways to strengthen the integrity and vitality of their educational philosophy while also meeting the demands of external accountability. In the models of school improvement we explored, the pupils and their involvement in their learning were in the foreground of our conversations. So was an emphasis on the particular community context of the schools involved. This in turn had implications for the curriculum, its design, content and structure.

Through narrative, action enquiry and qualitative approaches we developed school improvement activity that complemented and added to the public measures of national tests and tables. The pedagogical approaches we developed had an effect on how we understood the role of school leadership and the purposes of schooling. It became a priority to understand how leaders develop their capability to actively lead the shift to authentic, lively, active learning. As Capra (2007: 13) notes: 'This shift encourages educators to serve as facilitators and fellow learners alongside students. It encourages a shift from "transmissive" expert-based teaching and learning to transformative, community-based learning.'

Three primary schools from three different parts of England have extended and developed this approach to school improvement for the book. They are Limeside Primary School in Oldham, Malorees Infant School in Brent, and St Vigor and St John Primary School in Somerset. They are schools that are creative and innovative about how they have interpreted the letter of the law as well as having excellent results and inspections. It is their journey to becoming more adventurous that is the story told here. The schools worked with INSI on different projects: the Oldham Networked Learning Community (2004–06), the Improvement In Action Project (2001–10), and the Somerset Learning about Learning initiative (2002–03). They have presented their work to other practitioners and are all leading practitioners in and beyond their communities.

Five senior members of staff have come together in a research and study group. They have visited each other and shared their philosophy for primary education. They have had extensive dialogues about the nature of their practice, how it got to be the way it is and how to continue to develop it. They have continued to research and develop what they were doing while we have been preparing the book. So the book reflects not just a study of practice but also observations about the process of change as we increasingly constructed the nature of adventurous school improvement. In the process, the contributors have had more space than normal to develop their collective thinking and to become increasingly adventurous. They have also had fun!

Between 2007 and 2011 the project team held three retreats a year in the East End of London. We reflected, talked, shared practice, developed theory and edited the writing up of our project. When they first joined the project, the schools already promoted active, exciting learning and saw themselves, their pupils, their parents and community as learners and leaders of learning. They are schools that know their pupils and their communities are on an adventure in their learning and that they all need each other to be part of the process. They are schools that wanted to understand more about what they were already doing and improve on it. During the retreats we gradually documented the features of adventure that emerged in our enquiry. We also had an enquiry about the nature of the leadership that was creating adventurous schooling.

Each school has taken a different metaphor in their writing to convey their adventure: illuminating, flying and growing. Our discussions were all recorded in detail and each time we met we noted what we were learning. About half way through the process we began to construct what we were about as akin to adventurous and the concept of the adventurous school emerged.

A working assumption in this book, as in *The Intelligent School* (MacGilchrist *et al.*, 2004), is that successful schools are ones that know how to take responsibility for their own destiny. Alongside accountability to national norms they also define quite firmly the nature and scope of their own goals. If they are to become creative, productive, living places for children to learn and thrive, they need to take charge and let the children learn to do the same. While working together, colleagues have identified how they have been creating their own paths into the future rather than following prescribed directives. Stepping outside conventional norms, befriending change and living with the unknown are themselves 'adventurous' ways of creating new directions:

> *The future is not a result of choices among alternative paths offered by the present, but a place that is created – created first in the mind and will, created next in activity. The future is not some place we are going to, but one we are creating. The paths are not to be found, but made and the activity of making them changes both the maker and the destination.*
>
> (Scharr, 2008: 112; cited in Udall and Turner, 2008)

It has become increasingly apparent during this project that the current use of the term 'standards' that has become simply conjoined to attainment outcomes is very limiting and in danger of shutting down innovation. It can narrow a school's view of the nature and purpose not only of learning but also more fundamentally of their school. It can stop the development of lively enquiry and create compliance. In setting their goals the schools also have been identifying their own standards and success criteria.

We discussed at length what primary schools could become if leaders led learning in more adventurous ways; we identified existing examples of adventurous learning. We noted that if these approaches were to take root and represent a different approach for primary education, then fundamental changes in mindsets and ways of seeing what they are about would be needed. Early on we went back to first principles and framed four fundamental questions to enable us to understand what the shift in mindset was about:

- What do we want most for children now and for their future, and why?
- What values, vision, activities, and therefore organisation, will best achieve that?

- What is the role of the school in relation to its community and how is each community present in the school?
- What kind of curriculum design brings life to learning and will best serve children?

Once the theme of adventure emerged, we wanted to investigate the nature and form of adventurous schools, to find out what it might take to change the current paradigm and what the three schools were doing already that could contribute. We built our enquiry by setting out the following assertions that helped to identify the philosophy of the book:

- Twenty-first century primary education requires a focus and commitment to learning and enquiry that complements performance measures and tests and which genuinely includes and values everyone and takes place in the context of the community.
- Children need to have more than just a 'voice' in school; their participation, engagement and contribution are central, and take place in the context of their whole life and their community. This set of contextual relationships, for a child, is a key factor in determining what a school does.
- The use of the term 'high standards' as a catch-all needs to be understood and used as part of a bigger playing field than just the basic literacies, important as those are.
- The curriculum for each school can be designed in a way that recognises the lived experience of the learners, the community context of their lives and the school, and builds upwards from the Early Years' Foundation Stage.
- Learning with and alongside the parents and community is a source of renewal and creativity and strengthens the bonds that need to extend across the boundary of home and school.[1]
- A major priority for the first part of the twenty-first century is for our children to engage in activity that promotes community sustainability and renewal.
- In summary, colleagues identified that they were already on the road of adventure but as a result of working on this enquiry this became more deliberate and explicit. This included:

  - taking charge of the direction and purpose of their school and their change process;
  - working more explicitly from their values and beliefs;
  - involving learners more fully in their learning, clarifying what learning means and enabling it to happen through real and purposeful experiences;
  - working much more proactively with their community;

- o taking charge of designing and developing the curriculum; and
- o seeing school improvement as a process of questing, journeying and open-ended exploration.

These principles and what they look like in action, together with our reflections about them, became the building blocks of our enquiry.

Despite success, the three schools have felt isolated; despite their accomplished status they have the challenge of maintaining success, responding to multiple pressures and managing the dominant assumptions and voices which they do not always feel reflect their own. In this project they have felt supported to share and compare their visions, and they have felt safe to name and explore the thorny issues and challenges that have to be lived each day when you are aiming to cultivate a spirit and climate of adventure.

What have we learnt about the nature of the adventurous school?

This book is a son or daughter of *The Intelligent School* (MacGilchrist *et al.*, 2004) in which we argued that at the start of the twenty-first century we are still preoccupied with preparing students for a world that is no longer the one that exists. Whitaker (1997: 143) noted that: 'Many of the structures and processes that have sustained educational development since the beginning of this [the twentieth] century may no longer be appropriate to the changed and continually changing circumstances of this one.'

Many would argue that at this point in human history we need more than ever to release creativity and ingenuity and that educational institutions could take a more proactive lead. As Senge *et al.* state (2010: 10): 'It is folly to think that the changes needed in the coming years will not involve fundamental shifts in the ways institutions function, individually and collectively.'

The reforms of the past two decades have in many ways reinforced the original blueprint of the industrial school, a blueprint that has an impulse to create passive consumers rather than co-creators (Lodge and Reed, 2003). Many young people are simply turned off school and as we write there are approximately one million young people not in education, employment or training. An 8 year old told one of us recently that if they don't understand the purpose for their learning in the classroom, especially when it is difficult, they don't enjoy doing it.

In *The Intelligent School* the authors argued that there is an urgent need for schools to move from an industrial model of organisation to a more organic and relational model. If the industrial model emphasises conformity, control and standardisation then a school based on an organic model is formed more from interrelationship, co-creation and living experience. It is more contextually alert and responsive than its predecessor, which has tended to set itself apart behind its gates and do business with its communities on its own terms.

A school with a more organic, connected approach is better placed to help young people grow and evolve and have positive experiences of themselves. It engages students in their life experience rather than protecting and cutting them off from it. In adventurous schools the adventure takes place in and with the community, and building new relationships is part of the adventure. This is a shift away from the image of a school as an ivory tower that dispenses instruction and only minimally involves parents to one where the school is not just open to and in service to the needs of the children and their families, but involves them far more actively. Everyone is seeking to build positive life goals with young people along with the choices and actions to make those real:

> If we are to be a nation of lifelong learners, school has to become a place where students take charge of their learning for life – where they become eager constructors of knowledge, and view the entire world around them as a rich and welcome resource.
>
> (Eckert et al., 1996: 8)

An adventurous school is one then that understands the necessity and urgency for this shift in approach and is testing out and realising what this means in practice. The adventurous school has a primary purpose not only of creating real, engaging, learning for life but also of supporting children, no matter how young, to enter the flow and form of their lives in a way which helps them realise they are in the driving seat and have a contribution to make. The adventurous school also has a view of the world that is about change: diversity, interdependence and co-operation rather than a world of linear thinking, competition, homogeneity and stasis.

If *The Intelligent School* explored and outlined the theoretical territory of putting learners and their learning at the heart of schooling and identified the implications for practice, then *The Adventurous School* is doing the reverse. It focuses on the stories of practice and the day-to-day challenge of bringing about new ways and thinking on the ground. Through the various dialogues, narratives and action enquiry, we have brought to the surface a different way of thinking. We then tried to understand the nature of the experience, the significance of what we were uncovering and the nature of the change process that is at work. Most importantly we noted any new ways of being and relating created by the practitioner leaders as they go about their day job. The book tells the story of some of the changes that began to lead to a different approach. We have tried to describe the intentions and processes of adventure as well as to understand the traps and distracters. Learning how to evolve from one paradigm of primary education to another has become part of the adventure. Stories of schools that do more than just raise standards are few and far between. This book is about ordinary, successful schools that are changing their script; they are learning to tell a different story of what they are about and creating new models for education in the process. 'If theories are maps of a terrain, models are the ships that take the inquirer into the specifics of a certain unknown' (Olds, 1992: 25).

Our co-enquiry has helped us to see that adventurous schools puts the pupils, their lives and world at the foreground of what they do. Their primary focus is to enable children to know and feel in relationship with themselves, each other, their family and world; to know they can become an author of their life as well as an actor in it. An adventurous school enhances rather than comes between the natural relationship children have with their experience. It challenges the taken-for-granted assumption of the traditional school that separates children from their world and teaches them to be passive and compliant. Pupils learn from early on to experience the connection between themselves and their world, and they learn to make decisions and choices that teach them responsibility and accountability to each other and to understand the effect of their thoughts and actions on the human as well as the non-human world. Their intellectual development takes place in a context where they learn that who they are and what they do matter. These intentions in action create so much more than just a culture of care and concern. A strong emphasis on the pupils in relationship to each other and their world creates what Rifkin (2010) terms 'empathetic sociability'. Empathy is a core skill in a world where appreciating and valuing difference is of vital importance.

The leaders of these schools have been engaging in the design of day-to-day activity so there is an alignment between this primary purpose and all their operating procedures. Nothing is taken for granted; everything is up for continual examination. Their goals affect and change the values and operations of the school, what the adults think they are there to do and how they achieve their outcomes.

Learning and enquiry as a process is the primary way that this is achieved and has a particular meaning; it is about participation and knowledge creation not just response and knowledge acquisition. Pupils are part of a community in the adventurous school where they contribute actively to a curriculum based on real experience of the world, the locality and the community, where they pose and experience problems and design and test real solutions. They learn to be enterprising and creative and find out where their interests and expertise lie. This approach to learning is based on an understanding that the relationship individuals have with the world is social and relational; experience, first-hand sources and critical reflection are primary. This is different to the traditional approaches that even in primary school are still often abstract, virtual and disconnected and where learning is predominantly named as 'work'. Children are in a living relationship with their world that can be made sense of, questioned, enquired into and broadened by the school. Children, no matter how young, can be part of inventing and creating new knowledge and a new world. They are participating and creating, not just receiving and being told.

The adventurous school provides the living experience and making sense of life that is the basis of effective and authentic education. The adventure is about transforming from within and creating space for children to imagine and create other worlds and possibilities. It represents a move from a response that has been largely reactive, for keeping going and for *survival*, to *transformation* that is responsive, proactive and for the future. Out-of-date ideas are spotted, named and stopped in their tracks.

Adventurous, participative learning has its own demands and rigour. This pedagogical approach is not a return to the perceived idyll of a pre-National Curriculum world, though it draws on inspiration from the best of the tradition. The approach is evolving from the best of the past 20 years in primary schools where there are things to harvest and build on as well as features that now need discarding. It gradually became obvious to the group as part of our first enquiry that what we were trying to articulate could be described as an adventure. These features came to mind to illustrate and clarify what adventure meant to us:

- the capacity to imagine what might be, how things could be different, to seize opportunities;
- developing a confident spirit and a hardy disposition;
- having a map to help you plan the route and a compass to guide you but not being static or rigid about the journey and being prepared to face the unknown;
- evolving, being on a journey, moving on, taking risks;
- living and lively exploration;
- questing, questioning, enquiring, not knowing all the answers; and
- travelling with others, knowing guides and mentors you can trust and how they assist you on the way.

Making the adventure happen: Where do you start?

As we have already noted we did not set out with the intention of describing what we have been doing in this project as an adventure. Colleagues from the schools came together initially with the intention of meeting each other, learning, exchanging experiences of success, seeing what was held in common and what was different. At some point we realised that we had moved from our original working title for the book that was 'Inside the Learning Primary

School'. For a start we were as much concerned with the outside as the inside, the communities of the schools and the broader social contexts for learning. Connecting to the future meant we wanted to challenge ourselves as much as possible to pay attention to what was emergent in our enquiry and not just staying safe in what we already knew.

In the process of getting to know each school, colleagues found out quite early on that they had some powerful guiding principles underpinning what they already did (Figure 1.1). First, this included deep respect, care and inclusion for those at the heart of the enterprise, who were not only the children but their parents and carers too. Second, providing exciting learning experiences was equally important to the three schools and all of them had a strong, existing pedagogy of active and collaborative learning in real contexts that had connections for children to their community and to their world. Third, each school had a belief system that all children can learn, be successful and achieve given the right opportunities and environment and not only that, they can, from an early age, take charge of their learning and lead the learning of others.

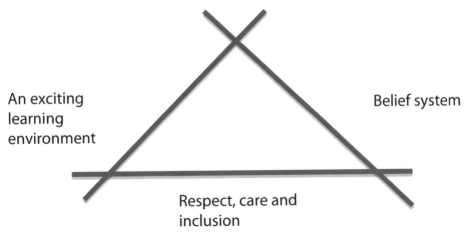

An exciting learning environment

Belief system

Respect, care and inclusion

Figure 1.1: The principles the schools had in common that underpinned our first enquiry

As we worked together, these beliefs and principles were examined more closely. We began to see that the three schools shared a purpose that was far broader than the current expectations of ensuring the attainment, well-being and safety of the pupils. They wanted children to have an educational experience that was authentic;[2] that enabled them to see and feel their control of their learning, to be empathic and in community with each other. The ethical position that each school was working from in relation to their children became clearer as the project developed.

In the next enquiry we began to unpack what authentic learning would be like in practice. We started by identifying what we most wanted for children and framed it as follows. We wanted them to have experiences and successes that gave them a sense of purpose, place, creativity, contribution and celebration; to provide them with every opportunity to develop who they are, why they are here and what they want to creatively contribute to their world both now and for the future (Figure 1.2). This meant being a school that encourages children to ask:

- Why am I here?
- What's going on in my world?
- How can I contribute?

This kind of school understands it is empowering rather than controlling, as it gives children the reins of their life and helps them learn how to make choices and about responsibility.

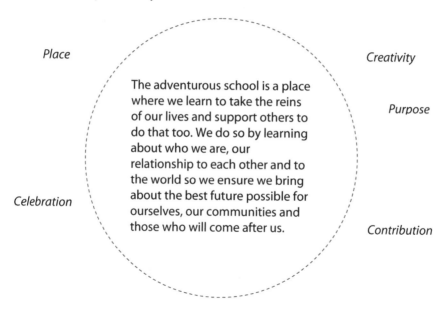

Place

Creativity

Purpose

The adventurous school is a place where we learn to take the reins of our lives and support others to do that too. We do so by learning about who we are, our relationship to each other and to the world so we ensure we bring about the best future possible for ourselves, our communities and those who will come after us.

Celebration

Contribution

Figure 1.2: The purposes of an adventurous school

The outline of the book

Chapter 1 provides the context for the book by exploring the territory and 'the call to adventure'. It addresses three underlying themes of purpose, pedagogy and power in current educational discourse and how these need to be surfaced and renewed if the school system is to evolve to a more contemporary paradigm. These three, we argue, can subvert change and innovation if they remain unexamined. This chapter is based on much of our discussion during the project.

The next chapters are written by the schools and are in Parts 1, 2 and 3. Each part explores a theme as it is enacted in each school. There is an overview first and the story from each school to follow. There are many ways that we could have framed the content of the chapters about the schools, and we selected three main aspects of the conversations that we have had. These are vision, community and curriculum (Parts 1, 2 and 3, respectively). Understanding how a school develops each of these and the connections and interdependence between them has been an important part of our enquiry. In thinking about their interrelatedness we have seen how learning is core to each of them, infusing and serving them all, as well as being an outcome. We have noticed that creativity arises when these three are working together as a learning system. We have also noted that the three aspects are in working relationship with the three themes of purpose, pedagogy and power in Chapter 1, which we come back to towards the end of the book.

When whole-school learning is in place everyone starts to feel included and the sustainability of the community and its environment can be addressed from a stronger starting point. The adventure can then begin, the questing to encounter and work with the new, to make the unknown known, to be learning together how to co-create new knowledge and experience with the tools and skills we already have. The book concludes (Part 4) with what we have learnt about leadership, its characteristics and qualities and how it can be adventurous in itself.

These pages tell the story of how the three schools have experienced, expressed and understood the adventure they are on with their pupils and communities. We hope *The Adventurous School* will make a contribution to the educational innovation that is currently led by practitioners and school leaders. We hope that others will recognise the path the schools are on from their own experience and be encouraged by that as well as finding new ideas and examples to support them and that they might want to try. Above all we would hope the book will promote discussion and debate.

I (Jane Reed) am deeply indebted to all I have learnt from working in community with these exceptional colleagues, the fun we have had, the new knowledge we have built together from listening to each other, the insights we have shared and the transformations we have begun to see are possible.

Questions for discussion

- What does adventure mean to you?
- What is the adventure for your school?
- How do you relate to the characteristics of adventure outlined here?
- What characteristics of adventure are missing for you?

Notes

1. Readers might be interested to know of the Nowhere Foundation's Enhancing Children's Learning (Ecl) Project and website, which has interesting approaches and tools for working to enhance well-being, creativity and learning (http://www.now-here.com/#!/ecl).

2. Starratt (2004: 70) explores the nature of authenticity in a useful way for this book. He writes: 'To claim authenticity as the justification for narcissistic, self-preoccupation is to miss the point of freedom. Authenticity is the human challenge of connecting oneself to a wider world, of finding one's life in dialogue with this wider whole, of discovering that the deepest character of all beings ... is their relationality, their participation in the larger life around them.'

Chapter 1

The call to adventure: Context, change and challenge for the twenty-first century primary school

The vital step in the journey of changing anything is this: hearing within yourself the call to adventure and choosing to answer it.
(Johnstone, 2010: 20)

The context of the twenty-first century primary school

Two 11-year-old boys open the box the head teacher has just left in front of them. Inside are the component parts of a miniature wind turbine that will be fully functional once put together; when assembled it will operate safely in a classroom. They find the instructions, chatting about what they are about to do, and set about putting the wind machine together. They have much greater technical ability than most of us will ever have, as well as a very sophisticated capacity to work together and interpret the instructions for the task before them. The head teacher who set up the activity with them has long gone on to her next conversation, knowing these two will not only complete the assignment but learn much on the way and have a great deal of fun. In a short time the turbine is up and running in the open area onto which the Key Stage 2 classrooms open. In the break a large group of Year 6 children flock from their classroom to find out what the boys have been doing. They are all fascinated, gently trying to find out how it works, asking questions and attentive to the achievement of their mates. What was striking was that it seemed perfectly normal for these lads to be undertaking an activity like this outside their classroom, with no adult in sight for at least 30 minutes. They were totally absorbed by what they were doing, reflecting and chatting as they set out to see the completed wind machine.

This is sustainability week at St Vigor and St John Primary School in Somerset. The children in the school study a particular quest in depth each term and the normal timetable is changed so that it can happen. Among other things the pupils have been dressing trees, learning about recycling, studying and drawing the hedgerow, making paper from recycled materials and, most importantly, learning that there is an interdependence between caring for ourselves, our world and each other.

Let's contrast this happy, constructive activity with some of the features of life on their planet home at the moment. The second decade of the twenty-first century is a picture of contrasts, paradoxes and conundrums in a world that has quadrupled its population in 100 years. All the signs are that the relationship between the demands of its seven billion inhabitants and the resources needed to meet them are stretched very thin.[1] This is a world that continues to have a comfortable standard of life for many people and a life of hunger and continual poverty for many others.

The cost is not only to those remaining in poverty but also to the natural systems that sustain us. Lester Brown warns that the changes that will secure the future of human life need managing now with unprecedented speed (Brown, 2008). Writers and commentators (Orr, 1994; Bowers, 2001; O'Sullivan, 2001; Sterling, 2001; Reed, 2010; Clarke, 2011a) suggest education and learning will either lead us out of the challenges we face or prevent us from coping with them.

Our children are developing a global identity but in a world that is more socially divided, has a throw-away economy that can't be sustained, is full of resource conflicts and continues to have threats from terrorism as well as disease. In their lifetime the oil supply is likely to peak and then dwindle, and food and fuel will increasingly compete for land. Resources are being consumed more quickly than they can be regenerated and we are discharging greenhouse gases into the atmosphere faster than nature can absorb them. Despite the optimism of any educational adventure, we cannot ignore that these are the big challenges in its context. Challenges our children are going to have to face in their lifetimes.

As we began the enquiry leading to this book, we had just witnessed the destruction of New Orleans. Several thousand people across the West of England were also without both power and drinking water, many of their homes badly flooded as a result of the worst floods in living memory and almost two months of rain. This scenario was repeated in subsequent months in Cumbria and Cornwall. As we complete the book tornadoes and hurricanes have struck in Haiti, New Zealand and parts of the USA. It is not certain that any of this extreme weather was caused by climate change rather than just freak events but over the past five years these incidents have felt like a wake-up call. Other life-threatening and extensive floods have punctuated the time of writing, both here and around the world in Pakistan, Brazil and Queensland.

On 1 July 2011 *The Independent* newspaper reported on its front page that the scientific community were now admitting that these various events were to do with profound climatic changes across the globe.

Pupils in our primary schools live in a comparatively rich country but despite that, there is a growing gap between those with a good lifestyle and those in poverty (Palmer *et al.*, 2007). The current number of children living in poverty in the UK according to Barnardo's is almost four million (Barnardo's, 2011). Children in this study who were from poorer backgrounds already felt that they were not going to get as good a quality of schooling as those from better-off families.

The Cambridge Primary Review (Alexander, 2010) notes, on the positive side, that life expectancy has risen; children are generally in good health and are more culturally literate than their predecessors; incomes have increased; and well-being and positive behaviour feature more as part of their schooling. They also report that parents think childhood has become more stressful; children are under too much pressure at school; there is too much exposure to the negative influences of information technology; and there are fears for their safety in many neighbourhoods. Richard Louv's (2005) important study adds that children are experiencing what he terms 'nature deficit', losing their contact with the natural world and increasingly living in a virtual world.

Matthew Fox (2006: 9), the Catholic priest excommunicated by the Pope while he was a cardinal for his outspoken views, says: 'We are an endangered species. We are endangering ourselves, our planet, our future. Yet we are also, as a renowned scientist recently said, "the one species that can prevent its own extinction."'

In 2006 Forum for the Future commissioned a survey of young people, which illustrates the involvement of students in critical discussion about the issues (UCAS and Forum for the Future, 2007). James, who had at the time just become a student at Birmingham University, said: 'Only when the mindset of previous generations becomes extinct will real progress be made.' Maya, while on her gap year, said: 'Those with the power to promote change must do so immediately and must not be frozen in fear of the chaos that climate change threatens.'

Lester Brown proposes a Plan B (Brown, 2008). He argues that securing quality of life for our children means not only investing in education and health but also investing in a programme to reverse the trends that are undermining their future; and these concerns provide an important part of the context for schools globally in the twenty-first century. Senge *et al.* (2010) note that the contradictions between how nature works and how society works cannot continue indefinitely. Gershon (2009) echoes this and highlights the imperative to continually evolve our social systems in ways that reflect the changes in both our world and its development. He says:

We need to heal our wounds, transform our limiting beliefs and enrich our impoverished visions of possibility if we wish to change the conditions that have created our current world. Otherwise they will keep showing up in our children, parents, teachers, politicians, business leaders, clergy and social change agents. For our planet to evolve, we the people living on it need to evolve. This is a pre-requisite for any lasting transformative change.

(Gershon, 2009: 301)

Joanna Macy (2005), the American Buddhist and systems science teacher, describes the transition we are making as one from an industrial growth society to a life affirming society. She terms it 'the Great Turning'. In her words, we are not 'served by playing upon our fear or guilt but by an enthusiastic release of creativity and ingenuity such as happens when we feel ourselves called forward on a great adventure.'

So what is the call to adventure of the twenty-first century primary school?

Colleagues in this project have identified that though they may not be there yet, the adventure is towards new forms, frames and opportunities for learning that will both release and equip their learners for a creative, challenging future and support them in being part of 'the Great Turning'. In our conversations the project group identified and discussed three undercurrents in the context of education at the moment. These are purpose, pedagogy and power. The call to adventure can be helped or hindered by the way these are thought about, enacted and connected to each other. Each carry influential - often unexamined and engrained - cultural assumptions that maintain the dominant discourses and forms of conventional education. In this project we have realised that the adventurous school is trying to confront the subtle impact these assumptions, and the habits related to them, can have on efforts to change, innovate and bring about renewal for twenty-first century education.

Purpose

The context of a school is like a sea that everyone swims in. Central directives have largely defined that context for many schools in recent years and this has become a constraint. Obeying rules and regulations has been more important than asking questions of deeper purpose and relevance. The context of a school both globally and locally affects children's lives and futures, but schools can still often feel too pressurised to diagnose and engage with their context more effectively.

This book argues that an adventurous school gives priority to reading its context and uses a particular type of spectacles or binoculars to do so. As

Reed and Stoll (2000: 130) observe: 'Being able to read the context is a critical skill in effective school improvement.' These spectacles have strong lenses that can focus on a wider perspective than they have done before. The lenses pick up colour and tone more accurately, they can detect movement and activity in the field both near at hand and further away. They can pick up on signs of danger to which they might need to alert the children; they develop ways of dealing with them in the classroom. This contextual knowledge provides feedback and helps define with greater accuracy a school's purpose; it supports the school in clarifying their goals in the competing sea of purposes they have to deal with. These spectacles also have the capability to develop the active skill of foresight and future spotting. Twenty-first century children need to develop what Wals (2007) terms an 'eco-cultural' understanding of their world and not just a purely cultural and social one. They need to understand the risks to human life of not living within the carrying capacity of the larger systems on which human life depends. Hicks and Holden (1995) argue that we lack guiding visions for the future and that this results in a loss of direction for education.

James Martin (2006) identifies today's children as the 'transition generation'. Founder of the James Martin 21st Century School at the University of Oxford, he established the school's mission as one which will 'identify and find solutions to the biggest challenges facing humanity in the 21st century and to find the biggest opportunities' (Martin, 2006: xi). He comments that: 'This could be humanity's last century, or it could be the century in which civilisation sets sail towards a far more spectacular future' (2006: 3).

Martin compares our challenges to a deep river canyon with a bottleneck at its centre and humanity as river rafters heading downstream. As we go into the canyon, he says, we will have to cope with an accelerating rate of change. He is under no illusion that we are heading for the bottleneck and that our political leaders in their slowness to respond are not making the time in the canyon an easy one. At the narrowest part of the canyon, the world's population will be at its highest and the world's resources under the greatest stress. Martin takes a predominantly positive and optimistic stance and argues that understanding the meaning of the twenty-first century will give meaning to the lives of young people; he is convinced this is as an exciting a time to be alive as a young person as any other in our history. 'The job of the Transition Generation is to take humanity through the canyon with as little mayhem as possible into what we hope will be smoother waters beyond' (Martin, 2006: 8).

As writer and commentator David Orr comments:

Those now being educated will have to do what we, the present generation, have been unwilling or unable to do. They must begin the work of repairing the damage done to the earth in the past 200 years of industrialisation, while they reduce worsening social and racial inequities. No generation has ever faced a more daunting agenda.

(Orr, 1994: 27)

Clarke (2011a) notes: 'As we have sought greater literacy in the traditional sense, we have become functionally illiterate ecologically. We need a radical rediscovery of our educational purpose, a renaissance of the educational enterprise for our urban age.'

So, how fit for purpose are our current primary schools? What sort of schools do the 'transition generation' need?

Scharmer (2009: 3) observes: 'We pour considerable amounts of money into our educational systems, but we haven't been able to create schools and institutions of higher education that develop people's innate capacity to sense and shape their future.'

In his work Clarke (2011b) calls for the development of 'sustainable community': 'This involves stepping beyond the constraints of the school environment and connecting to the wider community, service and business sectors, then reconnecting schools into new configurations.'

It is only 140 years since it became compulsory for children to go to school and the norms and forms of the industrial primary school were first established. Throughout their history the purpose of primary schools has been the subject of many debates and discussions. The Cambridge Primary Review (Alexander, 2010) notes that through its short lifetime primary education has been in almost continual transition. By the middle of the last century young children's learning in English primary schools held the attention and regard of educators throughout the world. However, this fame was short lived. The thinking of the time, epitomised in the Plowden Report (1967), was at best 'opaque' about how learning in primary schools should be organised and conducted (Lowe, 2007: 46).

The goals of the post-industrial English primary school have represented a mix of purposes, which for the past decade or so have centred on public discourse about the importance of raising standards for the new 'knowledge' economy in the 'core' competencies of numeracy and literacy and enabling England to compete more successfully in global markets. A more explicit goal of educating for social and environmental responsibility and awareness has been largely sidelined into aspects of citizenship and geographical education. Wrigley comments:

It is truly ironic, at a time when industrial management consultants are drawing upon complexity theory, that government agencies are trying to impose an archaic and mechanistic model of linear rationality on schools…The central processes of education are undermined by language that doesn't articulate moral purpose…The

> *discourse of performativity, of efficiently fulfilling specific targets is deeply corrosive of education.*
>
> (Wrigley, 2003: 47)

While we were writing this book we marked more than 20 years since the Education Reform agenda of the late 1980s, when the perceived lack of planned progression and shared 'standards' brought about a new policy agenda that was more politically driven and interventionist than it had been. The National Curriculum and end of key stage assessments marked the end of the mid-twentieth century primary school as it was and the beginning of a much more centralised, regulated and bureaucratic system. The schools in this project are aware that they have been judged by their results and inspected more than ever before.

The three schools have been successful partly because they have been sailing against the tide. Inspection reports have noted and welcomed their creativity. The schools have always seen achievement in literacy and numeracy as crucial but embedded in a broad and rich curriculum. They have all at times felt under pressure to narrow their focus to what was the more commonplace accountability agenda. While it has had some benefits, colleagues at the start of our project described the last few years as a hard journey. It has caused a form of professional dislocation and loss of purpose. They reported that those who have trained as teachers more recently know nothing different than the formulas and recipes of prescription. The time for change is now, if schools are going to have any role in education that will help us out of the bottleneck that Martin (2006) has identified; but as Claxton (2008: 23) comments: 'It is as if we hold the basic institution of the school in such reverence that we simply cannot conceive of ever doing more than tinkering with it.' The children's writer Michael Morpurgo noted the same tendency in his 2011 Richard Dimbleby lecture when he said: 'We endlessly jiggle the system and call it reform.'

The greatest hope for the adventure for education in the twenty-first century is to find ways to influence the often unnoticed, deepest currents in the river flowing towards the 'bottleneck', in order that humanity can pass through it safely in the coming decades.

In the school change-and-improvement literature of the past 20 years there are a range of suggestions for what is needed to create a larger sense of purpose for schools and for them to provide the opportunities that will give that sense to students. In their reflections of current school improvement practices Reed and Lodge (2006: 59) argue that schools will: 'become artefacts of a bygone age unless there is a concerted effort to challenge the present instrumentalist discourses and pitch the thinking into the future agenda.' They identify three ages of school improvement in the past 30 years: first, a focus on school level change; second, a focus on teachers; and third, the development of pupil agency. They critique top-down approaches as encouraging an overemphasis on the perspectives of politicians, teachers and leaders rather than those of the pupils.

Wrigley, however, notes that:

> The political pressure of target setting and accountability is mentioned (in the literature) perhaps as an unfortunate obstacle in the way of authentic change, but there is no sustained attempt to analyse which way our educational ship is being driven ... what if our schools need a change of direction as much as a boost in capacity?
>
> (Wrigley, 2003: 176)

Stoll *et al.* challenge the reductionism of contemporary policy and argue for a more ecological paradigm for schools:

> An alternate view emerges from fields such as quantum physics, molecular biology, Gestalt psychology and ecology. All these disciplines have challenged the conventional rationale paradigm. Their proponents have argued that rationality must be balanced by an ecological approach that looks at human and natural systems holistically rather than through knowing them by their parts – that we need to examine the inter-relationships and interconnections among components of a system
>
> (Stoll *et al.*, 2003: 15)

Hargreaves and Fink comment:

> The prominence and urgency of having to think about and commit to sustainability in our environment highlights the necessity of promoting sustainability in other areas of our lives. Foremost among these are leadership and education, where our consuming obsession with reaching higher and higher standards within shorter and shorter time lines is exhausting our teachers and leaders.
>
> (Hargreaves and Fink, 2006: 2)

Mitchell and Sackney in their work on schools as learning communities similarly note that:

> The learning community acknowledges the organic nature of learning for educators and students, and it positions educational improvement as a natural consequence of a natural view of a natural process. It represents an alternative set of assumptions, beliefs, values, practices, structures, and understandings that, if held by enough people and supported in enough places, could break the iron cage of the mechanistic worldview.
>
> (Mitchell and Sackney, 2000: 133)

Senge *et al.* are clear about the change in purpose that is needed for schools:

> *If I had one wish for all institutions, and the institution called school in particular, it is that we dedicate ourselves to allowing them to be what they would naturally become which is human communities, not machines. Living beings who continually ask the questions: why am I here? What is going on in my world? How might I best contribute?*
>
> (Senge et al., 2000: 58)

They reflect that machine age thinking became the foundation for organisational models that reflected standardisation, uniformity, rote and drill:

> *The result of this machine age thinking was a model of school separate from daily life, governed in an authoritarian manner oriented above all to produce a standardised product and as dependent on maintaining control as the armies of Frederick the Great ... other countries had their own local indigenous texts, both written and oral. They learnt about weather and climate, but not for the sake of altering or controlling the seasons. They learnt about the world to understand and fit into it, not to command or control it.*
>
> (p.31)

This section has identified why it is urgent to discuss renewed goals for primary education. Purpose is probably the most pivotal of the three undercurrents that we identified in our discussions. The research and forums that the Cambridge Primary Review has set up are a welcome response to that need. The schools' chapters demonstrate the ways in which they are updating their purpose and how this manifests in particular through their school vision.

Pedagogy

The first section of this chapter argued why the twenty-first century primary school needs to have the capacity to respond to environmental as well as social issues and that they need to use a wide lens to be able to accurately respond to their context. As Hargreaves and Fink (2006: 9) assert: 'Sustainability isn't just a metaphor borrowed from environmental science. It's a fundamental principle for enriching and preserving the richness and interconnection of life, and learning lies at the heart of high-quality life.'

At the heart of the adventurous school are learners and learning; there are also the learning contexts, environments and challenges that engage children in ways that help them to take the reins of their lives and engage with others on the path. To get us through the 'bottleneck' described by James Martin (2006) it is not just the purpose of a school that needs broadening. To manifest the purposes suggested in the first section, consideration needs to be given to the way we think about learning, the way in which it is organised and designed, and the social contribution that it makes. A major question for this project has been what we mean by learning, how adventurous, relevant and real is it, and how can it take a central place in a school system dominated by high-stakes testing?

We have already argued that much of the founding industrial form for primary education remains intact, reinforced by a long period of central regulation, direction and bureaucratisation. This is nowhere more the case than in the pedagogical structures and artefacts of classrooms. Unexamined assumptions about what learning is also persist, and so do views on what its purposes are. The Cambridge Primary Review refers despondently to 'the neo-elementary condition' that they perceive English primary schools embody as a result of instrumentality and utilitarianism and the 'state view of learning' that they now enshrine (Alexander, 2010: 39).

In their work on the leadership of learning, Kaser and Halbert (2009) comment ironically that a shift to focusing on learning is still new work for many schools. While many teachers may focus on it as individuals, learning as a social skill that makes sense of experience in community is not yet an ambition for the school system as a whole. Learning that actively fosters participation and develops agency, rather than simply remembering facts and information for tests and examinations, is still submerged, ill defined, and competing with other demands. Olson (2003: 4–5) observes: 'Pedagogy refers primarily to the practices of teaching, not to the broader question of why teaching is required in the first place.'

Perkins argues the importance of learning by 'wholes' and in his recent work discusses an approach to the 'whole game of learning'. He comments:

> imagine a world where almost any adult had a kind of energetic if simple sense of civic engagement or ecological responsibility or avoidance of prejudice. Starting from the baseline of today's indifference and neglect, these 'games' do not have to be played in a very sophisticated way to do substantial good! The world would be a better place if in areas like these most people achieved average mediocrity rather than passive erudition.
>
> (Perkins, 2009: 22)

Several colleagues who have been working with us on our projects comment that they were trained in curriculum content and delivery rather than pedagogical processes. One young teacher in her second year remarked 'they taught me to be a performing monkey when I was training'! 'Learning for life' is still often associated with the more relaxed and optional aspects of formal education. It has tended to be seen as what you do *after* getting qualifications. Despite the attempts of several projects in the past decade and a major Economic and Social Research Council (ESRC) research programme, enabling classroom learning to become more learner driven has not become a real priority. There has been little time given to the professional enquiry that might ask what it means to create the pedagogic and organisational processes that will enable more creative approaches to flourish in any coherent way.

Learning remains a loose term because it is too easily confused with teaching, work or performance (Watkins, 2010). Learning can be an empty term because in its fuller sense it conflicts with the dominant orthodoxies or is perceived to take the eye off the ball of high standards. Roland Barth (1990, 2001) has been a strong advocate of models of school improvement that are learning focused. He distinguishes between improvement that monitors and controls adult and student behaviour and assures the attainment of prescribed skills and targets and improvement that creates the conditions for everyone to become a community of learners.

As we reflected in our discussions, the project group argued that a step into the territory of more adventurous, empowering learning does not need to be a big one. As Senge *et al.* (2000) say, school is a living system, resonating with life, youth and energy, rather than a factory or machine with rules to follow and facts to absorb. For many children this cultural difference makes the difference between becoming a learner and being just an attainer, between a positive and negative experience of being at school, from being a statistic in a league table, a cog in a machine and being treated as a human being, the difference between being connected to or disconnected from the world.

The adventure of becoming a school that genuinely offers learning for life, argued colleagues from these three schools, is to behave as if a school is alive and to confront the traditional assumptions and patterns that have limited its vitality. The next step, and this is the challenge, is then to create a culture rich with artefacts, processes, structures and new patterns that are themselves alive and worthy of being called learning. Learning and knowledge that are not part of a lived enquiry gradually become inert and set; they become formulas to follow and copy rather than experiences to be investigated and examined. Colleagues involved with this project were very alert to the dangers in the last ten years of reverting to a view of learning that would disempower their pupils and make no connections for them to their own experience. The development of their own adventurous selves came partly from their own professional disinclination to reflect these dangers in their own practice. They would be the first to say they haven't yet achieved this aspiration fully in their practice but it is certainly at the forefront of their thinking.

The 'assembly-line' school, as Senge *et al.* (2000: 32) refer to it, created many of the problems that parents and children still deal with in school. Uniformity resulted in an assumption that everyone learns in the same way, those who didn't learn at the speed of the assembly line were labelled as slow or dumb. The authority put in the hands of the teacher gave them total responsibility for motivation and the engagement of the pupils. The pupils became the products rather than the creators of the learning. As Nicholls and Hazzard (1993: 24) state: 'A community of Adventurous Scholars will not spring spontaneously from this soil.'

Sackney and Walker (2006) comment that schools operating under clockwork assumptions foster compliance as a priority over learning and that compliance breeds dependence and passivity, not community and agency. Colleagues on the project report a concern about the dependence among contemporary practitioners on pedagogical packages and off-the-shelf solutions. When reporting in a local continuing professional development (CPD) meeting that her school had a new curriculum, a fellow educator asked 'Oh! Where did you get it from?'

The Cambridge Primary Review (Alexander, 2010) notes that pupils in England are more tested than anywhere else in the world. As well as creating compliance, dependence and passivity, the requirements of an external agenda has reinforced a model of teaching as a way of 'delivering' the curriculum at the expense of the engagement of pupils in learning. The logic has prevailed that if teaching is effective, attainment at a good standard will follow. As we dig into the experience of the past two decades, the processes of learning that add up to more than just a response to teaching have got absorbed in this logic and ended up in rather a weak and neglected position. Olson (2003: 20) citing Ravitch (2000) comments that: 'Well-meaning reforms often had the effect of reducing student responsibility and accountability.'

In their work Carnell and Lodge (2002), Watkins (2005), Dweck (2006) and Claxton (2008) have been encouraging practitioners to swim against the tide and develop more of a focus on learning but, as Olson (2003) notes, the mindsets that need to change run very deep.

Watkins (2005) challenges us to be clear what we mean by 'learning': is it simply a response to teaching, is it an individual act of meaning making or is it collaborating and participating as a community? Hallmarks of community he identifies as agency, belonging, cohesion and diversity; each of which we can see being developed on the ground in the schools' chapters. In their work Watkins *et al.* (2007) outline the processes of active, collaborative and learner-driven learning as ones that particularly promote effective learning. Carnell and Lodge (2002: 42) explore the promotion of rich learning environments for twenty-first century classrooms. They see the encouragement of the following as central:

- a shift in responsibility from teachers to young people;
- a focus on learning and a learning language;
- a shift in the teacher's role from a behaviour manager to a learning manager;
- a shift in the young people's role as a researcher and learning partner with other learners;

- an emphasis on reciprocal teaching and learning;
- a view that the territory of the classroom is a shared learning space; and
- more permeable classroom boundaries.

Perkins (2009) argues for the conceptual road of learning to be one that is understood as a process of making sense of and constructing larger and larger 'wholes' as increasingly complex connections are made through using and applying our knowledge. 'If much of what we taught highlighted understandings of wide scope, with enlightenment, empowerment and responsibility in the foreground, there is every reason to think youngsters would retain more, understand more and use more of what they learned'(p.61).

This section has discussed the importance of examining the assumptions that underpin and limit the development of pedagogy in an adventurous school. The schools discuss their pedagogy in Part 3 (their curriculum chapters) but it is also there in Part 1 (the vision chapters) and Part 2 (the community chapters) too.

Power

The previous sections in this chapter have identified that an adventurous school gives attention to revitalising both the purposes and the pedagogies that are needed to realise goals fit for the twenty-first century. It has identified some of the existing structures and assumptions that inhibit the development of adventurous practice. These two in turn draw on a third partner to support and nourish or, alternatively, undermine them. This is power.

'One feature that distinguishes humans from other animals – perhaps as characteristic as speech or upright posture – is the fact that we find so many ways to oppress and exploit each other' (Csikszentmihalyi, 1993: 89). Csikszentmihalyi is describing here the negative consequences of a model of power that is still in common use in our culture. In our collective mental models of what power is, power is still often perceived as a commodity one party has *over* another.

Because of their age and stage of life, children through history have not traditionally been viewed as being able to contribute or have equal agency with adults, although this is beginning to change now. For example control of pupils for conformity has been a dominant assumption through the history of schooling, and in a performance culture that form of control continues to be a very necessary commodity. Cooke-Sather notes that:

> *Adults' basic distrust of young people and insistence on being in control of education has meant not only that students are not authorised as knowers, they are de-humanised, reduced to products,*

and thus devoid of those qualities that would make them authorities: trustworthiness and legitimacy as knowers.

(Cooke-Sather, 2002: 5)

Watkins (2005: 113) points out that: 'The dominant model of running a classroom uses a gross simplification of what we know about learning and this shows up clearly in the forms of social structure that you see in most classrooms today.'

Sarason (2004: 82) asks: 'Who writes the constitution of the classroom? The answer to which there was no exception was that teachers wrote the constitution of the classroom.'

In his work on power, Johnstone (2010) notes that the 'do as I say or I will bash you' approach to power can create fear that blocks more creative uses of power and undermines confidence to think differently. In his work he sets out a series of shifts in how we understand the nature of power that are the basis of a more positive shared approach.

There has been a growing expectation in the past 20 years that children and young people are more involved in making decisions about things that affect them (UN, 1989). The 'pupil voice' movement has been a major response from the school improvement field to this growing recognition. However, as McMahon and Portelli (2004) point out, the shifts in power that result from more focus on student engagement continue to vary across a traditional/democratic spectrum.

As Frost observes:

Any attempts to listen more attentively to students' concerns, to widen their participation in school life, or to recognise their latent leadership potential need to take into account the persisting effects of divisive practices and structures of schools and the way in which structures and power dynamics work together to constrain agency for young people.

(Frost, 2008: 355)

Lodge (2008) argues that it is more appropriate to use the term student 'participation' than 'voice'. She argues that all students have the capacity to play an active role in school; and that schools need to create the opportunities for students to have a say and be heard and to be attentive and responsive. Schools, she argues, should acknowledge the inequality in power relationships.

Cooke-Sather reflects that 'authorising' students' perspectives is an empowering process:

As the pace of life accelerates, the population becomes increasingly diverse and the media more complex, more than ever before, we educators and educational researchers must seriously question the assumption that we know more than the young people of today about how they learn or what they need to learn in preparation for the decades ahead.

(Cooke-Sather, 2002: 3)

Our enquiries have led us to see that an adventurous school is working with a positive model of power. It is a model of power that is shared between adults and children, based on trust, and includes everyone. A model of power that knows everyone can contribute and be successful and that the success of each part of the community, of each member, is the success and power of the whole.

Johnstone (2010) terms this power 'with', distinguishing it from power 'over' and power 'through'. Power used in this way can support a school in the adventure of realising its potential, creating a constantly evolving world of possibilities. Everyone is invited to take their place and participate as a member of the community. When the road is challenging, the school leaders can draw on the power that is being created collectively. Positive power can create energy and enthusiasm and contribute to success. Power is used for the good of the whole, not to defend or assert territory or personal reputation. This kind of power is based on and fosters a sense of belonging, safety, interdependence and responsibility between people rather than isolation, finger pointing and blame. Positive power creates cycles of positive effect; growth and change produce optimism that feeds further change and growth. Participants are not just members of an organisation; they are there for each other and they share the power between them.

As Nicholls and Hazzard observe:

Whether or not we acknowledge it, students are curriculum theorists and critics of schooling. If they are drawn into the conversation about the purpose and practices of education, we may all learn useful lessons. Children can change our priorities and shape our stories in unexpected ways. Education can become an adventure in which teachers, researchers and children together learn new questions as well as answers, so that their lessons are never complete.

(Nicholls and Hazzard, 1993: 8)

D. Whitmore (personal communication 2010) also argues for empowerment rather than control for young people and identifies that supporting young people with the means to grow and evolve rather than just controlling their behaviour supports their making beneficial choices. She argues that young people need positive experiences of themselves that build esteem and aspiration. Building life goals and the actions to make those real will promote higher attainment.

Gershon (2009) identifies that having a sense of personal empowerment in our lives and work creates more caring and compassionate human beings; who then want to contribute more to the good of the whole. He notes that the forms of learning and growth cultures that are needed now in society's organisations are often thought to be present but that they rarely are.

One of the earliest and most influential school improvement studies to look at school culture in this way and that examined the benefits of positive power for teachers was Rosenholtz's (1989) influential research into schools in the USA in the late 1980s. Here she found that there were certain characteristics of 'moving' or 'learning enriched' schools as opposed to 'stuck' schools or 'learning impoverished' schools. The moving schools took power and sought freedom *to* focus on their own priorities; the stuck schools did not see the power that they had and were seeking freedom *from* external demands (Stoll and Fink, 1996: 85).

'Moving schools' (of which the adventurous school is an example) have particular cultural characteristics that make a difference to student outcomes and are based on empowerment strategies. They encourage collaboration in reality and not just in name, and create an environment in which teachers share ideas and solutions to problems and learn together about educational practice. Barth (1990, 2001) also advocates models of shared power. He identifies the norms of a community of learners where adults and students together are learning from each other. He too says that schools can have the capacity to take charge of themselves, if the need and the purpose are clear, and that what needs to be improved is the school culture, the quality of relationships and the nature and quality of learning experiences.

In the field of community development, there has also been much discussion about how to give more power and control to those whose community it is. Bawden *et al.* (2007: 133) comment that: 'Humanity is caught, it seems, in systems of governance that radically constrain rather than unleash our collective learning capacities.'

In a study of neighbourhood transformation, James (2007) identifies four factors that promote local empowerment:

- flexible structures reflecting real need and circumstance;
- the processes that support change;
- enthusiastic individuals that make change a reality; and
- a local culture that puts neighbourhood empowerment centre stage.

A report on social venturing asserts the importance of providing opportunities for people to take charge of transformation. It affirms that this is done by creating relationships that are ones that 'affirm what it means to be a human being' (Murray *et al.*, 2009: 8).

The implications for the schools in this book

Since we began writing, the ropes that kept the edifice of reform tied down tightly, that interpreted its requirements very literally in a constraining, prescriptive way, have relaxed a bit and lost some of their grip. Creative, open-ended thinking is more prevalent than when this project began. Primary schools have been the focus of two major reports (Rose, 2009; Alexander, 2010) which have followed on from the findings of the 1995 Primary Assessment, Curriculum and Experience (PACE) study. The *Independent Review of the Primary Curriculum* (Rose, 2009) provided a new framework for thinking about and designing the primary curriculum, and the Cambridge Primary Review (Alexander, 2010) is the most important review of primary education for over 40 years. Discussions about purpose, pedagogy and power are more likely to be happening now in school communities than they have for some time. However, a new political administration is about to revise the National Curriculum again and at the time of writing we are not sure what this will mean for schools.

Colleagues involved in this project discussed the impact on them of the requirement to make a continuous response to the policy context of the last two decades: the combined impact on their school of the National Curriculum, the Primary Strategy, end of key stage assessments, inspection, target setting, performance tables and a code of practice for special educational needs to name the main elements. They agreed that initially they have given them a form of 'provisional licence' to run a school and that this is not at all the same as the full licence they want or have to earn. They feel they only have a certain degree of independence but, like learning how to drive competently, running a school can only be done on the job. It involves understanding how to manage and respond to (not just lead) a complex, sometimes challenging, combination of different people's needs: the needs of their community, the learning of their pupils, the professional development needs of their staff and the organisational development processes and structures of their school. Attending to those aspects will help keep the provisional licence and turn it into a full one. They also agree that despite the loosening of the prescriptions, they still have to comply with external demands. They admit that the taking of the full licence for themselves has been a necessary part of their success and creativity. Seizing the opportunity to take full charge is the first step, the creating of the mindset, the taking of responsibility that enables adventurous practice to begin.

They were in agreement that one of the main benefits of the past 20 years has been better subject knowledge among primary teachers, particularly in subjects such as design technology. There has been useful exemplification in schemes of work and staff are better equipped to teach literacy and numeracy. Generally, standards and expectations have been raised as a result of these improvements. Planning that included learning outcomes, intentions and success criteria has helped to provide a structure for the curriculum, albeit a limited one. Much more is known about how to assess progress, using national standards for comparison. The Code of Practice has been very positive in driving and highlighting the inclusion agenda. *Excellence and Enjoyment* (DCSF, 2003) and the recent reviews of primary education gave permission for more creative and exploratory approaches.

The downside, they agreed, has not quite outweighed the benefits, but almost. Colleagues described the overwhelming amount that they have had to respond to. They have had to deal regularly with too much happening too quickly, that hasn't allowed for 'bedding in' or implementation time for the initiatives. It hasn't allowed time to respond fully to what was needed from the perspective of their school; it has taken time away from thinking about the whole. This has meant constantly being vigilant about fragmentation of effort and offer to the children. They are critical about staff training for central initiatives, which together with the materials to go with them have been too often of a poor quality. To make matters worse, they think, the pedagogy of the previous national training programme has created a dependency among staff rather than enabling them to think for themselves.

Even though creativity has been encouraged, inspection has and continues to have a restricting effect and to be intimidating. It has felt punitive and based on deficit rather than possibility. We have come to understand that becoming adventurous in a school is a way of both taking back control *and* giving children a central and active role in their own learning in more than name. This brings purpose, pedagogy and power together. Adventure is going from the known, normal and accepted ways of doing things; it is questioning the conventional and taking it further, out of the comfort zone of what is known. Adventure aims to explore and create new learning and new knowledge through a deliberate focus on novelty and experimentation. It is about questioning what is taken for granted and moving it on, recombining existing elements in new ways (Mulgan, 2007a).

The vision, values and practices described in the following pages are about enabling children not just to become scholars and philosophers but also to feel connected to and concerned for a world that needs them. These three schools are involved in the creation of cultures that are not weighed down by outdated or narrow ideas of what they are there to do and assumptions about schooling that no longer serve their students. Colleagues may not be explicit about the exact ways they are constructing different views of purpose, pedagogy and power. They would say themselves, they are in many ways only setting out on the adventure of fundamental change and shaking off the shackles of top-down control.

They are, however, quite clear that they are not developing scholars in the way that our medieval mind originally intended, set apart from daily life in a world of ideas and books alone. Rather, they want children to be the scholars of the street and park, who are learning in school in order to make sense of their world and their potential contribution, and philosophers who are questing after the truth that will serve rather than undermine their future.

Questions for discussion

- To what extent is the purpose of your school influenced by global issues and challenges that young people will face as they grow up?
- Do you need to update the pedagogy in your school to meet the challenges and opportunities of twenty-first century life?
- What models of power currently operate in your school and how might they need to change?

Note

1. The number of people on the planet reached seven billion in early November 2011.

Part 1

VISION

Reflections on the vision chapters

A vision is a long line of possibility radiating outwards. It invites infinite expression, development and proliferation within its definitional framework.

(Zander and Zander, 2000: 170)

The importance of vision to school improvement has often been noted (Stoll and Fink, 1996) but the development and use of a vision in a busy school can be a bit of a mystery or even a cliché. Too often it is just a statement at the start of policies and publicity, which is rarely referred to. How does it become an integral, all-encompassing part of day-to-day life, influencing all decisions and practices? During the writing of this book the schools involved have thought in depth about the vision that they hold for their schools and how it serves and influences their practice. We concluded that without having a deeper sense of purpose for our children in their lives, a vision would be a superficial self-serving waste of time. A vision gives meaning, character and momentum to a purpose that may otherwise remain hidden or not even expressed. It brings the call to adventure to life.

The first thing to emerge from our enquiry was the importance of having a vision to the success of an adventurous school. A vision, we have concluded, is the way the call to adventure is articulated. It is an important expression of how a school sees their role, of their particular commitment to every child, their learning and their community. It is the visible manifestation of their purpose. Sergiovanni (2005: 59) points out that: 'Effective visions obligate people who share them.'

We discussed how dealing with the pressures of external accountability, league tables and inspections has become the primary vision and purpose for many schools. Children have slipped, perhaps unintentionally, into the background rather than the foreground of the vision for their school. They are probably not very active either in helping to realise the vision or even know what it is.

A vision in an adventurous school, we concluded, seeks to define the school's aspirations for children. It highlights how, in order to become the best learners, children have an active relationship both to their world and to their life within it. It identifies for each school the role the education and learning they provide has in empowering children to create their own futures. It is a statement of beliefs and intent, a way of describing the identity of each school and what they stand for.

Zander and Zander (2000) describe a vision like the tonality of a group or orchestra: it sets the key in which the music of the learning adventure is played. As such, it creates a form of contract between school, the children and community to provide the best opportunities and experiences so pupils can grow, learn and find their sense of themselves and connect to their life path. In identifying and describing purpose in this way, the schools take the first step towards creating the future they are envisioning. In the process they are also describing the approach to pedagogy and power that support their vision.

Senge *et al.* (2000) note another reason for having a vision. They name the dual awareness in any purpose between where we want to be and where we are; this creates a tension between the current reality of a school and its envisioned future. Articulating a vision immediately highlights a dissonance between the two, creating an impetus to move towards the desired future. So the adventure lies in exploring and really knowing a school's aspirations and values. They help illuminate the gap between vision and current practice and catalyse movement into the new. Change becomes a more natural, inevitable consequence rather than a process of orders and instructions:

> This dual awareness – what you want and what you have – often creates a state of tension that, by its nature, seeks resolution. The most natural desired resolution of this tension is for your reality to move closer to what you want.
>
> (Senge *et al.*, 2000: 59)

A vision isn't just a dream either; it is a working philosophy, which provides purpose and direction for everyone's learning. It serves as a compass to determine the route for the adventure. Once any journey is embarked on, it is a way of recognising whether the path you are travelling on is the right one. It also provides the impetus for creating your own path into the future. So a vision holds and makes explicit the intentions for the school community, as they shed light on, fly above and grow their purpose.

Without shared purpose and direction any adventure is likely to be short lived or even an escape from engagement in the reality of the world. The schools involved in this enquiry have found that a strong vision has given them clarity and control, enabling them to take risks and make decisions for themselves. Their adventure has been in part about discovering where they want to go, but once identified, their vision has given them an empowering drive and determination based on the insight that the direction is right and they are moving forward with integrity.

Fink (2005: 27) points out: 'Perhaps a better way of thinking about a vision is to expand it to include voice because it involves dialogue and must be shared before it can be a call to joint action.' A vision will remain an expression of a dream and aspiration unless the whole school community owns it. More than that: the whole community must also hold it and breathe life into it. It has to become the ground that everybody walks and acts on and must therefore reflect the needs of each school's particular community. Through their actions together, the development of their shared purpose, the community begins to join in with co-constructing the reality of the vision.

Visions are challenging to realise, if indeed they can ever be fully realised. They are always changing and shifting as the organisation grows and responds to its call to adventure. The interpretation of a vision changes as the collective understanding of what it looks like in practice and its possibilities evolve, the purpose comes to life. To facilitate this, the curriculum provides the learning opportunities that embody and realise the values and skills that each school cherishes. The vision will manifest in the curriculum and children will draw on it to forge their own paths.

Each of the schools whose story is told in this book has been working on its vision for about ten years, constantly revising, reviewing and building on it. They have continued to make sense of what it means for their daily life and the implications that emerging insights have for the lives of their children. They have taken the images of growth, flying and illumination to embody and try to epitomise their primary purpose. The journey to understand their vision has been as much a part of the adventure as the actual realising of it. As Wheatley and Kellner-Rogers (1999: 56) put it: 'Every self is visionary. It wants to create a world where it can thrive. So it is with organizations ... At the heart of every organization is a self-reaching out to new possibilities.'

So a vision enables a school to identify, crystallise and express its potential and purpose. In Figure P1.1 you can see the way in which the purpose and vision are in continual relationship with each other, nourishing the values, entitlements and experiences. The adventure is setting out on a journey to bring the vision to life; and bring life to the vision; it's an exploration with the children and their families of the power and pedagogy needed for their purpose. This is the journey that each school describes in the following three chapters of Part 1.

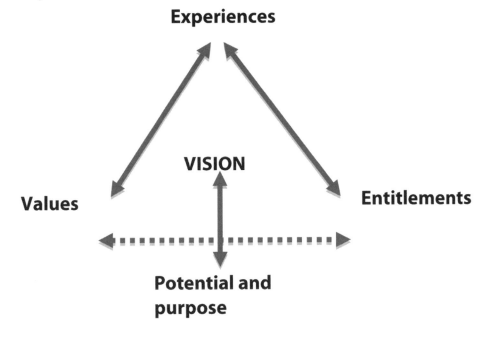

Figure P1.1: The central elements of a vision in an adventurous school

Chapter 2

Let them fly: Limeside Primary School

He who would learn to fly one day must first learn to stand and walk and run and climb and dance; one cannot fly into flying.

(Nietzsche, 1885)

Introduction

What greater adventure can there be than to take off and fly? Flying opens up the world. It can take you anywhere. Flying to ever more distant heights and places has long been a dream for humanity. Our ultimate aim at Limeside is for our children to develop the skills, confidence and independence to fly within and beyond their immediate world. Although flying can be enjoyable in its own right, we also want children to fly with purpose so that they can recognise the elements of the world that are worthy of admiration and those that need improving. Essentially the purpose of our school is that the life journeys and adventures of our pupils will contribute in some way to making the world better. This is a long-term dream but our vision helps us to understand how we might contribute to this, what it might look like in practice and what kind of skills, attitudes, beliefs and values this might entail.

Limeside is a one-form entry primary school, situated in the middle of a predominantly white British housing estate, with high levels of social and economic deprivation. The school is a large red-brick 1930s building, sandwiched between rows of terraced housing. In 2000 the Office for Standards in Education, Children's Services and Skills (Ofsted) put the school into special measures for two years. During that time achievement and behaviour started to improve. The children developed a growing sense of pride in their school and themselves. Our vision needed to build on these initial shoots of pride. The Limeside vision had to be very personal to the area and the school itself. Understanding exactly what our vision entailed was an adventure in itself, an adventure that never ends as new experiences constantly create different insights into what is important for our children and our community. Realising our vision is a further, never-ending adventure.

In this chapter we present the journey of our vision development so far. It began with an exploration into what we really believed was important for our school and increasingly (as our understanding of the school's role in the community grew) our community. Doing this created a feeling of excitement and energy. It helped us create a clear sense of our purpose and map values and behaviours that would determine the opportunities that we would provide for children. From there we created a multisensory vision statement exploring what these might look like in practice. The rest of the chapter examines some of the methods we used to make this happen and to ensure our values remain prominent in daily school life.

What is flying?

One of the school's guiding principles is the belief that anything is possible. However, the possible will not just happen. To achieve it takes personal effort, active involvement, determination and self-belief. Limeside's vision has to help children and adults adopt such an enabling, empowering can-do and will-do culture. They need to believe that they can influence their future and take responsibility for doing so.

However, when it came out of special measures, the school was still very much a place where education was done to the children. It was a passive process. As long as children attended and did as they were told, they were being educated. It was probably a comment by an Ofsted inspector in the follow-up inspection 18 months after the school was removed from special measures that had the most impact on our values. She explained that we were holding the children too tightly. We needed to give them more independence and trust them. In short we needed 'to let them fly'.

This was a great starting point. Flying became synonymous with taking control. It was about playing a role in deciding the speed, direction and destination of learning. It also implied an element of freedom but mutual responsibility. Just as geese take it in turns to lead a V formation, we understood that different people, children included, must sometimes take the lead, but each goose is important no matter where in the formation they fly. In the same way as geese support each other in reaching their destination, children should also help and encourage each other.

Flying is also a very active process. Our flyers were not going to be passengers in an aircraft built and controlled by others. Instead they needed to take it in turns to pilot the plane and crew it. It was a doing process. It involved energy, efficacy and involvement. Being active was also imbued with a sense of responsibility. A crew works more effectively if everyone plays their part. It also required courage to step away from the more commonplace models and practices but it was exciting. The Limeside crew was going to be instrumental in building their future and deciding how it would look.

Our vision is based on what flying might look like in many different spheres: academically, socially, artistically, spiritually and emotionally. It encompasses the whole community because children cannot fly in isolation. They need others to support and believe in them. Perhaps one of the most exciting things about our vision lies here. What began as a dream for children has evolved into a dream for the community as a whole. It has had knock-on effects on the wider community, staff, governors, parents and local residents. As children have achieved more, the social capital and the expectations of the community have also seemed to increase. They too seem to fly. At the same time, we have learnt more about the specifics of our community, deepening our understanding of what is particularly important for our school, our children and our citizens.

Capturing our vision

- What is important for *our* children now and in the future?
- What do *our* children, *our* community and ultimately *our* world need?

We began with a reflection based around these questions. After much spirited and heartfelt dialogue the following main principles emerged.

Our children play an active role in their own learning

Initial attempts to introduce greater responsibility through Assessment for Learning practices were paying dividends. We could see that our children were capable of evaluating and determining their learning paths and deserved more. We want them to imbue their learning with energy, interest and passion. We want them to take responsibility for themselves and others, to understand themselves and others as learners and thus become more effective and critical in their learning adventures.

Our children play an active role in and with their local community

Community can be understood at a variety of levels. Within the school, children need to be involved in decision making, taking responsibility and contributing ideas. However, the skills they develop must not stop at the school gates. We need our children to take them out into their family lives and community. We hope that they will care enough to get involved. Perhaps this element of our vision is best encapsulated by Emily (Year 6), who took herself to speak at the tenants and residents meeting one evening because she 'needed' to give her views about the development of the local park.

Limeside lies at the heart of a predominantly white area in a town of largely racially segregated communities. Opportunities to meet and understand people from other cultures are therefore vital; we want our children to become active ambassadors for their own and other cultures. Our children need to fly alongside people whom they have traditionally viewed as different. Meeting people and exploring ideas and customs from different areas and traditions is a vital part of the adventure we want to have.

Our children play an active role in their future

Living in Limeside could easily be very insular. All the services people need are on their doorstep. We want children to see and aspire to all the possibilities that the modern world offers. We want to equip them with the confidence and self-belief to decide what they want to achieve and go for it. We want them to understand that learning is the key that opens the door to wider future possibilities.

We are also aware that our children are unique individuals, filled with potential to develop in many different ways. Enabling children to actively create and play a role in their own future must acknowledge and build on their different strengths, interests and enthusiasms. It involves valuing diversity and difference. In a community with strong traditions it can take courage to choose to differ from the norm. To play an active role in the future also depends on having physical, mental and spiritual strength, something to draw on when faced with challenges. These all needed to be aspects of our vision.

Our children play an active role in the future of the world

Our children are not only instrumental in creating their own future but also in creating the future of the planet. This includes both the human-made and the natural world and understanding the relationship between them. It embraces the somewhat clichéd but nevertheless true ideal of making the world a better place. The contribution our children make can be big or small but our ultimate wish is that they do something. Just as we aim for them to care enough to get involved in their community, our vision centres on our children taking responsibility and action in the wider world now and in the future. We aim that they will care enough, feel empowered and skilled enough to respond to threats and injustices to people and to nature.

Once we had identified the core purpose of our school, we set about listing the values, attitudes and dispositions that underpin the above principles. What elements would be important if we were to realise these statements? A whole professional learning day was dedicated to exploring these values, generating our vision and clarifying our purpose. All staff and any governors available were invited. We drew pictures of our ideals, described dreams and gave voice to passions and convictions. There was a buzz of excitement, as though restating our purpose reconnected people to the feelings that had drawn them into teaching in the first place. The list was long and brought many deep beliefs to the surface again.

During the years of National Curriculum and national strategies very little time seemed to have been spent in dialogue about the purpose of education. As a teaching profession, it was easy to slip into a pattern of compliance as different government directives were issued. Much time was dedicated to new strategies and national initiatives, with their focus on a narrow view of attainment. Little time was spared for examining the wider role of schools in developing the next generation and the skills and mindsets they would need. Now it felt like we as a staff were becoming more active and reclaiming our school, and the direction it would take. In framing our vision we were beginning to actively set the course for our own Limeside adventure. As a team of staff and governors, we were beginning to fly.

Some of the values, attitudes and dispositions we initially identified:

independence, questioning, love of learning, creativity, self-esteem, happiness, health, key skills, motivation, respect, caring communication, pride, passion, love of nature, experiences, close relationships, never giving up, enthusiasm, empathy, adaptability, tolerance, curiosity, resilience, own interests, interdependence, confidence, practical skills, self-belief, ability to solve problems, compassion

---

Grounding our vision

The words in our vision and values were emotive but in many ways they were still abstract. We needed to ground them in our daily life. We needed an image of what they would look like in action. What would we see, hear and feel if our ideals were in place? Together we took an imaginary journey through our ideal future. What would we see, what would we hear, what would we sense and feel if we were to wander through Limeside Primary as it incorporated and realised all these values? The multisensory picture we formulated became our vision statement (see below). It incorporated the elements suggested by the whole team. It was solution focused, based on the best future we as a team could imagine. It provided us with a clear understanding of the sorts of learning opportunities we would need to offer. We gave it high prominence. It is displayed on the back of school folders and we employed a professional graphic designer to create posters to display throughout the school.

Limeside's Vision Statement

Imagine a stimulating place ringing with the sound of laughter. See confident, reflective and playful learners, filled with their own sense of purpose and self-belief. Watch as they enjoy the challenge of new experiences, pose questions and solve problems. Listen in, as they discuss the skills they are using and plan what they need to do next.

Admire the high levels of academic, sporting and artistic achievement, as everyone strives to be the best that they can. Notice how the needs, interests and talents of all are valued and supported. Join us in celebrating success at every level, as all learners discover and develop their own passions, potential and individuality.

Prepare to take some risks as you take part in the creative breadth of exciting curriculum experiences. Hear the buzz of enthusiastic talk, generated by people of all ages learning from each other. See how learning extends beyond the school gates, to embrace the outdoors and wider community. Acknowledge, in particular, how learners draw appropriately on abundant ICT [information and communication technology] to enhance their achievements.

Enjoy the security and the harmony of a group of people who nurture and care for each other. Sense their respect for people from different backgrounds and cultures, for society and for the natural world.

Notice the exemplary behaviour, as learners assume responsibility for making choices and consider how their actions affect others. Watch as they are empowered to rise to any challenges in the future.

Sense everyone's pride in themselves, each other and their school.

This is **Limeside Primary School**, a place where everyone **SHINEs** with possibility.

Realising our vision

Writing our vision was the easy part; the next part of the adventure was realising it and making it part of everyday life. There were initially two vital elements in making our vision come to life for the whole school community, particularly children and parents. The first is the concept of the 'wizard learner' who embodies the skills, attitudes and dispositions for learning, and the second is the distillation of key social elements into our version of a mission statement: SHINE.

Wizards and wizardry

Our learning wizard embodies the idea that learning is active, special, magical, powerful and fun – an adventure in itself. Throughout history, scholarship and wizardry have been closely linked. Magic, science and the quest for knowledge have been entwined with each other. Goethe's Faust, a scholar and magician, sold his soul in return for the opportunity to learn about the mysteries of the universe. Tolkien's Gandalf was a wizard, who despite his powers and wisdom still had to research and learn from experience in order to understand how to destroy the one ring. More recently, Harry Potter is on a continual quest to master his wizardry and to develop and draw on his skills to aid him in his adventures. Of course wizards also have the skills and knowledge to fly with confidence and direction.

As they walk through the school doors, the first thing any visitor meets is the Limeside wizard learner. He is an expert learner, who knows and practises everything there is to know about learning. He is master of learning skills such as: risk taking, asking relevant questions, taking responsibility, learning from mistakes, persevering even when it seems challenging. He embodies the learning ethos of the school.

Each week, Celebration Assembly starts by the head teacher announcing this week's wizard, someone who has done something special to promote their learning. They sit on the stage, dressed in a cape and hat. This is a high prestige award, which commands utmost respect. Even the toughest Year 6 boy is eager to don the wizard robes. Their photograph is displayed in the entrance hall alongside a certificate detailing exactly why they have been awarded the title of wizard. It has increased the level of discussion about learning throughout the school community. Children report back to their parents about who the wizard was. Parents tell the head teacher about the learning children have been doing at home. Staff report examples of significant learning to the head teacher so one of their class receives the award.

This award also illustrates the idea of learning for all. Staff have also been crowned the learning wizard, in recognition of significant learning experiences for them. For example one teacher managed to learn to play a short tune on a clarinet. Another exemplified the idea that learning involves taking significant risks when he did a charity parachute jump. In our annual Presentation Evening the highest achieving children are dressed in wizard gowns and hats to receive their awards from the mayor and receive graduation-type photographs to mark the occasion.

Wizardry is not just confined to formal gatherings. Each class was equipped with wizard puppets and cloaks so that children can use them to reflect on their learning at the end of lessons. The focus of plenaries changed from what we learnt to how we learnt. They became more evaluative, focusing on areas for improvement and ways forward. At a recent visioning day for governors and friends of the school, we traced the path of the school through time. One former pupil, who is now a parent governor, commented that the black formal teacher gowns they associated with the past regime have now been replaced by purple cloaks and pointed wizard hats. Indeed it is not unusual now to catch a glimpse of a purple-clad child walking down the corridor, on their way to show someone else examples of their learning or indeed to teach someone else what they have learnt. However, the idea of learning wizardry did not just stop with the pupils and staff. Parents have bought into the wizard concept. They join the Celebration Assembly acknowledging with us the different aspects of learning that are recognised.

Over the past few years, there has been a change of attitude among parents that has spread into the wider community. As our vision has opened new ways of thinking and possibilities to them, they have developed the 'language' and concepts to enable them to think differently. As the children have gone home using key ideas and phrases from the vision, these have spread to their parents. For example parents now endorse the notion of a wizard learner and recognise the qualities he embodies.

The following responses are from parents in response to the question: 'How do you think the learning wizard helps your children?'

'It teaches them to work hard and when you find something hard, try harder. You have to keep trying when things go wrong. Ask questions, help others.'

'It makes them be proud of themselves for learning. It helps him talk about what he is doing and learning and think and say what he needs to do next.'

'It makes them keep trying and pushes the children to learn new and harder things. If they make mistakes, they learn from them. It gives them goals and helps them want to achieve.'

'When a child has got the wizard learner, they are buzzing and it makes them want to do it again.'

Shine

The second main way we convey our values is through our own version of a mission statement 'SHINE':

S *ocially responsible*

H *igh achievers*

I *ndependent*

N *urtured*

E *mpowered to meet life's challenges*

Again, this is given a high profile. A weekly SHINE award is presented at the Celebration Assembly to someone who has embodied some of these qualities. They too have a special chair on the stage. Photographs of all the SHINE children are displayed on a special board and children wear various colours of SHINE badges with pride. Everyone sees shining as an integral part of their school. It is something they are proud of and often compliment each other on.

Katie (Year 4) sums up their feelings and the central role of SHINE in a piece of unsolicited home reflection.

How to be a SHINE

Try your best about everything. If you're finding it hard then find a place where you're sensible and follow others. Get teachers' attention with your beautiful actions, ideas and questions. Remember that you are responsible. Be kind and look after others. Then you might find yourself to be a SHINE. It might take everything but it really is worth it being on the stage in front of all your grandparents, mums and dads, anyone. You have a photo and a badge and you get your name on a newsletter.

Popularising the vision

Almost without realising it, every school develops their own particular catchphrases. At Limeside we have consciously adopted ideas that exemplify our values into school-wide sayings. Phrases from favourite stories and songs are built into our everyday language. For instance the children cite 'Learn and you will teach, Teach and you will learn' from Disney's 'Son of Man' song, when they help each other. These sayings have become our 'guiding ideas' (Senge *et al.*, 2000: 26), and by constantly articulating them we are building the culture of our school. In this way, values such as risk taking and learning from mistakes have become established norms for everyone in the school and are truly embedded. They make elements of our vision audible and tangible in our everyday discourse.

Year 4 children produced the following glossary of Limeside's sayings.

Limeside glossary

Be a radiator – Be friendly, cheerful, honest, funny and make other people happy, look for the best in everything, laugh lots.

Turn a corner – I used to be naughty in Year 2 but I turned a corner and now I am good. It means keep learning and trying and never give up. Every piece of learning you do you turn a corner. You learn from your mistakes and copy other people's good behaviour.

Don't be a passenger – Means don't just sit there, be a learner, and that's called a driver. Take part in everything you do.

Fly – You are up and away and doing your learning because your learning is powerful. You fly when you do something hard. Be confident for yourself. Take a risk. If you are a bit wobbly about something, just start and have a go. Never stop trying.

Reach for the stars – Aim high in everything: your behaviour, your learning, being helpful, being confident and being truthful. We reach for the stars because we are stars and we shine like the sun.

Growing your own – Grow your own learning, confidence, friends and grow other people's learning, confidence and friends and making our community safe and better.

Believe in yourself – Know that you can do it even if other people say you can't. Like when my dad said drama is for girls but I do it because I know I am good at it.

Go the extra mile – Don't just do what your teacher tells you, follow what you are doing as far as you can because it's good to learn new things and it is the way to get to your dreams.

Put your bricks in the wall – Building up your learning is like you are building a house and sometimes you have to put the bottom bricks down first and it is hard to understand if you are missing a brick.

What if we could all be wizards? What if we could all SHINE?

These guiding phrases have been instrumental in school but have also served to spread our values and belief in the school and its community into the wider area. Working with the local housing association, we published a book entitled *What If ...?* (Contour Housing Group and Limeside Primary School, 2007). Each page is headed by one of our guiding ideas and contains art and written responses that were generated by the school, community members, local residents and nearby business people. It was our first truly collaborative undertaking with the community. Both school and housing association were equal partners. It gave us a true chance to create shared values with other people working in the community, to explain what was important for us and to see how it related to what was important to others. More importantly, however, is the way this is helping to take our vision beyond the school gates and how people not initially connected with the school are becoming part of it.

Trying to realise the vision by working on projects like the *What If ...?* book has brought the immediate school community into close contact with representatives from the wider community such as housing and regeneration officers. Through this we have come to recognise common interdependent aims, values and visions. For example we share aspirations for developing better community agency and inter-community understanding. This has helped us work collaboratively with them (see Chapter 5).

Many leadership courses stress the need for a shared vision to promote school improvement, often meaning little more than the head teacher sharing his or her ideals and other people signing up to them. Our vision is truly shared because it is the product of many minds and values and has brought people together to share their understanding of what these mean in practice.

> *The game plays the game; the poem writes the poem; we can't tell the dancer from the dance.*
>
> *Less and less do you need to force things,*
>
> *Until finally you arrive at non-action.*
>
> *When nothing is done*
>
> *Nothing is left undone.*
>
> (Mitchell, 1988: viii)

Our vision has become an integral part of everything we do in school and provides the map and justification for all we embark on. Most interesting perhaps is the way that our collective understanding of what our vision actually means in practice is constantly deepening and making us even more aware of our purpose. While we are continually evolving in line with our ideal world, our concept of what this looks like is always shifting. As we live out experiences consistent with our vision, our insight and our ambition grows. Our dreams become greater and more becomes possible. For instance, after a day of thinking and dialogue around the area of personalisation, the Senior Leadership Team (SLT) emerged with a much deeper understanding of what '*Join us in celebrating success at every level as learners discover and develop their own passions, potential and individuality*' could look like. We planned to create 'goal-den' time (to replace Golden Time) during which children would have an opportunity to work on an extended project, in mixed age groups, focused around different types of activities such as art, drama, music, writing, dance, etc. Thus children and staff would have opportunities to follow their interests and passions collaboratively in greater depth than is often possible.

Living and deepening our vision – some examples

Every new academic year used to begin with the reading of the vision. Now we go one step further and live it as a way of deepening our understanding of a particular aspect of the vision. Initially we focused on exploring experiential, creative and spiritual learning. Staff, and those governors and representatives from the housing association who could join us, were told to turn up with waterproofs and wellies; otherwise what was about to happen was a surprise. A short mystery coach ride took us all to Alderley Edge, a wood associated with wizards. Legends suggest that King Arthur and his band of knights sleep under this wood, awaiting a call to rescue England when necessary.

The coach stopped at the Wizard Walk, where coffee and pastries were served. A short walk took us to the 'Grounding' at the Druid's Circle, a circle of about 20 large boulders. Sat on the stones, we read our vision and enquired into what spirituality and finding our place in the world meant to us. The rest of the day was given over to groups developing a presentation about their spiritual responses. These were shared in the 'mixing pot of enlightenment'. For example one group chose an oak tree with clearly defined roots to visually represent life's journey. The oak tree symbolised the ultimate goal of self-fulfilment, realisation and belief. People were asked to place themselves physically as to where they felt they were at that present moment. After a time of reflection they then had the opportunity to move further towards the oak tree – and they did. There had been a shift in self-realisation.

Classes later experienced the same adventure. Year 2, for example, dressed as wizards and tracked down a secret wizard's well in Alderley Edge. They listened to and told stories in the wood and planted their own magic seeds, making a wish for the world as they did so.

The following year the first staff development day involved another magical mystery tour. This time the coach stopped at a small, rural opera house, where a composer and recording technician were waiting to help staff compose, sing and record the lyrics and tune of a song to express the

---

'The world is ours to conquer,
The future's in our hands,
The world is ours to conquer
Across all different lands.

Help us fly, help us find our wings,
No matter where we go
No matter what life brings...'

The hall rings out with children's voices singing proudly. A composer pounds out the music at the piano. A journalist photographs the occasion. This is the first public airing of 'Wings', the Limeside song, written by the staff as a gift to the children and now a firm favourite in the school's repertoire of music.

Limeside values and vision. As with all adventurers, our adult team was initially apprehensive but experienced many of the elements and values we aim to promote in our children during that day. We find that revisiting our purpose and values together in an unusual context gives a greater insight into the steps we need to take in the joint adventure of moving into the ever-changing reality of our vision.

How do others contribute to our vision?

It is hard to identify exactly how others contribute to our vision, as ideas and understanding seem to grow naturally. As people become involved in the school they seem to grow it organically and become part of it. For instance an enterprise consultant, used to the hard reality of setting up small businesses, has become a key player in realising the role enterprise needs to play in enabling children to fly. It seems that the values and aims resonate with others and they too become excited and caught up in the adventure.

We have a few formal structures that promote the values and aims of our vision. We use questionnaires to canvass children's and parents' views and a school council. The children complete a learning treasure hunt with their parents and give their opinion on how they might want to change elements of school life. Each context for learning provides opportunities for the children to steer the direction of learning by suggesting the questions they would like to investigate (see Chapter 8).

> Please can the school council book the conference room next Tuesday playtime? We need to discuss our ideas for having a friendship week.
>
> Also we've had an idea for the play. We don't want to do anything little like *Cinderella* last year. We think we should aim for the sky and do *Phantom of the Opera*.
>
> Paul (Year 6), school council member

Much of the development seems to happen informally and to come from the children or to arise from small opportunities or ideas that might previously have been laughed off as zany. Possibly the biggest adventure for Limeside has been in being prepared to take risks in order to follow these up. The centrality of our vision helps us identify the right direction in which to fly. However, the adventure lies in not knowing exactly where we will land.

Next steps

Given that our ultimate aim is for children to fly in order to be able to actively change the world for the better, what kind of values and qualities would they need in order to do this? At the time of writing we are moving increasingly to developing a values-based education. The topics we are choosing to support learning must earn their place according to the contribution they can make to exploring somewhat abstract concepts. While our vision statement serves us well, it is largely predicated on a skills-based approach to learning and growth. Values and beliefs are part of our vision but are somewhat implicit. We now need to give them an added emphasis and priority. How we can do this and give them higher prominence in the school is our next challenge.

Currently we are beginning to identify six manifestations of our values (almost like avatars or Philip Pullman's daemons). Each persona will embody a set of values, attitudes and beliefs. The personae are adventurer/ entrepreneur, carer, spirit, citizen, creator and wizard/achiever. We hope the idea of connecting with different manifestations of their belief system will help children identify and develop the associated values and give them a higher prominence when designing learning opportunities. Certainly, as we are implementing our new curriculum, we are consciously designing opportunities for the whole school to explore values through philosophy, assemblies and inherently by the topics chosen.

Our vision statement is also largely centred locally. Starting with our immediate area was important but now we need to become more global in our wishes, actions and aspirations. Our wish is for children to play an active role in the future of the world; to make this happen we need to embark on more global projects. Again this awareness is feeding into our new curriculum planning:

> *Hear the buzz of enthusiastic talk, generated by people of all ages learning from each other. See how learning extends beyond the school gates, to embrace the outdoors and wider community.*
> Limeside Primary School Vision statement (see above)

A final principle for our vision has also emerged through our growing understanding and partnership with the local community. We have come to an understanding that it is not just our children who must play an active role with and in the community but also the school as a whole. In working actively with partners in the community, we can do our bit towards improving the world locally. In fact we are expanding our vision to see the school as a social enterprise. Here lies the greatest challenge and the greatest possibility. At the time of writing, we are stood at a threshold relating to the school's future. The local authority is facing severe cutbacks, the services we have up to now taken for granted will have to be re-sourced or at the very least traded. The school is now facing more independence and with this comes the potential to become yet more central to the community – an ideal that we explore further in Chapter 5. In many ways it feels like our vision is just taking off or as our *What If …?* book ponders: What if this was just the beginning?

Conclusion

A favourite anonymous quotation compares a vision to seeing the masterpiece before even mixing the colours. The Limeside masterpiece would be an active, responsible member of society who contributes to the future world. However, this is a long-term and abstract dream. Our vision also has to identify the colours, or the skills, the attitudes and the values that need mixing, particularly in relation to our own community. The colours we select and the way we choose to mix them is what gives Limeside and each school its individuality. Determining these colours empowers us to respond creatively with integrity to new ideas, whether they are government directives, children's suggestions or unforeseen opportunities. Being clear and blatant about our vision and values helps us to be confident and effective about the direction we should take. It helps us determine the opportunities we should provide and gives us the rationale and justification for why we act as we do. However, it is hard to mix colours without suitable tools. Part of the success of our visioning has been in developing the methods to make it happen daily and to keep the colours visible and prominent in everyday life.

In the course of writing this book, it has become increasingly clear that our vision is not a constant. Our understanding of what it entails is always evolving. Limeside's vision has grown in scope as we have become more certain of our purpose and confident and active as a school. It seems to have developed through time from a focus on the local child in their immediate setting to an aspiration for them to become citizens of the globe. It has expanded to encompass the school as playing an active role within the local and potentially global community. Perhaps this is an indication that we have truly started to fly. After all, throw a stone and you can predict with some confidence where it will land: *let them fly* and people have the freedom to determine their own place to land.

Chapter 3

Creating a learning community where everyone can thrive: Malorees Infant School

One way or another, we all have to find what best fosters the flowering of our humanity in this contemporary life, and dedicate ourselves to that.

(Campbell *et al.*, 1988)

Introduction

An infant school stands at just the beginning of the educational adventure but it is in these first few years that we nourish the roots that will enable our children to flower and flourish throughout their lives.

In this chapter we describe how we moved away from the more traditional view of education as a race to get ahead (with winners and losers) and began to see it more as an adventure that explores and develops children as people, their ideas, learning potential and understanding of the wider world. We examine how we began to take more responsibility for our own direction, building a school with its own individual identity that tries to nurture and inspire our children and help each and every one of them to thrive. We describe how we developed the 'vision jigsaw' to encapsulate what our values would look like in practice and help us to plot learning opportunities that would promote our vision.

Malorees Infant School is a two-form entry infant school near Kilburn in Brent, North West London, which is one of the most multicultural boroughs in the country. We share a site with our neighbouring junior school, to which most of our children transfer at the end of Year 2. Almost all walks of life are represented in our intake and we are proud of the inclusive and diverse nature of our school. Although we are an inner-city school we are privileged to be situated within attractive, spacious grounds, surrounded by beautiful trees.

The majority of Malorees Infant School's parents report in questionnaires and at parent–teacher meetings that their children love school. As a first school this positive attitude is the crucial foundation for everything that follows. Without it there is little hope of our children gaining their entitlement to a future filled with possibility. Our community is very varied, socially, academically and ethnically, so it is particularly important that all of our families have the same expectation of exciting and unlimited potential for our children and that this is clearly stated in our vision. We don't think any less of a slower growing plant, knowing that in good time it too will blossom. Equally some of our children are not ready yet to excel in terms of national academic benchmarks but that doesn't mean that, given the right start, they won't in the future or that they can't shine now in terms of social and emotional development, creativity and attitudes to learning. To promote these we have been developing a vision based on thinking and social skills, a more creative curriculum, a growing emphasis on outdoor learning, and closer links with our families and community.

By the late 1990s Malorees Infant School was already a successful, popular, north inner-London school at the top end of the local league tables. However, the National Curriculum years and latterly Literacy and Numeracy Strategies had taken their toll and the curriculum, based around the strategies and the Qualifications and Curriculum Authority (QCA) schemes of work, was not always the nourishment that fosters the growth we were looking for. Looking back, teachers had increasingly lost the ownership to interpret the curriculum in the way that they felt best served the children. For some time, however, there has been a strong emphasis in the school on the creative arts delivered in a welcoming, inclusive and diverse community with very supportive parents and carers.

> One looks back with appreciation to the brilliant teachers, but with gratitude to those who touched our human feelings. The curriculum is so much necessary raw material, but warmth is the vital element for the growing plant and for the soul of the child.
>
> (Jung, 1954)

At Malorees Infant School our vision is centrally about creating a safe, nurturing environment in which all children are happy, motivated, confident and successful. Our goal is to bring this about in reality so that it is not just an aspiration. We know that children learn best when they enjoy learning through an inspiring curriculum. We want to lay a foundation of positive attitudes and experiences that our children can make use of and build on throughout their future lives.

Our core beliefs can be expressed through the image of a seed that is planted and nurtured in rich soil, well watered and fed with enriching compost in a warm garden. When it is planted out in the woods it is ready and strong enough to survive on its own and grow and flourish. What will it grow into? The possibilities are limitless and the choice is theirs.	
	Drawing by a Year 2 child

The learning journey at Malorees

Change during recent years at Malorees evolved organically through development on three different fronts: promoting a vision and values-led culture; learning that has the children as its focus; and developing the outdoor learning environment of the school. The momentum of progress in one area helped to increase confidence in another and led to the most important transformation of all, that of taking responsibility for our own direction rather than sticking rigidly to a path imposed by others.

A values-led culture

At this point our vision was still implicit but there was a clear consensus of shared aims and values. We knew we were aiming to nurture children who were emotionally resilient and confident in the ownership of their own learning. We were aiming to grow an abundant garden full of a multitude of different plants, so we would need to promote above all a celebration of our differences as well as understanding, tolerance, co-operation and collaboration, which would support each other's growth and opportunities for individuality. This started by developing an understanding of the importance of emotional literacy for ourselves as well as the children through a focus on learning, circle times and systems for positive behaviour management. Personal, social, and health education (PSHE) started to be taught more rigorously, with emotions and relationships discussed and explored with the children. Rules, rewards and sanctions were made much more consistent across the school and were also made explicit to the children in the expectation that they would feel more responsible and in control.

Partly as a result of a change of leadership, decision making became more collegiate and transparent with a strong emphasis on shared responsibility to support the school ethos. Professional development became increasingly led by the needs of staff and children. We gradually began to reclaim the confidence to make decisions for ourselves and put the child and learning back at the centre.

A focus on learning

Another impetus for change came from 'Improvement in Action', a project led by the International Network for School Improvement (INSI) at the Institute of Education, London, in which local authorities led groups of schools in developing action research projects in their schools to investigate and develop children's learning. Altogether six members of staff have attended the Brent-led year-long course, and our head teacher co-ran the course for two years. The project, entitled locally 'The Learning Project', engaged with a range of current ideas promoting a learning rather than a teaching or performance model of school improvement. A key process in the project is to listen to children's own views and insights into their learning. This is underpinned by a view that the child should be viewed as much of an expert about their learning as the teacher, if not more so.

This led to a culture being created in the school where learning itself is frequently discussed with the children, one example being the use of class 'learning logs' in which children can log their learning on a daily basis. One of the research projects we ran was a term-long art experiment in collaborative paired learning, pairing a Year 2 class with a Year 1 class and observing the effects on children with low self-esteem and difficulties engaging with their learning. Our observations were accompanied by the children's own voices that were noted in comments and questionnaires. The Learning Project has been pivotal in bringing about a deeper reflection on the aims and purposes of the school and in reminding us of the visions we had when we first became teachers.

Learning to grow – the outdoor environment

We also felt it important to be explicit about how much we value everyone in our school and one way to demonstrate this has been to create an increasingly attractive and stimulating physical environment. Although the school is situated in spacious and attractive grounds, we felt that these resources were underdeveloped and underused and we wanted to maximise and enrich learning opportunities to include outdoor learning more extensively. Partly this was due to an understanding of the physicality of young children and an awareness of the health and emotional benefits of being outdoors, particularly for some of our children who live very urban, indoor lives dominated by technology. Partly it was due to an imperative we had to stimulate the children's interest in nature and the environment with the purpose of inspiring them to focus on sustainable futures for the planet and how they are going to contribute to that goal.

Our focus on the outdoors was a big step on the adventure for our school and for our vision, a major undertaking that involved participation from children, staff, parents and governors. It began back in 1999 and took a period of five years to achieve, though it is still ongoing. One of our starting points involved clearing and redesigning a very overgrown orchard area that couldn't be used as it was overrun with cow parsley and brambles with no pathways. A group of parents, including a local park keeper, were galvanised to hack back the undergrowth, lay bark chip paths, create an amphitheatre with a circle of tree trunks and dig a pond for frogs and water snails. Over time they turned it into a beautiful, tranquil place for exploring nature, which has continued to be developed and cherished in recent years.

Ahmed and Haseeb are in their element in the orchard, searching for tiny creatures, absorbed and focused, sharing their findings with anyone and everyone. Nothing else fascinates them to the same extent; they struggle to concentrate in the classroom, but their passion for nature builds their self-esteem and creates a launch pad for the first small shoots of a love of learning.

We also refurbished the playground area to create varied and stimulating opportunities for learning and play, adding secluded seating, role-play areas, climbing frames, a stage and planting. Each classroom now has an outdoor area semi-partitioned from the playground to enable groups to undertake class learning activities outdoors. The outdoor area for the reception classes is an integral part of their classrooms now and they run a free-flow system without a morning break. This is to enable the children to have uninterrupted learning opportunities indoors and outdoors.

At the time of writing, an underused space is being transformed into a sensory garden to further extend opportunities for the children with inbuilt musical instruments, a willow den and a stage area. The intention is to incorporate children's artwork, possibly ceramics, and create a quiet and reflective space for them to explore and enjoy.

Taking the lead

However, the most fundamental and far-reaching change was a change in the attitude of the Senior Leadership Team. We began to look at plotting our own course, exploring possibilities within the overall map of initiatives laid down at that time by local and central government. If our school was designing an adventure rather than a race, it was up to us to take responsibility for packing our rucksacks and choosing our directions and making that explicit in our vision. This sense of ownership was further inspired by our enquiries with colleagues from Limeside and St Vigor and St John described in this book. Having time away from school to discuss and reflect on the 'bigger picture' is a luxury for practitioners; it is vital for a re-think of fundamental aims and purposes.

When we joined the project that led to this book, excellent practice was occurring in the school. New ideas were being trialled in classrooms, professional development was organised based on Assessment for Learning creativity and thinking skills, resources were being acquired to develop a more hands-on curriculum, medium-term planning was being updated to be more cross-curricular and relevant to the interests of the children, and an increasingly positive ethos was being developed. However, development was still rather fragmented and not all staff had a clear idea of what others were doing or where the school was really headed. Our aims and purposes, although documented, were not sufficiently explicit and accessible to all. We needed to work together to create a clearer vision.

The vision jigsaw

A day was set aside as we joined this project, late in 2006, to involve all staff, including support staff, in trying to come to a new consensus about the aims and purposes of our school as a place that provides effective early education. It was important to try to map out what we were aiming for and how all the developments taking place in the school fitted together in the pursuit of that goal. The day was very useful and resulted in the 'vision jigsaw'. Staff 'mind showered' what they felt was important for our particular school and ideas were grouped and phrased to reflect a shared view. We were committed to a vision growing from the whole staff, one that they felt ownership of rather than yet another imposed initiative. There was unanimous resistance to a straight-jacketed, performance-orientated view, and a feeling that now was very much the time to develop a more adventurous model which would inspire both staff and children. The image of the vision jigsaw (Figure 3.1) incorporates our attitudes for lifelong learning. It places emotional and social intelligence as equal partners with the acquisition of skills and knowledge in effective learning and early education.

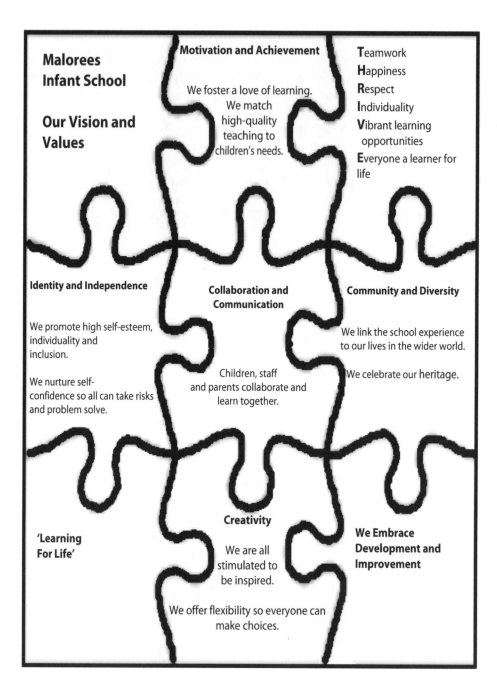

Figure 3.1: The vision jigsaw

The following are the principles on which the vision jigsaw is based. It is a map of the seven elements of the value system that now underpins the philosophy we have put in place to enable our learning community and all its members to thrive as learners and as citizens of the twenty-first century.

Learning for life

During a class discussion about global warming one of our Year 2 children came up with an inventive suggestion: shift the earth slightly further from the sun. At the end of the lesson he said to a member of staff, 'I'm going to think about this for the rest of my life.' We want to plant the seeds that will inspire and enable our children to grow up to solve global warming and also create world peace, cure cancer and achieve nuclear fusion.

We would like the best of the pupils' experience of Malorees to stay with them throughout their lives. We are not just preparing them with adequate skills and knowledge for Key Stage 2; we are hopefully inspiring our children with the confidence and enthusiasm to go out into the world and view learning as a lifelong adventure. Connecting their learning through real experiences of the world is an important part of what we do – if we're learning about explorers we too go exploring, if we want to set up a bookshop in the role-play area the children need to do a research visit to a bookshop first.

We embrace development and improvement

Our vision jigsaw has not remained static. We have added 'learning for life' and 'we embrace development and improvement' as we are firmly committed to our practice at Malorees being open to innovation and change. We want a buzz in the air, an environment where we are excited and stimulated by our colleagues' adventures in teaching and learning. The children of the twenty-first century will need to be adaptable and find new ways of doing things and we have a responsibility to set an example ourselves and develop our sense of adventure.

One example of change included professional development on Philosophy for Children (P4C). We set up philosophy classes for all Year 2 children and now also some reception children. One of the key benefits of P4C is that children begin to understand that they need not all hold the same opinions, that disagreement and difference are stimulating and that everyone has a right to their own beliefs. Not everyone in the garden need be a daffodil – we are not about uniformity; in fact, as in our wild garden, cultivating diversity is essential.

Another example is that our deputy head led a Teacher Learning Community with a group of five teachers from our own school and two other local schools, where the teachers met monthly to share, try out and progress ideas for classroom practice around Assessment for Learning. This has given us opportunities to experiment with strategies, take risks and adapt ideas for ourselves.

Teachers are also increasingly planning to include the parent community in learning opportunities. Initiatives include 'Family Learning Days' where parents learn alongside children on practical problem-solving tasks, using reporting and communicating to parents as a 'finale' for themed projects, and family show-and-tell sessions.

Collaboration and communication: Children, staff and parents collaborate and learn together

> In the smallest room in the school a shy 6 year old is divulging her fondest wishes and hopes for the future into a tape recorder to be professionally edited and published on CD, her portrait and autobiographical details on the sleeve. This project, led by a parent who is a professional storyteller and broadcaster, was part of a recent Arts Week entitled 'Who Am I?' – a powerful three-way learning experience for children, staff and parents.

Central to our vision are staff learning with each other, the children and their parents. The shift is in the wording. It is only more recently that we have begun to treat ourselves as learners as well as teachers; this has been an emergent theme in the learning projects that we have been on. As a small school it has usually been possible for major decisions to be arrived at by consensus, bringing everyone on board.

We also have a good tradition of parental involvement in classrooms as well as for fund-raising and social events. We are now extending our collaboration with parents to encourage them to take an even more active part in the learning journey we are taking with their children. If this is to be a truly collaborative effort we are aware that parental ideas may sometimes take us beyond our comfort zone and not necessarily reflect our expectations. A Parent Forum has been set up to try to dig deeper into parents' views and create an opportunity for opinions to be aired.

Another exciting element of our vision of collaboration is children learning together. Collaborative projects that promote paired, group and whole-class tasks have a great deal to offer. They can develop emotional intelligence, build self-esteem, deepen understanding through explanation, extend speaking and listening skills and develop leadership and peace-making skills.

> Antonio comes to mind: on entry to the class he had a poor self-image as a learner that presented as negativity, reluctance to commit to a task and a tendency to dominate and put others down. After a year of intensive work on collaborative learning, not only was he addressing a challenge with enthusiasm, he had also emerged as one of the most effective 'teachers' in the classroom, having developed the skill of sensitively leading a partner towards understanding rather than feeding them an answer.

Community and diversity: We link the experience of being in school to our lives in the wider world; We celebrate our heritage

Some snapshots ... A tall Sudanese 7 year old proudly demonstrates how to use a Muslim prayer mat, a little blond boy chats in Swedish to some visiting Scandinavian educators, a tiny Japanese 5 year old teaches a student teacher how to do origami, the class answers the register in a dozen languages.

Malorees' racial and social diversity is one of its greatest strengths. Every child's culture and heritage needs to be overtly affirmed and celebrated in our school as children learn to embrace the rich variety of people in the world. We take as many opportunities as possible to do this in a variety of curriculum areas and especially in our displays of learning. We need to ensure that no child or family believes their potential is limited by their racial or social identity.

We also try to raise the profile of the local community, which we discuss in Chapter 6, and our place in a wider world particularly with regard to sustainability. We have been forging closer links with a local Muslim primary school with visits to an exhibition about Islam and a visit from them when they performed an assembly for us about Eid Ul-Adha.

Identity and independence: We promote high self-esteem, individuality and inclusion; We nurture self-confidence so all can take risks and problem solve

At Malorees we believe in inclusion and learning without limits. Ability groupings are no longer the norm or gathered only for specific learning tasks. Rigidly differentiated tasks are increasingly being replaced with open-ended investigations and optional challenges so that those who achieve more slowly are not denied a chance to do well. This has had a very noticeable effect on how children feel about themselves and as a result on the performance and motivation of children who might once have underachieved. Risk taking and learning from mistakes is increasingly being planned for and encouraged throughout the curriculum. We have a positive behaviour management policy and we try to involve children in solving behavioural problems when they occur, trying to keep a clear separation between the undesirable behaviour and the children themselves. We listen to children, take on their ideas and give them responsibility. Visitors to our school invariably comment on the friendliness of the children and how articulate they are.

Motivation and achievement: We foster a love of learning; We match high-quality teaching to children's needs

We all know that children who feel successful are much more likely to enjoy learning and be motivated to learn more. Through refocusing teaching and learning on progress and process rather than achievement and product, every child can be successful; in fact the 'lower attainers' often achieve more. We support children to move forward in their learning at the same time as making them feel proud of what they have achieved. Their achievement and awareness of it will be greatly enhanced if children are taught to understand how they learn, the strategies they can adopt to support their learning, and if they are offered opportunities to reflect on what they have learnt and where they need to develop further. We have been building up their understanding of their learning through developing their vocabulary to think and talk about how they learn through the use of Assessment for Learning strategies and the use of the 'wizard walls' to encourage positive attitudes to learning, an idea 'borrowed' from Limeside Primary School. Overt discussions about learning are becoming an integral part of everyday life and through these we try to make children aware of how much they are 'growing'.

> Reflective feedback from children on their most enjoyable learning over the year used to be dominated by outings, performances, PE and Arts Week. However, at the end of the first year after the introduction of our new creative curriculum over half of the Year 2 class cited their hands-on, open-ended collaborative science challenges as their favourite activity.

Creativity: We are all stimulated to be inspired; We offer flexibility so everyone can make choices

At Malorees we want to be creative in our approach to our curriculum and our teaching. We believe it is important to present ideas in exciting and novel ways to stimulate curiosity, awe and wonder of the wider world. This necessitates a spirit of adventure among the teaching staff and a degree of risk taking.

> Darren exhibited challenging behaviour, in fact he was currently working with a specialist from the Brent Behaviour Team to improve his social skills, but before posing his question to the Chinese princess, he intuitively put his palms together on his chest and took a low bow. The Chinese princess was in fact the class's student teacher dressed up in character to take part in a question-and-answer session to deepen the children's understanding of the Willow Pattern Story. This was part of a term-long China project that culminated in a class performance. Every child suspended their disbelief and addressed their visitor as if she were an honoured princess.

Similarly, we are trying to offer more opportunities for the children to find their own ways of developing their creativity, making choices, being involved in setting up an enquiry, finding their own ways to use materials/music/ideas. Children who can confidently perform closed tasks may do well in national tests but will not develop the mindset to solve the world's problems.

> No one would have predicted that Lloyd would have shown such creative leadership in dance. Following some specialist tuition in Bollywood-style dance moves, the children were asked to improvise a short sequence in groups of three or four. Lloyd's group comprised

some of the most inhibited boys in the class, but in no time at all he had them rehearsing a tight little routine and they really appeared to be enjoying themselves! At Malorees we want to give children the opportunities to surprise us and exceed our expectations.

A mantra for the school

The vision jigsaw as a whole is difficult to hold in your head so we ran two professional development sessions for the whole staff to return to the vision jigsaw and try to summarise it. We also wanted to revisit our beliefs in view of new staff joining the school, who had not been involved in the initial process. We decided that a succinct 'mantra' would unite us all, help with decision making and cast light on everything we do. There was a very clear shared consensus that we all wanted it to include our emphasis on emotional nurture and active and exciting learning opportunities to equip the children with the skills and attitudes to move forward enthusiastically on their continuing learning journey. The image of growth from a seed fitted our philosophy, our environment and the age of our children. We finally agreed on **THRIVE**: **T**eamwork, **H**appiness, **R**espect, **I**ndividuality, **V**ibrant learning opportunities, **E**veryone a learner for life. This mantra matches closely with the image of the seed planted in our school grounds, thriving in our nurturing environment, full of potential now and for the future.

Next steps

We have been very keen to also involve the children in the shaping of our shared vision for the school. For some time the school council has contributed to change. There has of course been the familiar focus on improving the school toilets (designing posters and suggesting 'a shiny golden floor that people would want to keep clean') and a school meals survey to improve provision. But they have also been involved in choosing priorities for the weekly whole-school attitude focus. An example in their own choice of words is: 'We should work on respecting each other like they are as important as you.' They have also encouraged the school to look outward by organising a 'popcorn club' to raise money for natural disasters and other charities, and sponsoring ex-pupils' citizenship projects. They raised consciousness about endangered species at an assembly and did research at the zoo resulting in the adoption of a penguin. However, this is all fairly small scale.

We are aiming to spread this level of involvement to include all the children in shaping their school and taking part in decision making on a far greater scale. One example of this is playtimes, in particular lunchtime, which a small proportion of children do not always enjoy. Ideas are being trialled to offer a range of activities in the playground including sports, dance, arts and crafts, and 'buddy clubs'. The children's feedback from these experiments will shape future provision. We recently introduced a draft child-friendly school development plan to the school council and are planning to use their feedback to design a succinct, visual version that we can share with the whole school community, including the children.

We are also looking for new ways to support our staff to thrive through offering opportunities for creativity and choice. We have undertaken training in coaching for all staff to develop their ability to problem solve and to support them to take ownership of their own challenges. Similarly we have employed a counsellor with whom staff can consult to help them deal with personal issues that are impacting on their working lives.

We are also incorporating the United Nations Convention on the Rights of the Child (UNCRC) into our future school development and planning. This will enhance our existing vision by promoting a more outward-looking community that prepares our children to be effective global citizens. Our 'golden rules' have been replaced with a range of charters called 'promises' and 'commitments', which outline the rights and corresponding responsibilities of different groups in our school community (children, staff, parents, visitors and governors). Each classroom has a 'promise tree' that includes up to eight green leaves labelled with the children's rights (to learn, to play, to be safe). Every class then decides together and agrees what their corresponding responsibilities should be. We felt it was important for the children's ownership and understanding that they should be closely involved in the formulation of the wording of the responsibilities. This initiative is still very much 'work in progress' but our aim is for concerns to be viewed and discussed in terms of infringing others' rights and not fulfilling our own responsibilities, giving children a moral structure that if fully internalised will become a lifelong guide.

A closer understanding with and from our children's families is an ongoing priority for the future. Our vision jigsaw and promise trees have been introduced to all parents with a general school questionnaire and responses solicited. Parents' feedback has been very positive: many remarked on how accessible it was and that it was a meaningful representation of their experience of the school. But we cannot be complacent and are continually looking for new ways to draw families into our school community (see Chapter 6). Of course as new parents join the school we need to keep working on opportunities for them to understand our values. Similarly we acknowledge that as the direction of the school evolves we need to periodically review and refresh our vision to maintain a dynamic energy.

We followed up our work on our vision with a second professional learning day with the whole staff exploring the idea of 'an inspiring curriculum', bearing in mind the vision that we had developed. This resulted in our second jigsaw, the 'learning opportunities jigsaw', which mapped aims into practice, listing effective learning opportunities that would exemplify our values (see Chapter 9, p. 150).

Conclusion

We are aware that schools have had 'aims and purposes' on the first page of their prospectuses for a very long time. The sort of thing we have put on paper, albeit through a useful collaborative exercise and in a more user-friendly design, is not, on its own, going to revolutionise practice in the classrooms. It has been essential to create opportunities to revisit and deepen our understanding of our vision and purpose, trying to ensure that everyone is heading in the same direction, with the same adventurous spirit. Not every staff member will 'buy into' the vision at the same point, so the work will always be in progress in much the same way as gardening is a continuous process. Strengthening teamwork is a key aspect to enable those who are fully on board to help everyone to contribute and take ownership of the future.

A strong, clear vision is an invaluable guide at all times but particularly when there are difficulties to navigate. Over the years our school has had a steady increase in numbers of children with quite complex and challenging special needs. At a factory farm where crop yield is the top priority these children would constitute an obstacle to success. Our vision is of a more organic cottage garden where not all the carrots need to grow straight, not all the roses need to be pink. The vision reminds you of what is important.

Decision making at the school now has a basis in a shared philosophy. Will a new initiative promote or hinder our aims? Can it be adapted to support our vision more effectively? Our vision jigsaw serves as a compass for our learning adventure at Malorees. It gives us direction while allowing us flexibility to choose our paths in the light of individual needs and strengths, opportunities and ideas.

Chapter 4

People make your place: St Vigor and St John Primary School

It is our light, not our darkness that most frightens us.

We ask ourselves, who am I to be brilliant, gorgeous, talented, fabulous?

Actually, who are you not to be? ... Your playing small does not serve the world.

(Williamson, 1992: 190)

Introduction

As you come into the front of our school, our vision is the first thing you will see. It is a star, a guiding star that shows us the way. Alongside the star we describe the purpose, beliefs, entitlement and methodologies that are enshrined within our vision. We talk about the purpose of our school in terms of what we want our learners to achieve, their sense of place in the world, their contribution and participation. This includes: being healthy, safe and happy; being skilled, creative and critical builders and shapers; being bringers of hope, love, care and peace; being curious, being open minded and ethical and being able to 'shine' in a future world we cannot yet imagine but which we actively want to participate in the building of. Here lies the source of our adventure, an adventure that needs courage and resilience. We want our school to be a place where ideas can be realised, developed and shared, and in many ways to act as a 'beacon' of learning for all who join us on the journey. 'Thousands of candles can be lit from a single candle and the life of the candle will not be shortened' (Buddha).

Our beliefs relate to the essential elements of human nature we want to foster. They also cover the ethical learning that is significant to us as well as how we want our school to operate. They include the values of love and care, our belief in an 'I can' culture and a belief in inclusion, equality and high standards for all. We frequently re-examine as a school the entitlement all our learners have as human beings and therefore the entitlement they have to learning so they can recognise and release their humanity. For us, they include a right to be loved, listened to, cared for, to be encouraged to take ownership and responsibility and to achieve. Our methodologies describe how we aim to realise our purpose, beliefs and entitlements through enquiry, inspirational stimuli, learning to lead and community participation.

In this chapter we will describe some of the key steps we have taken in order to define, articulate and facilitate this vision, the initiatives that have influenced the process and the direction we have taken as a result. It is the story of our team and our community and how we have co-constructed a vision for our school that has successful learners right at its centre. We describe some of the key models for learning we have developed over time and how these have been brought together through the development of our 'star vision'. We describe how the adventure of developing a meaningful vision has grown from a desire to describe and examine the purpose of learning at our school and the ethical dimension that underlies it.

If you want to walk fast, walk alone.

If you want to walk far, walk together.
African proverb (Clifton Diocese, 2012)

St Vigor and St John Primary School is a voluntary aided Church of England school situated on the northern edge of Somerset. It lies in a stunning rural location about 15 miles south of Bath and Bristol and serves the villages of Stratton-on-the-Fosse, Chilcompton and smaller hamlets between. It has a one-form entry and currently 215 children of primary-school age (4–11 years) and a 30-place nursery (90 on role) in the Children's Centre on site.

The journey to create, articulate and put in place the vision of our school started over ten years ago, with a small core of like-minded people who had a belief that 'collectively all things were possible', including an aspirational vision for children and their education. Every new initiative and idea was rehearsed, tried and tested by this growing collective. The core group included the leadership team, which made it more possible to encourage, cajole or even tell people, with a smile, to take risks.

This support networking was essential and so was the celebration of success. A growth in the way we harness our staff's diverse skills and the momentum of success itself has acted as a potent driver for more and more creative ways of facilitating our vision of education for children. Every school has a group of individuals who drive and form the direction of learning in their place and indeed illuminate, as they do so, the adventures in learning that their school engages with. For us, it has been the *collective* growth of ideas and aspirations that has led us to become the school we are today.

We have often tried to analyse what has led to success for us as a school. There are indicators such as high achievement, good behaviour and excellent resources but these don't necessarily convey the vision that guides us. Over time and through experience we have reminded ourselves that the quality and attributes of many schools are related to the belief systems of the people in them. Therefore we began to spend more and more time shining light right into the corners of who we are and what we believe in. Consequently we agreed and established the key beliefs which we, with our community, think are the most important in ensuring success for all our learners.

So, who are 'we' and what are we like? What is our philosophy and identity? We are people who behave in particular ways and we have grouped these behaviours into four key areas, acknowledging that an understanding of our behaviour directly informs our beliefs and conversely an understanding of our beliefs directly informs our behaviour. These four areas are relationships, ethics, questing and connectedness.

> *Your own acts and behaviours tell the world who you are and at the same time what kind of society you think it should be.*
>
> (Ai WeiWei, 2010)

Relationship behaviours that inform our beliefs

We are a community of team players; we take risks together and have support structures that are deeply rooted to enable this. We believe everyone has an important role to play and we emphasise and celebrate this with all our staff, children, parents and school community. We love and care for each other and talk about this love and care openly. As far as we can, we try to take important decisions together and enable groups and committees to take responsibility for specific areas of school life. This includes the learning in classrooms. We actively engage with learning about the skills and attitudes that are essential for the formation of good relationships and try to live that talk. For example our children first learn about values by thinking about how valuable *they* are. In our reception class, one of the first things our children create and share is an identity 'map' that describes who they are, their favourite things and the people who are important to them. We always celebrate with much clapping, flags and parties!

Ethical behaviours that inform our beliefs

We are 'bothered' – desiring the best and investing energy and commitment to seek this. We have a clearly articulated value system that is shared with our school community, and the courage to practise it in reality. Central to these values is the concept of 'love'. We talk about love in all its guises in an open and straightforward way. In many ways, we want to be *different* as a school and have an individual and identifiable perspective as a learning community – acknowledging that each person and therefore each school is unique within a shared set of values. The adventure of the learning journey may be different for each individual in our school but we make sure that each child has an equal opportunity to make this journey and that the quality, worth and nature of the adventure are supported by an ethical framework. Every half term, the whole school chooses two of our stated values to focus on. We do this through opportunities such as circle time, PSHE sessions, and conversations as well as in assemblies.

Questing behaviours that inform our beliefs

We quest – we ask questions all the time, the 'why' question being the favourite. Our quests take us on adventures in our learning, adventures within the curriculum we provide, adventures in the opportunities we enable, adventures in the activities our children engage with, and adventures in the visions we have for our school. We have a go, take risks and turn ideas into reality with clear criteria for success. We have high energy (usually!) and ways of refreshing it. Most of all we believe our quests to be exciting and worthwhile. As well as our half-termly research quests that all classes engage with, we hold termly whole-school quests that engage us all in the exploration of important concepts such as sustainability, democracy and belief. We always plan to involve parents and other community members in these investigations.

Connectedness behaviours that inform our beliefs

We think in creative and adventurous ways, making space for the process so we can make connections across all we do. These connections help all aspects of learning to become real, relevant, purposeful and personal. The need to make real, tangible connections to the wider national and global community and environment while also making connections to thinkers in other parts of the world is central to our vision. For example we recently held a global breakfast where the journey of different foods was mapped and issues to do with interdependence and the notion of a global citizen were discussed. This event gave us a real opportunity to examine the importance of local resources and allowed children not only to make connections to their place but also to perceive how people in places far away connect to their own lives. We are, most of all, rooted in our *own* community … its quirks and its delights. We want our children to develop a pride in their own place as well as seeking opportunities for learning beyond it. For us, this is sustainability in a nutshell.

What is remarkable about these behaviours is their contagious nature and over time they have become increasingly apparent in our community of learners. It is as if our behaviour gives permission for others to find these attributes in themselves. Their importance is described in our curriculum chapter (Chapter 10). The curriculum is the key way that these behaviours are developed, enhanced and evaluated in our school.

> As part of a whole-school initiative on healthy attitudes to food and eating, a group of 12 parents were empowered to make decisions and lead activities in school. They were given the opportunity to work with a professional chef to inspire and teach them skills. They presented ideas at assemblies, had a budget and ran a number of workshops with children on adventurous eating without staff direction. These included adventurous pizza cooking in our homemade oven, preparing healthy lunch boxes and a broad range of cooking with apples as part of Somerset Apple Week.

Learners go on journeys

Our journey towards understanding what we wanted for our children and of really clarifying our philosophy was initially influenced by a combination of the following four ideas and policies. These four key ideas have fundamentally influenced the vision of our school and have provided us with inspiration and direction within our learning journey:

- ideas within *Excellence and Enjoyment* (DCSF, 2003);
- our four 'cornerstones' of learning;
- enabling children to learn to learn; and
- the concept of a 'lead learner'.

Ideas within *Excellence and Enjoyment*

The document *Excellence and Enjoyment* was produced by the Department for Children, Schools and Families (DCSF) in 2003 and set out a vision for the future of primary education built on what had already been achieved. This vision described a sector where high standards are obtained through a rich, varied and exciting curriculum that develops children in a range of ways. As well as giving our school permission and freedom to create for itself a meaningful and relevant curriculum for our children, we particularly took on board the principles for learning and teaching. We re-wrote these and embedding them within our own vision was one of the first steps on the pathway of becoming a more adventurous school.

We agreed it was vital at St Vigor and St John that we ensure every child succeeds in a culture of inclusion and high expectation. Part of this success relies on the need for all our learners to have a basic skill entitlement, encompassed within their identity as a learner. Basic skills are the fundamental tool kit that all learners need in order to embark on adventurous learning. We liken them to the essentials you put in your pockets when setting off on a trek where the unexpected might occur.

We also agree that children have a learning identity and learning interests unique to them. We aim for our teaching to provide an appropriate framework for the development of opportunities that enable personalised learning success across the curriculum. It is a curriculum where children are able to build on and connect their learning through activities that cross subject divides. To inspire learning, provision needs to be vivid, exciting, real and relevant to children's needs. It has been increasingly important for us that the processes of learning are made visible and talked about. How children learn is not a secret: children need to learn about themselves and others as learners in order to self-reflect and make decisions about their learning progress.

All of the principles within *Excellence and Enjoyment* were significant but one principle in particular, the 'what, why and how of learning', emerged as one of our more important creative tools. This principle maintains the idea that every learner should know what, why and how they are learning. We thought about it in the way shown in Figure 4.1.

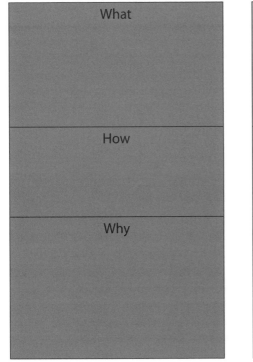
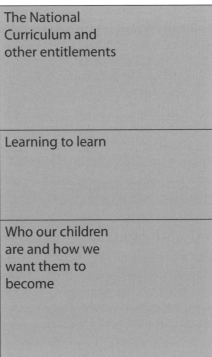

Figure 4.1: The what, how and why of learning

The 'why' of learning – the four cornerstones

Understanding 'why' children need to learn, and for what purpose, became the important idea behind the development of our 'four cornerstones'. These cornerstones built a picture for us of what we considered were four essential requisites in order to be a good learner and therefore informed our resulting curriculum design. They have become an essential tool in enabling our vision for learning to become tangible and visible to our school community. We articulate the four cornerstones in our vision as identity, communication, problem solving and creativity. The following examples help to illustrate them in practice.

Identity

Learners need to know who they are and how they learn within the personal and wider contexts of their world.

In a whole-school focus week on diversity we shared stories about ourselves by making a 'Me box'. These boxes contained objects that have special significance.

'This is my special tractor. My Mum and Dad gave it to me for my birthday. It's like the ones you see on the road out here. My little sister plays with it too. She rolls it round the floor. I have my favourite book in my box because I like the story.'

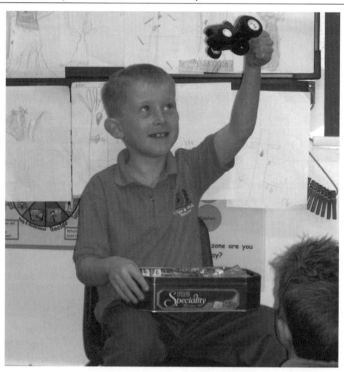

Communication

Learners need to be effective in the way they tell, show, question, debate and inspire using a wide variety of techniques and media.

> Year 6 children created a dance piece that communicated ideas about what it was like to be different and have a special talent.
>
> 'Being different means that people, just like apples, can look different on the outside but we all have similarities on the inside. We all feel, we all think, we all love, we can all be hurt. I saw that being different could be a good thing.'
>
> James, Year 5

Problem solving

Learners need to develop the skills of enquiry and issue resolution. They need to be able to identify problems, plan lines of enquiry interdependently and apply the skills and understanding they develop in their learning to a variety of situations and contexts.

> Year 2 children were challenged to solve the problem of snails eating the lettuces they had planted in their garden.
>
> 'I tried to stop the snail eating my lettuces by making a giant bird to hang over. It scares the snails. I think the lettuce was eaten a little bit and the big bird helped a little. But the snail was full.'
>
> Emily, Year 2

Creativity

Learners need to be enabled to develop their own ideas in order to promote and develop their own personal conceptual frameworks and also enhance those of others.

> Children in Year 1 played with clay to discover ways of making changes. The hall floor was covered with paper and balls of clay were thrown, rolled, mixed with water and used to draw with.
>
> 'Look, my clay is sticking to the paper! When I mix water with it, it slides about and comes off. I add more and more water and the paper gets all holey and the clay slips about.'
>
> Hugh, Year 1

The impact of the four cornerstones in our vision is clearly seen in our enquiry approach to curriculum provision that we describe further in Chapter 10. Each year group, on a termly basis, within a six-term year, undertakes an enquiry or quest through a research question, which particularly focuses on one of the four cornerstone areas.

For example our reception class developed a quest entitled 'How can we create an exciting maths learning trail for the local playgroup?' ensuring a focus on problem solving. Our Year 2 class asked 'How can I be a good storyteller?' ensuring a focus on creativity. One of the research questions for Year 4 was 'How can I communicate my understanding of friction using ICT?' This obviously has a focus within communication.

Although any of the four cornerstones could potentially provide a focus, one usually has a stronger and more obvious link to the learning enquiry. Generally, the cornerstones have enabled children and staff to see purpose behind their learning, provided a vocabulary about learning and assisted teachers in the planning of related understanding, skills and attitudes.

The cornerstones also help determine the success of our termly focus weeks, which develop both our and our children's thinking in challenging areas. The example in Figure 4.2 illustrates a focus week for the whole school devoted to further understanding the concept of belief in its widest context.

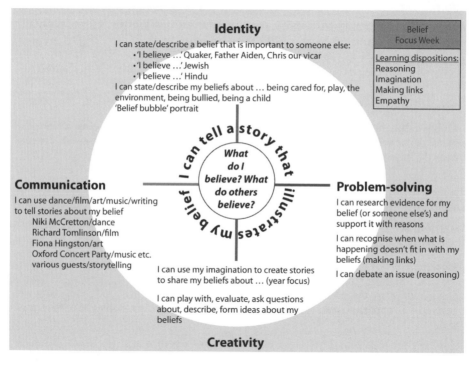

Figure 4.2: Cornerstone plan for a focus week on 'belief'

About three years ago, having come this far with our vision, we hit a snag and a gap in our thinking. We had devoted much time to developing a curriculum that was compatible with the National Curriculum. We were also beginning to enable children to develop aspects of those essentials we called the four cornerstones. But there was something missing. We were still not teaching children in an explicit way 'how to learn'. It was not yet a strong enough part of our vision. So we embarked on another quest to find a way to enable this wisdom to be learnt in a clear, manageable and explicit manner.

The 'how' of learning – learning to learn

We were very influenced by Guy Claxton's work *Building Learning Power* (Claxton, 2002). It provided a framework in our vision that helped us to make learning visible and put it at the centre of all we do. The methodology focuses on 17 learning dispositions which we found to be particularly effective in enabling all learners to develop a specific, shared vocabulary based on learning and the nature of learning. It was amazing how quickly learning became the subject of discussions when children were provided with the language to help them form those discussions. We initially chose one learning disposition per half term to focus on across the whole school. Each term, at a staff meeting, we discussed and defined what this disposition might 'look like' as part of the learning within the classroom. We shared how each disposition might develop and progress as children get older. Children and staff became skilled at understanding and recognising the learning dispositions and realising opportunities for their development in everyday experiences. Most of all, a more developed vocabulary of learning was established throughout the school.

> 'It shows us and teaches us how to learn all the ingredients about being a good learner, like linking, managing distractions, collaboration and planning. If you're a good manager of distractions you have to use your looking, concentrating, listening skills. So if someone was having golden time outside then you'd need to be concentrating on your learning and how to do it really well. They're all about being a better learner.'
>
> Alfred, Year 6

Developing the idea of being a 'lead learner'

After giving children further control over their learning through the ideas in *Building Learning Power*, we developed the notion of 'lead learner'. It was an extremely important leap forward in our visioning and developed our staff and children's understanding of how an individual can influence the learning of others. We developed it as part of a 'big idea' funded by some work associated with the government's 'sustaining success' initiatives. The 'idea' affirmed a belief that everyone, parents, staff and children, can be a leader of learning. The example of others leads us through the process of our lifelong learning journey. What seemed to be important to us was that learners should learn first of all to be good learners in their own right (fledgling learners) and then should be empowered, encouraged and given opportunity to lead and enlighten the learning of others. This part of the process, 'the leading', should be recognised to be 'of worth' and we felt it should be promoted and enabled through the learning of a specific skill set. We were all too aware of the issues of dependency learning and the problems of independence, especially for children who find learning difficult.

'Being a lead learner is all about demonstrating and showing how you can learn, being able to set an example and helping. All these things make you a lead learner. We have lead learner hands to help us remember. I had a lead learner badge for helping others to find things out for themselves. I didn't show them the answer; I let them do it, but helped them.'

Isaac, Year 5

'Lead learners make other lead learners. They help other people. If people come up to me and want help I would do it. You've got to be kind and helpful. You've got to think and use your brain really hard about it.'

Edna, Year 1

So the idea of a lead learner in our vision developed into a clear set of beliefs and methodologies that are briefly summarised below.

We believe that *all* learners are entitled to:

- information relating to what, why and how they learn;
- support, love and care at a personal and group level to develop resilience and personal belief to take on the challenges of learning;
- direction and enlightenment in terms of a shared vision and milestones of learning – a beacon on the way; and
- involvement which ensures ownership and a vested interest in successful learning so that learners feel valued as part of an inclusive process.

We also believe that being a lead learner is not a separate entity from being a learner itself; one grows from the other and is a continuous dynamic. Some of our ideas about how you might recognise this are summarised below.

Learners can learn by:		*Lead* learners should learn how to:
Actively listening and therefore be able to share information	←→	Tell, so that other learners can create key information and skills
Acting on inspiration and therefore be able to pursue a difficult idea	←→	Inspire, so that others can fly with an exciting agenda
Following a model to develop a key skill such as being able to work effectively in a group	←→	Model, so that others can take the best of a skill or value and use it for themselves
Responding to being coached and therefore be able to find a solution to a specific problem for themselves	←→	Coach, so that others can be empowered to solve problems for themselves and pass that on

Learners can learn by:		*Lead* learners should learn how to:
Responding to being mentored and using expert advice to improve a piece of learning (e.g. a play script)	←→	Mentor, so that through expert knowledge or skill, others can also be skilled
Acting on a strong provocation such as the outdoors, or watching a piece of theatre to, for example, create a dance to perform in a theatre themselves	←→	Enable, by providing environments and provocations that provide excellent contexts for learning

Figure 4.3: Learners and lead learners

Lead learners are proactive, well-informed, confident, purposeful individuals who take every opportunity to be included and embrace others in learning success.

Our children share in our vision by having a five-fingered 'helping hand' that enables them to think of the lead learner concept in more simplistic terms. It describes a lead learner as someone who makes things better, sets a good example, encourages and helps everyone, loves learning and inspires others, and cares about people and places who are part of the learning community. It is not, however, just our children who we see as lead learners; staff, parents, governors and other members of our community have opportunities to lead the learning of others. For example our parent partnership group has recently led a campaign to have a crossing installed on the road outside school.

We hold weekly lead learner assemblies and award our unique badges. Children vote for the person who they feel has made the most significant lead learner contribution to the class that week. Here are some examples.

Ben was so enthusiastic about bugs that everyone wants to find out about them.

(inspire) Year R

James has set up a special website to help you be organised about your home learning.

(mentoring) Year 6

Jasmine helped Jack with his maths today but was careful not to tell him the answers.

(coaching) Year 4

The need to revisit our vision

Over time, we were beginning to accumulate so many ideas about how children learn and how we should enable this to happen that we were in danger of no longer being clear, effective or directional in what we were doing. We also wanted to incorporate our newest thinking about the central place of environmental sustainability and the key values that underpinned it. There was an urgent need to re-vision. This was more difficult than we thought and resulted in many staff discussions. We like images and we played with multiple images such as growing trees, life rings and compasses but no image would quite embrace our thinking and aspiration. The breakthrough finally came when we used an experienced coach and with seemingly little effort an image and an interrogatory tool emerged. It seemed no coincidence that an appropriate image for us manifested itself in the café of Salisbury Cathedral – our vision star.

The 'vision star'

We fell in love with the star because its imagery was so strong. We thought of it as a 'guiding star' and therefore a 'light' for our learning journey. It links well with our concept of 'Shines', which are certificates that we give to celebrate our children's and adults' achievements, and also with our understanding about 'lead learners', who should be motivated not only to be splendid learners in their own right but to 'shine' their learning onto others. Learning, after all, is about a quest for enlightenment and each small light makes the pathway clearer.

Stars can also represent something of awe, wonder and thinking about possibilities. Our star helps us re-emphasise the nature of our quest and that the vision for our school and curriculum needs to be seen in that same light of awe, wonder and possibility – not in terms of prescription, formula limitations and control. The word 'adventure' springs to mind! A star seemed a suitable image to represent the constantly changing notion of a vision – one that has unlimited scope for expansion, one that reflects important truths and signposts to our whole school community.

The vision star encourages us to discuss, share and question the way we are as a school, not to prescribe it. It allows for innovation and questfulness, as we can use it in many contexts and at many different levels. It was to prove, for example, a useful tool in helping us to describe the purpose and nature of our new Children's Centre as it evolved. Stars have traditionally been a guide for adventurers when they are facing the unknown or darkness; they provide a sense of direction. The star became a tool of both representation and interrogation. Using its four points we were able to articulate four key questions about the nature of our vision:

1. Why and for what *purpose* do we want this vision?
2. What important *beliefs* underpin it?
3. With this vision in mind, what is the basic *entitlement* for our school community?
4. What *methodologies* will we use to realise this vision?

The connection between these questions and our original 'what, why, how' analysis is not chance. It is the beliefs, value and ethics that have grown in immense importance for us in the intervening years and now play a more fundamental part in what we decide. This didn't give us the vision in so many words but once we could articulate our key beliefs, what our purposes were and what basic entitlements were important for the children, the jigsaw fell into place. Methodologies follow when you know what you really want for your children. Figure 4.4 shows the fundamental strands of the vision star.

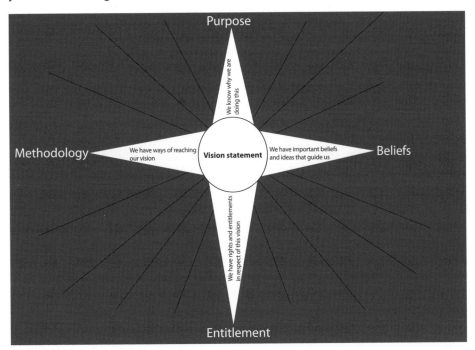

Figure 4.4: The fundamental strands of the vision star

A whole-staff professional training day and some further discussion were needed to make a final leap to an articulated vision statement. We already had some central elements of the vision that we wanted to include. First, it needed to include our idea about lead learners. We were also excited about previous learning that we had undertaken about the concept of sustainability, which had become important to our school community. We needed to articulate what sustainability meant to us, and how we could place it centrally in our vision. Linked to this, we had become increasingly convinced of the need for our children to fully utilise the outdoor environment in their learning, to make real links to their place as they develop a sense of local identity. A whole week of work with the school and community on sustainability had resulted in our own definition of what we feel it is. Simply, we say our community of lead learners should be able to:

- love and care for themselves;
- love and care for their community, both local and global; and
- love and care for the environment.

We wanted to be like this – we wanted to be sustainable and we wanted to declare it.

Another facet of our thinking was to include the idea of co-construction – the idea of building things together in an inclusive way. So many of the successful elements of our school related to our ability to be creative and solve problems using the power of the team. We were anxious that this sense of co-construction should relate to our learning community in the widest sense, to involve children, parents, grandparents, village residents and other stakeholders in discussions about the purpose and significance of our evolving school. The words 'we' and 'building' were essential in our vision statement.

Finally and most importantly we wanted to include the word 'adventurous' because it describes many of our approaches to curriculum design and the way we are. It is often the missing element when children struggle with risk taking and independently constructing their learning. For us, the notion of adventurousness resonates with our ideas of freedom in learning, of being different and of the ability to tap into the potential creativity necessary for learners to be successful in the future. As we said at the beginning, we want our school to be adventurous in its journey. In the process it has also become a beacon for learning – casting light on the path our children are taking and resourcing its direction. This is now realised in a clearly articulated statement: 'We are building a sustainable community of adventurous lead learners.'

We developed the interesting idea of incorporating the key school improvement priorities into our vision star .The spicules or 'gaseous extrusions' on our star represent them. They are much more temporary and will evolve, fade or even grow brighter depending on our needs in furthering our vision over the passage of time. For example in 2008 (Figure 4.5) we made a special study of 'invisible' children in order to ensure they made appropriate progress and could become effective lead learners. We were also advancing our concept of sustainability by empowering a greater ownership of the green agendas by an enlarged, classes-based school council.

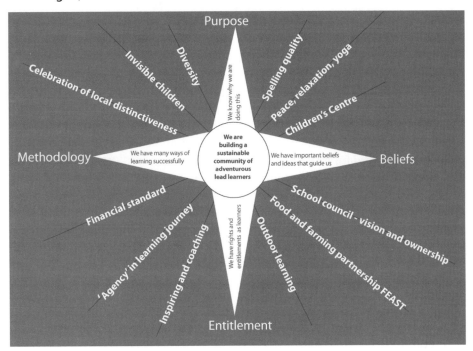

Figure 4.5: Our 2008 vision star

Next steps

The models we use to communicate our school vision are important for us as they provide a way to describe, examine and share our thoughts and ideas. Ultimately they help us to articulate our purpose, what we are here for as a school community. There is always a need to be aware of how this is communicated to all our stakeholders and how meaningful it is. Future steps for us will include the need to explore how our vision, and particularly the four behaviours described at the beginning of the chapter, become known, owned and 'lived' by all. As stated above, learning is not secret and the best learning comes when agendas are visible and shared. It is relatively easy to talk about important behaviours but more difficult to embed these in what we do every day in a way that is understood and owned by all.

Conclusion

Schools, including ours, are constantly changing establishments. Agendas come and go; sometimes they are presented from external sources such as the government or local authority, sometimes from within school. There are times when our school's direction seems planned and controlled and times when it seems organic and self-propelling. There are times of consolidation and implementation and times of innovation and experimentation. These moments are not static or isolated; they are all interacting. Our adventure as a school is the journey we take through these times and how we sustain and develop our community within them.

Most importantly, the journey itself creates, sustains and enlivens our school community along with the creation of a vision and goal for future thought, direction and inspiration. Our staff, pupils and, as much as possible, parents and friends are involved in what could be seen as a constantly evolving and developing mission. Fundamentally, forming our vision has involved our community in a search for purpose, identity, possibility and quality. Resilience is an important disposition to have on any journey but not perhaps as important as curiosity and a willingness and desire to seek new worlds or truths. An obvious parallel can be recalled in the story of the Magi who undertook a perilous star-led journey to discover a new fundamental truth that would change the meaning of their lives.

Questions for discussion

- Does the vision for your school reflect its true purpose?
- What would make your vision more adventurous?
- How can a vision move beyond a simple statement of purpose and belief?
- How can everyone own a vision?

Part 2

COMMUNITY

Reflections on the community chapters

> *Our lives are lived amidst the architectural expressions of displacement; the shopping mall, apartment, neon-strip, freeway, glass office tower and homogenised development – none of which encourage much sense of rootedness, responsibility and belonging.*
>
> (Orr, 1992: 127)

What is the relationship an adventurous school has with its community? It is a relationship that is very pivotal and can help to provide a sense of rootedness and belonging in an increasingly disparate and often fragmented context. A relationship with the families, locality, neighbourhood and district offers so much more than just a working partnership or drawing on the skills of those beyond the official boundary of a school. It provides new ways of seeing purpose, relationships, scope and sites of learning. Clarke (2011a: 7) points out that: 'Growing community through place, relationship, action and interest connects people, idea, place and action in ways that the earlier idea of single site based solutions seemed to inhibit.'

A way of thinking about community has emerged while we have been writing the book. It is one that can create a new sense of the relationships that people have with their place and their purpose (Birney and Reed, 2009). It is a relationship that increases and values diversity. The relationship that a school has with its community deepens purpose, manifests its approach to power and affects the way it sees pedagogy.

Children of primary-school age who are growing up in the first decades of the twenty-first century are citizens of the world in ways that their ancestors could not have dreamt possible. They have a greater sense of identity and connection than previous generations of young children and are quite used to emailing their friends in schools on different continents or sharing their projects and photos via Internet links they have made with schools in different parts of the world. Children now are citizens of the world beyond the narrow models that once defined what it is to be a pupil, models that have tended to separate and confine their learning. They are also better informed about social and environmental issues than previous generations.

To focus their learning, twenty-first century children benefit from learning in context, being posed with real problems and asked to solve real issues. This is a more grounded view of school scholarship and success than the traditional one, and it expands conventional academic goals. It involves learning and leading that are community based and practical. Children in adventurous schools are the potential scholars of the street, park and allotment not just the academy and the office.

Education professionals still often perceive the 'outside' of a school in a traditional way. While situated in a particular community, a school is often set apart, its implicit role seen as compensating or remedying for deficit in the community. Wrigley (2003: 241) notes that: 'Given the mission of Victorian public education to domesticate the unruly offspring of the industrial working class, parents tended to be seen as the enemy rather than potential collaborators.'

Busy with the demands of the day to day, schools have tended to be distanced from and uninvolved in their neighbourhood in anything but a superficial way. One of us was involved in leading an introductory course to school leadership recently. Almost all the participants admitted that they had never taken a walk into the immediate vicinity of their school for the explicit reason of understanding its context; and had only a very hazy sense of what and who was there.

There has also been an increasing move recently to overprotect children by safeguarding them. The negative effect of this can be that children become closed off from the world as the main focus for their learning. More 'fenced in' (one of the schools with a large perimeter has had to be completely re-fenced) than ever because of safeguarding regulations, an adventurous school is challenged to live with a more flexible set of boundaries and a wider sense of purpose than its traditional counterpart.

As suggested in Chapter 1, the twenty-first century brings particular challenges for communities both locally and globally; but as James Martin (2006) suggests, if we can navigate our way through the particular combination of environmental and social issues facing us, there will be wonderful opportunities for the new to emerge and for human beings to create different possibilities for ourselves and the flourishing of our future. In the process the traditional role of the school and how it sees the territory beyond itself needs to change and its boundaries alter in the process.

The community is not just a resource to 'get on side'. The adventurous school has an educational approach that provides children with a profound sense of place, purpose, responsibility and belonging to the world and neighbourhood, of teaching them how to engage and contribute. Taking a community perspective seriously means a shift from the dominant 'us and them' mentality of the twentieth-century school, a shift from 'doing to', to learning, acting and 'working with'. One of the aims of the Cambridge Primary Review (Alexander, 2010: 262) is to celebrate culture and community, which is 'an explicit steer towards both the regeneration of communal life and an education in which mutuality in learning as well as relationships is axiomatic'.

Community cohesion as a theme in recent educational discourse has been useful in identifying commonality and belonging, providing similar life opportunities and strong and positive relationships as the basis of community ethics. Work on public-sector innovation has also been helpful (Mongon and Leadbeater, 2010) in clarifying that schools are more likely to provide effective public value if they:

- draw their community into what they do;
- reach out to work in their immediate social networks;
- work with their wider community to create social capital and cohesion; and
- provide services with no immediate feedback to themselves.

The adventurous school is engaged in creating public value by paying attention to the effects of fragmentation and fragility, by valuing diversity and creating efficacy. To do this, school and community work together and create social capital and cohesion by identifying and building on community strengths. This is akin to the models of 'social productivity' currently being discussed by the Royal Society of Arts (RSA, 2011). Really knowing the community, seeing it as an asset, enjoying its quirks and working with challenges is the daily work of the adventurous school. The adventure becomes a willingness to do and see things differently. Education has a role in the unknown of the field not just in the certainty of the ivory tower. Fielding (2007) argues that a school community that is person centred ensures that personal relations take priority over the functional aspects of organisational life.

A child comes first from their family and community, and learning together with them gives meaning to what they do in school. It develops the reciprocity that guards against the institutional mentality that schools have put between themselves and those on the outside. Parents and community members increase their trust and participation when they have a real involvement and their contribution is valued and authentic. A virtuous reciprocal cycle can then result.

Parents may be only surviving or be 'up against it' in their locality but the following pages demonstrate the efficacy and empowerment they can experience when engaging in and with their child's school that treats them as co-creator rather than victim, that trusts and respects them and creates shared investment and shared expertise in the education of their children. As Wrigley points out (2003: 152): 'We would do well to explore the concept of the learning community in a more grounded sense, involving what happens outside the walls of the school as well as within.'

Clarke (2011a) notes:

> *Scratch the surface of the normally functioning compliant school and in many cases you quickly recognize schools are full of inquisitive people managing a vibrant internal conversation about living, connection, creativity, and possibility; a similar picture exists outside the school gate. Our suggestion is that these places manage this despite of, and not because of, the prevailing externally defined conditions and parameters of performance and community expectation.*

(Clarke, 2011a: 120)

The schools illustrate and develop different aspects of these reflections in the following pages. Each chapter in this section takes a slightly different aspect of how the schools see the nature of the relationship they are developing with their community. The chapters also suggest the way in which this relationship alters the way they see purpose, power and pedagogy.

Chapter 5

Flying together: Limeside Primary School

Let us remember

That as many hands build a house

So many hearts make a school
(Extract from our Friday Celebration Assembly school prayer)

Introduction

Limeside Primary School sits in the centre of a red-brick 1930s former council estate, which is now owned by a housing association. The building itself is a large, two-storey box, with 1930s' tiled walls, parquet flooring and the original separate boys' and girls' entrances. It was built to educate over 600 children but falling roles mean that it is now one-form entry. It is sandwiched between the terraced rows of Third and Fourth Avenues running north to south and Seventh and Eighth Avenues running east to west.

Limeside is an area of high social and economic deprivation. Only 6.5 per cent of adults in the ward have accessed higher education. The number of children entitled to free school meals is consistently high at around 50 per cent. The school population hovered consistently around 98 per cent white British for many years. The area is situated to the south of Oldham, a town with a history of segregated ethnic communities. The challenges of this were brought to national attention in May 2001, when young white and Asian people clashed violently in three days of rioting.

The local community has strong traditions and tight bonds. We have several families who are the third generation educated at our school. Many families have close relatives living on the estate. As families grow they move up to a house with more bedrooms. The majority of services needed by local residents are provided on the estate: doctors, shops, rent offices, etc. are very close by. Families are close, with a strong sense of honour and loyalty.

Traditionally it has been easy for educators to disrespect poorer communities and have lower expectations of their children. However, this community has depth and strength. The people are loyal, close and have a strong sense of pride. The kind of day-to-day challenges many face make them adept at thinking on their feet and solving problems and they are strongly resilient. As one governor explained at a recent visioning day, Limeside is a 'gutsy community, filled with gutsy people who need a gutsy school'. Such attributes equip the community well to take part in our shared adventure.

As discussed in Chapter 2 our written vision statement for learning at Limeside encompasses images of intergenerational learning extending beyond the school gate. Harmonious relationships, respect for differences, caring for and understanding others are all important elements of this vision. Although this statement was originally developed with children in mind, as we have developed partnerships and greater understanding and respect for the community, we have come to realise that the same values and aspirations are relevant for everyone. We have moved from a mental model that saw the school as doing things for the community to one in which we learn, work and act with them. The adventure for Limeside is encapsulated in this change of emphasis. It lies in acknowledging and honouring the reciprocal responsibilities and partnership between school and community. It is about learning to understand what it means to truly fly together.

In this chapter we explore some of the ways in which this has happened. We start with trying to understand the implications of Limeside's specific context for our children and their families. If our vision of a community of active flyers is to be realised, what in particular do we need to do? Next we explore some of the actions we have taken as a result of this understanding. At the same time we try to understand how these actions have embraced our community members, so that what initially began as an adventure for our school has expanded to include many more co-adventurers, including people who would previously have had little involvement with the school.

For us the notion of community operates on many levels and is closely linked with an individual's identity. It is like a series of ripples, with the person at the centre (Figure 5.1). An individual is a member of a family, a school, the local area, the town, a country and finally a citizen of the world community. As with dropping a stone into water, each ripple has an influence on the others. A strong sense of self-worth and self-efficacy in one circle contributes to a stronger identity in the next ripple. We want our children, our parents and our community members to understand and celebrate who they are and the role they play at all these levels, but also to respect and understand others and their interconnectivity. For us community cohesion is about valuing diversity within all these spheres while recognising the commonality and mutuality between them. In the Limeside community the inner family and to some extent the local ripples are well developed. The challenge lies in connecting to the outer rings.

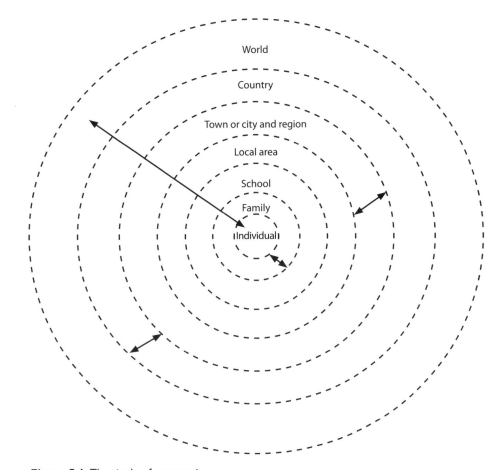

Figure 5.1: The ripple of community

Building a positive sense of identity in any layer has an influence on the other spheres of community. Each ripple is interconnected. At the same time, within each sphere there is commonality, connections and diversity.

Given the Limeside context, what are the main implications for the school?

First, the school sits in the centre of the community and should be a part of that community. In 2004, Ofsted described the school as a beacon within the community and a beacon of hope for the community. While encouraging, this still set the school apart. Somehow the barriers that see school as a place set apart from the rest of life for our children and their families need breaking down. Our school is not just in the community but must become an integral part of that community and the community must become the school.

There is no 'us and them'. We want what happens within the building to continue outside the gates. Limeside Primary School should contribute to the community as well as take from it. It is a two-way relationship: the success of our children is closely linked to the success of the community and vice versa.

To facilitate this, the adult community needs to feel more comfortable, active and involved in education and learning. The previous school experiences of parents and community members have often left a legacy of negative associations with education. They must feel more positive and confident about connecting with it, feel the vitality of learning, and enjoy the experience for themselves as well as their children. The school building itself is a fairly austere red-brick box, which dominates the streets – its appearance, despite many attempts to soften it, suggests educational tradition and associations of authority and ivory-tower separation. We have to welcome the community in to join with us on the learning adventure. Perhaps a measure of the success of this so far lies in a description, proffered by a consultant who has worked closely with the school over a number of years. She described Limeside as a former house that has now become a home.

The second main implication centres on the school's role in promoting community cohesion. Schools have been identified as one of the key players in bringing together distinct communities with different ethnic origins within Oldham. Limeside had already engaged in several different projects to forge links with a partner primary school with a predominantly Asian heritage population. However, this was only scratching the surface of the challenge. What began as a way to bring children together needed to expand to bring together parents and community members in the hope that people from different backgrounds will fly together.

Finally, there is a need to broaden ambitions. The Chair of Governors talks passionately to the children about the days when they will return from Oxbridge as lawyers, politicians, even prime ministers. Somehow we need to help imbue our community with the same driving ambition and hope. Together we all need to believe in our children's potential but also in the potential of the area and its individuals.

How have we set about meeting some of these challenges?

Developing and growing the school community

> Unity
> I dreamed I stood in a studio,
> And watched two sculptors there.
> The clay they used was a child's mind,
> And they fashioned it with care.

One was a teacher; the tools used,
Were books and music and art.
One, a parent with guiding hands,
A gentle and loving heart.

Day after day the teacher toiled,
With a touch both deft and skilled.
The parent laboured side by side,
And all the values filled.

And when at last their task was done,
They looked at what they'd wrought.
The beautiful shape of the precious child,
Could neither be sold nor bought.

And each agreed it would have failed,
If one had worked alone.
For behind the parent stood the school,
And behind the teacher, home.

(Swarat, 1948)

In many ways this poem seems to sum up a shift in the attitude between the school and the parents. It encapsulates a true interdependence between home and school for the benefit of the child.

> It is the last day of the school year. A long line of slightly tearful Year 6 pupils take a final bow as their parents, children and staff applaud their leavers' assembly. The head teacher thanks the children and turns to the parents at the back of the hall. 'We are so proud of them but they are yours. You have done a marvellous job with them. Thank you for helping us to achieve so much together.'

West-Burnham *et al.* (2007: 74) recognise that: 'Differences between parents can be explained more by parental perceptions of their role, and their levels of confidence in fulfilling it, rather than primarily by their social status.'

Increased respect for parents has been a vital factor in creating the kind of community relations we now enjoy. It has been achieved by forging closer, more equal relationships with them and stressing the importance of their role in educating their children as much as possible. Part of the success lies in 'talking parents and community members up' and celebrating their achievements. For example parents who took part in special literacy and numeracy classes were presented with their certificates at our annual presentation evening alongside their children. Their achievements are recognised in our weekly Celebration Assembly and newsletter.

Removing the mystique around school has also played a role in developing confidence among parents and carers. In the past it could be argued that many schools, Limeside included, have created the illusion that teachers are the professionals who hold the only key to learning. Encouraging parents to recognise their role and believe in it, through celebrating home learning in all its guises, has contributed to helping parents develop their own sense of efficacy and engagement with the school. Children now have learning journals in which they are encouraged to reflect on their achievements at home as well as at school at a meta-level. Every week children flood Celebration Assembly with models, pictures and various achievements that they have created at home.

> 'I made a chocolate machine with my grandad but it was too big to fit in the taxi to bring it to school. I was a creative thinker because I had lots of ideas and I used my imagination. I had to change my ideas when I ran out of milk bottles but I didn't give up.'
>
> Matthew, aged 9, reflects in his learning journal on his experiments in response to a context for learning based round *Charlie and the Chocolate Factory*.

Perhaps the greatest factor in creating the partnership between school and parents and carers lies in a change of relationship. The school does its utmost to welcome parents in. The head teacher or deputy meet and greet every morning on the playground, and in the foyer. As one governor stated, this gives school a welcoming face to draw you in each morning. We see it as part of our role to nurture and help involve our parents but not in a patronising way. Previously, in transactional analysis terms, schools tended to assume the adult role, casting parents and carers into the role of a child; schools were the dominant, authority, expert figure. Now, our relationship is far more equal, established on adult-to-adult terms. We expect and believe in the capacity of parents to contribute actively. Our role is to include them, recognise their strengths and assume they will take on greater responsibility.

At the same time we help, encourage and support them, directing them to opportunities that may be relevant and building on their strengths. A recent small measure of success comes to mind. For a young mother life was difficult and she seemed nervous and fragile when her eldest daughter started nursery. Three years on this mother bursts into school each morning, with fresh examples of beautiful, creative artwork produced by her children with her at home. Her pride, enthusiasm and confidence shone out when she was asked to help in art lessons. It feels like she is finally taking off in her own right and as the mother finds her wings her children are also flying higher.

> 'Vote Creative Kids because all children love art. It's good to keep busy – it's FUN!'
>
> 'Thank you for listening to our presentation.'
>
> This was the summing up speech by Year 4 children from Limeside and our partner primary school, as they presented their business proposals to a group of council representatives, housing officers and real *Dragons' Den* winners in their own version of *Dragons' Den* to the applause of parents from both schools.

Appreciating and understanding other communities

One of the major recommendations in response to the Oldham riots in 2001 was to bring schools from different ethnic areas together. Link schools were established across the borough. Special activity days were planned so classes could experience joint arts or sports events. However, at one such event organised for Limeside and our partner school, the children from the two schools tended to remain apart. They were only just beginning to get over a sense of shyness and apprehension about meeting people from a different community, and starting to talk to each other, by the end of the event. We felt the children needed to develop more sustained contact with each other to form real friendships and deep understanding.

Therefore, we started bringing classes together over longer periods in situations where the children would have to talk and collaborate. We established a regular philosophy session for children from both schools in Year 2. They met weekly and discussed a variety of issues of their choosing. Deep understanding about shared values and differences developed and the children looked forward to meeting their philosophy friends. Representatives from the Year 2 Philosophy Crew spoke at adult conferences on topics such as social cohesion and 'Oldham against racism' with passion and understanding.

We also set up a business enterprise venture with Year 4 children from both schools. Mixed school groups had to invent, research, cost, market and create a business plan for a company to run from the schools. They then took their proposals to the housing association's head office, where they pitched their ideas to various business and local council executives and a real *Dragons' Den* winner in the boardroom. The local television station covered the event in their news bulletins and children were interviewed for local radio. To spread collaboration beyond just the children, we arranged shared transport to the venue and a buffet to bring both schools' parents together. Parents and children from both communities were thus given an insight into different spheres of the world of work and a chance to meet and talk to people with whom they would not normally come into contact.

Reciprocity between the school and the local community

At the starting point of this particular part of the adventure we tended to look at the community from the point of view of what they could give to the school. The community was there to support the school. We looked to them to provide money and maybe prizes for special events. Their role was to attend and support the activities we wanted to enact. They were there to support their children but we would advise them how. The real change in our community involvement occurred with a shift in attitude. We began to see the relationship as reciprocal and instead to concentrate on what we could give to the community. After all, the community give the school their most precious possessions, their children. Instead of maintaining a kind of ivory-tower distance we needed to become more ground-based, more part of the complex day-to-day life surrounding us. The development of breakfast club illustrates the shift in our thinking.

Every morning breakfast club opens at 8.30 a.m. This began as an initiative to encourage children to come to school on time and to ensure that they had had something to eat before they started trying to learn. Since then it has escalated and developed into a true community service. Now past pupils drop in for take-outs on their way to the local secondary school. Parents and family friends eat with their children and have even been known to come in for food and company when their child has been ill. The community police and local librarians drop in regularly. Once a week, the school nurse holds mini-consultations and advice sessions. A teaching assistant runs an outbranch for the local credit unions.

The initial benefits have magnified for the school. Breakfast club has now become a way to bring together people who were previously reluctant to talk to each other. The informality and friendly atmosphere makes it easier for parents, staff and other agencies to talk together. The emphasis on promoting well-being has extended beyond the basic principles of preventing hungry children to include the wider community and a much broader sense of what well-being entails. Plans are now in the pipeline to develop this further to incorporate a cyber café so that children can continue learning out of hours and adults can access computers. Recently two parent governors prepared the case and represented the school at a local council meeting to request funding so that we could further develop the canteen as a hub for community activities. As a result it is now used for holiday clubs, independent of the school; a local community worker uses it for church services; an ex-army bomb disposal expert is setting up a club to promote fitness and team building; and a dance troupe practises there weekly.

Working and learning within the wider community

'He was very nice Miss, but he's not really a philosopher. I had to tell him what a philosophical question was.'

This was a 7-year-old member of the Philosophy Crew, talking about the Regeneration Officer for the local housing association. Year 2 and Year 4 children had taken part in a philosophy session alongside representatives from the housing association's head office and representatives from the residents association.

The community is more than just the people attached in some way to the school. It has become increasingly important that the school plays a role in different areas of community life. We want to be part of the everyday life of Limeside. Just as our vision seeks to empower our children to play an active role in their community, the school needs to be active within the locality. This role needed to be more sustained than previous, somewhat tokenistic gestures, such as litter picking, carol singing or distributing harvest gifts. We want to be an active participant in the adventure of local life. To this end, the head teacher sits on the Area Committee and children contribute to tenants' and residents' meetings. We have established close links with housing association representatives and through them with other organisations. School staff and children introduced and supported housing association personnel to develop philosophy for communities and an enquiry approach within their organisation and the communities they serve. A teacher trained their staff and facilitated enquiries that brought housing association staff, children and adults from different communities together.

A striking example would be a philosophical enquiry that brought together adult residents from Limeside and a neighbouring, almost 100 per cent Bangladeshi, community. Despite initial apprehension and the need to work through an interpreter, people began to realise areas of commonality as they discussed questions arising from a picture of youths in hoodies. As James Williams, the Regeneration Manager at Contour Housing Group, reflected: 'The groups bonded well, both young and old. There was no problem with people listening to others speak, solely an understanding that they both wanted the same thing.'

People who had never met began to actively engage and learn from each other. Perhaps the most striking image from this came at the end of the enquiry. An elderly Bangladeshi man grasped the hand of Limeside's head teacher and through an interpreter explained that 'my son is your son and your son is my son'.

This has become a real partnership, perhaps best illustrated through the production of *What if . . . ?* (Contour Housing Group and Limeside Primary School, 2007) – the book created and published by the school, residents and housing association. It brought together school, housing, community and business representatives. It aimed to take a series of guiding ideas and explore what impact they had on the local community and what it would mean for the future. It involved various people aged from 2 to 90. Perhaps the most important element of all these initiatives has been their role in promoting understanding, trust and respect between areas of the community that would not otherwise have come together. Strikingly, co-operating in this way brought home the realisation that many organisations are working with a similar sense of purpose – we are all in the society-building business – although our immediate concerns may be significantly different.

'From this opportunity I have learnt that when I take a little step forward it only takes me to a little amount of achievement but with a lot of little steps and a huge amount of enthusiasm I can do great things. In the future, I will use this to do great (amazing) things in my life WHAT A GREAT TIME!!!

To make it even more exciting we qualified for our Level 2 certificates, this meant were on the way to be famous at the age of only 9 to 11 WOW!!'

This is taken from the final part of Annie's (Year 5) project planning diary.

Building aspirations

Some of our children come from families now facing their third generation of unemployment. Self-employment and enterprise ventures are under-represented in the locality compared with national norms. When the local housing association hired a small business consultant to help residents explore and set up their own enterprises, take-up was limited. Instead, the school used the professional's expertise to run the *Dragons' Den* project outlined above. When questioned about their future, children and families often envisage the next generation working and living to a similar pattern. Our ultimate aim is to encourage children to fly beyond what is known and accepted, to forge their own future adventure and to be active in creating the future adventure for the world. The community needs to see what this future could be and believe that their children can attain it. Somehow we need to widen everyone's views of the range of possibilities open to our children and to believe them to be attainable.

To address this, we set up an initiative in which a group of Year 5 and 6 children planned and put on an art exhibition, helped by a social enterprise company and a motivational coach. They organised transport for parents and other community members, refreshments, press releases and marketing. At the same time, they learnt about project planning and managed to achieve an AQA (Assessment and Qualifications Alliance) Level 2 certificate in contributing to a project, normally a post-16 qualification. The hope is that seeing what their children have already achieved will expand parents' expectations for themselves as well as their children. To encourage this, we take every opportunity to publish the school and community's achievements in the local press. It is a slow process and we don't reach all the parents but it is important to recognise and celebrate small changes.

> 'Miss, can we do business enterprise today? I've got to tell the others about the market research so we can decide on our designs. It's my job.'
>
> This is John (Year 3) greeting his teacher waving his project plan and highlighter pen.
>
> Year 3 are currently organising the summer fair and have been since December! They have researched different Christmas markets, and are designing products, having constructed their own aims, objectives and project plans complete with risk assessments.

Developing enterprise skills has become an increasingly important aspect of our vision and mission. We see it as a way to empower children and to create the active engagement and drive that are so vital a part of our mission to enable children to fly. At the time of writing we are collaborating with a local enterprise company to find ways to build this into all learning contexts. This will not just be about financial enterprise, but will also involve ways to promote self-motivation, drive, meta-reflection and self- and group responsibility. It involves developing many of the leadership skills and understanding often thought to be the province of business leaders. We hope that parents and other community members will be partners in this work and that it will further increase the ambition and creative agency of the community in the future.

Limeside and the community in a nutshell

> 'Help us spread our wings' sing children, parents, and staff.
>
> Sixty children dressed in green, yellow, red and blue waterproof ponchos transform from the shape of a caterpillar to form an enormous butterfly on the school playground. Above are representatives from the housing association and school who are filming the movements. The Mayor and Chief Executive of Contour Homes lead the applause before approximately 300 children, parents, representatives from local government, neighbours, governors, housing association staff, enterprise staff and members of the Maharishi community gather to wave at the camera.
>
> It's snowing and so cold that people are hugging each other but everyone is there participating and celebrating together.

This was the launch of our community book *What If …?* (2007). For 12 weeks, Year 6 children had planned and organised this celebration. They had rehearsed and enabled the rest of the school to perform a dance in which they made human shapes to symbolise the images and ideas in the book. They transformed from a world to a heart, from a bird to the sun, from a smile to a shout. The music and song were written by school staff and governors joined by some local workers during the vision day, described in Chapter 2. The children had been supported by regeneration and housing association staff, graphic designers, advertising agency employees, a life and motivational coach, a local dance specialist, governors, the school meals service – the list is extensive. By organising the event the children qualified for their contribution to the project planning certificate. They were only the second group of primary pupils to achieve this. The first were the art exhibition group the year before. After the performance the adults all congregated in the hall to eat specially iced 'What If …?' biscuits. It brought representatives from many local spheres together in an acknowledgement and celebration of what the community had achieved by working together. The local press described it as 'an example of how thinking differently has impacted on housing, the community, schools and businesses'.

Of course there have been difficulties and challenges for the community in this shift of attitude. Both school and parents still revert back to more traditional roles, particularly in times of pressure. At the time of writing, economic cutbacks are making life difficult and in times of crisis it can be more difficult to take action. We are finding that as relationships and trust between school and families grow, the school is being asked to help with increasingly complex situations. This is stretching our capacity and could, if we let it, divert us from a central purpose of learning. Some parents are harder to reach than others and we are now beginning to face the welcome but challenging prospect of relating to people who have English as an additional language. Also, safeguarding requirements have forced us to limit access to the building and grounds.

However, perhaps one mark of the loyalty and care the community now feels towards the school is epitomised by the fact that we don't have CCTV on site and incidents of vandalism are very rare; the neighbours watch out instead. Indeed when a small wooden owl was stolen from the Foundation Stage outdoor area, the community was shocked. By the next morning, it was back on its perch having allegedly been retrieved from a garage.

Next steps

At the time of writing, we are currently engaged in plans to forge a new pathway for our adventure. We are planning to further develop the school as a local hub by creating community growing opportunities, using the space around the edge of the playground as a resource for planting and harvesting food. The wish is that this will help catalyse children, families and local people into taking action to make Limeside greener, while awakening an interest about future food sourcing and security.

Most of our work so far has centred on our local community but we now need to help children understand their role as global citizens. The next challenge will be to develop a sense of identity and coherence within and between the outer ripples of our community model. This is particularly important as the school's population is beginning to change and we now welcome children who have recently arrived from Eastern Europe and African nations. It has implications for the breadth of heritages we wish to celebrate and it gives us the first-hand opportunities to do so. It is an important factor to feed into our new curriculum planning.

Our school building is a great resource that is underused. To fully realise our dream of being an integral part of the community, we need to open it up to more community groups. Plans are under way for community groups to use the canteen out of school hours. However, we are aware that there is a vast array of people in our local community with whom we still have little contact. Trying to create links between generations will be important. Our dream is to create true intergenerational learning opportunities that build on and extend beyond the short-term projects such as the *What If ...?* book.

Conclusion

Two years ago the school staff spent an enquiry day trying to understand the school's community in greater depth. The final group task was to find a way of drawing the school within that community. Our favourite idea was two pairs of cupped, interlinked hands, with a watch. It showed that the school and community had a practical, creative, 'doing' role within the area and yet also had a caring, embracing and encompassing role. The watch signified the ticking pulse of change and that practical changes would take time. The *What If ...?* launch would suggest that much of this is being realised, at least within the four inner spheres of our community ripples. At a recent visioning day a parent governor described the school as a fire – warm and welcoming so that it draws people in. Creating this atmosphere takes time, energy and continuity. One of our greatest assets has been the stability of staff, so that we really learn to know our community well.

Above all, it has become clear that by learning to understand and work with our community, we as a school have developed a clearer insight into our purpose at Limeside. In order to serve our children, we must also serve our community. This must inform the kind of curriculum opportunities we provide. It is, however, a purpose that goes beyond what has recently been seen as the remit of schools in that it centres around a sense of mutual responsibility that extends past our immediate children and families to the wider local community. It echoes but goes beyond Alexander's (2010) Cambridge review of primary education when he stresses the need for schools to contribute towards the regeneration of communal life. One of the principles underlying our vision is that children will care enough to want to get actively involved. Perhaps we should restate this to embrace the vision that school *and community* will care enough to get actively involved with each other. After all, as the children pray each week in Friday's Celebration Assembly:

Let us remember

That as many hands build a house

So many hearts make a school

Chapter 6

Varied invitations for a diverse community: Malorees Infant School

Small opportunities are often the beginning of great enterprises
(Demosthenes, Greek orator and politician in Athens
(384–322 BC) *Ad Leptinum* 162, cited in Harbottle, 1897)

Introduction

In this chapter we outline how we have implemented a range of small yet significant steps that together have facilitated an improved partnership with our school community. Our diversity is both a strength and challenge; our children have had a wide range of different early experiences, governed by very varied cultural norms and expectations. If Malorees' children are to THRIVE as we want them to they need to be fully engaged members of the school community with a strong sense of purpose, achievement and belonging. Being young doesn't prevent full participation. The strong learning identity built in school needs to extend beyond the building and into the home and the community, where so much valuable learning takes place.

To support this development a key element of our vision is to give more priority to the relationship we have with our community and the pivotal role we play in breaking down barriers. We describe our diverse community and the elements that make up an effective partnership. We then describe the innovations that we have introduced over time to develop that partnership.

In the past, school and home were kept very separate for many children. Their parents would leave them at the gate or come to the occasional event or parents' meeting, but that was all. The climate has been changing, with schools being encouraged to embrace opportunities to work with parents and outside agencies. This is a change we welcome. To do this effectively we need to extend membership of the school community to our children's families for real, so that home and school overlap and we build a closer and more mutually rewarding relationship in which the community and the wider world provide a location and resource for our adventure.

As a school we are on a learning journey to create more flexible boundaries and build a new 'synergy' which will enable families to learn with us and feel part of the whole community, extending 'school' learning into the home and bringing 'home' learning into school. This interdependence is crucial to the achievement of our vision and values – our young plants need a steady diet of nutrients at school and in the home. If we can communicate effectively with our parent community and share our messages about learning, the children's opportunities will increase enormously. 'Learners for life' need their learning to continue and spread throughout their whole life, wherever they may be, so it becomes the way they are, rather than merely the way they behave in school. We want our families to engage in rich conversations with children, to work together creatively to solve real-life problems, to encourage choices and decision making, not just to support them by more traditional methods such as setting sums and spellings.

We know the gap is beginning to be bridged when the children come into school with anecdotes or examples of learning they have done at home without being asked. This includes poems about kites to add to a display, an extension of a number sequence up into the tens of thousands, research on jellyfish, and the solution to a design technology problem. Similarly we know this gap is closing when parents report particularly interesting questions and conversations they have had with their children arising from lessons in school.

Our school community is central to our success. First, research through time has made it clear that parental involvement in their child's learning at home is a very powerful factor in children's achievement and attitudes. For example the work of Douglas (1964) over 40 years ago found that children were disadvantaged not by social class, but rather by lack of parents' interest. More recent research confirms this (Desforges with Abouchaar, 2003). Second, our local community is a key context for hands-on, real learning. Third, we also have the opportunity, and we would argue the responsibility, to support growth for other family members and the community around us. We recognise that there can be a lot of social and ethnic fragmentation in our locality but that in school we can offer opportunities for cultures to mix, for relationships to be formed and for everyone to belong. Sharing goals for all our children is a powerful tool for creating mutual respect and understanding.

What is our community like?

The broad social and ethnic diversity of our school community is our greatest asset. It is the particular context of the school that provides us with both tremendous scope and opportunity, combined with genuine challenges. We are a community infant school located in Brent, one of the most ethnically diverse and economically deprived boroughs in the country. Our families represent a wide spectrum of countries across the globe (with 40 home languages spoken and all six major religions represented) and they come from an equally broad spectrum of social/economic groups. About a third of our learners are learning English as an additional language, with again about a third having special educational needs. The number of children with statements of special needs has increased five-fold over the last five years and is well above the national average, with most classes supporting two children with statements for complex needs. Although we view this as a positive feature it has brought with it a number of pressures. Our community includes a strong core of middle-class professional families who have traditionally chosen our oversubscribed school over the years. Demographically the school is closely situated to Queen's Park, one of the most sought-after areas in the property market in London. Parents have very different working lives from each other, from skilled professionals to those in unskilled jobs and unemployment. We have children from families with up to five children living in one-bedroom flats and bed-and-breakfast accommodation, children in the care of the local authority, as well as children whose families live in expensive properties.

The area around the school is varied and has witnessed considerable change in recent years. The community itself comprises a wide range of privately owned housing and an equally wide range of social housing accommodation. Characteristically within Brent there are considerable pockets of deprivation. The immediate location around our school does not necessarily appear to reflect this as we are placed in spacious and appealing grounds, with attractive housing, yet we know from the home visits that we undertake with all new nursery children that a considerable number of our families are living in poverty. Undoubtedly it is this range of diversity, an inherent feature of living in London, which provides great richness. Alongside this there are destabilising factors, which include pressures around housing, education, unemployment, crime and community living.

In essence, the challenges we face are the same as for many schools, as the communities we all serve are constantly changing and evolving. Our school community is no exception. The social and ethnic diversity in our school provides harmony and collaboration – there is such a multiplicity of groups that no one stands out – but even so, there is occasional distrust, separation and isolation, with working-class families and non-fluent English speakers sometimes feeling intimidated by the English-speaking middle classes. On occasions tension and bad feeling can also occur within the community around competition for places at the school.

Creating a partnership

We have identified a range of elements that need to be put in place to achieve effective family membership of the school community. We need to ensure mutual trust, share our philosophy with them, listen to their views and find common ground, as far as possible, while valuing their diverse heritages and opinions. At the same time we need to provide plenty of opportunities for hands-on participation and contribution in school life and learning for the families. If the school ensures that these elements are in place it will still need the active and enthusiastic involvement of parents to create a real partnership (see Figure 6.1).

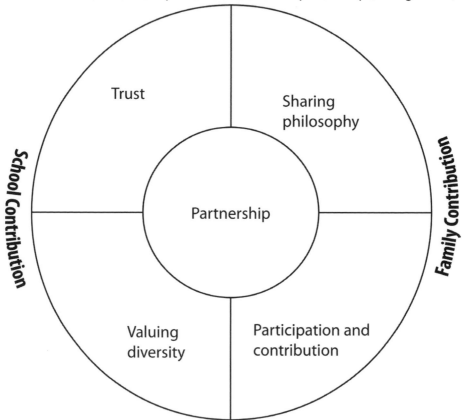

Figure 6.1: Creating a partnership

Trust

A partnership by definition is non-hierarchical and mutual. Traditionally schools have set the agenda, the curriculum and the rules and reported back to parents on progress, with the parents being allocated a very passive role. We appreciate that all parents take a risk entrusting their children to our care. What we want the parents to feel is that we acknowledge a *shared* investment in their child. Using the analogy of the child as a seed with limitless potential, the family could be viewed as bringing us their precious seedlings to be planted out in the garden. We then want to work in partnership to nurture them and help them to flourish.

Essential to this sharing of investment is mutual trust. Trust is not a given but will grow as we create knowledge, openness, dialogue and involvement together. Teachers need to develop the confidence and resilience to engage with and listen to parental requests, suggestions and even grumbles, without being defensive or threatened, recognising the insights that parents can share. The culture of 'them and us' needs to be broken down.

There has always been a strong culture in the school of good communication with parents via standard sources such as weekly newsletters, parent consultation evenings, curriculum meetings and assemblies. But we wanted to go beyond passive information sharing to develop dialogue and interaction. Therefore we have been instigating a range of new initiatives to find ways to listen to parents as well as to inform them.

We began by organising home visits with all new nursery families to emphasise the shared responsibility of home and school in the first stage of the child's education. Similarly, introductory conversations are set up with reception parents and staff to build a relationship from the very beginning as well as class tea parties in September for all the staff, children and families in every class to meet each other informally. After that there are the usual range of formal and informal meetings between teachers and parents. But even at these meetings it is all too easy to fall into traditional roles, with parents expecting to be told, not asked, and teachers having only limited expectations of the parents' contribution. It is not always easy to encourage parents to know that they can also be an educational expert.

We have therefore felt the need for additional opportunities to listen to families' views of our school but, like many who try to do this, only get a partial answer as we tend mainly to hear from a self-selecting group, those who attend meetings, fill in questionnaires and talk regularly with teachers. Responses to questionnaires include statements such as: 'I find Malorees Infants to be a very inclusive and nurturing environment for our young children. I enjoy being part of this community. As a working mum I try to participate as much as I am able.'

Which aspects of school do you think work well?

'Nurturing the children's respect for one another.'

'Excellent emphasis on social skills and caring for others.'

'Very good on encouraging artistic, expressive side. Good confidence building and sharing.'

Comments from a parental questionnaire, 2008

But what of the parents who we rarely see and from whom we get no feedback? We still have a small but crucial minority of families who rarely attend parent–teacher meetings or engage in home–school projects, let alone engage in shared learning opportunities. Some are wary of our more adventurous style of learning, giving the impression that they would prefer a school providing a much more formal education similar to their own, where learning really only takes place in school and is not the responsibility of parents at all. Sometimes this takes the form of resisting our attempts to enlist the support of outside agencies to help troubled children or those with special needs, and in these cases it is crucial we gain their trust for the benefit of the children concerned. For these families, instead of starting with developing partnership we try to build towards it through encouraging participation and contribution (see below).

To look below the surface we set up the Parent Forum in 2008, a group of 12 parents, chosen to represent a cross-section of our diverse community, to gauge views and act on parents' ideas. The group meets with no fixed agenda to share ideas on a range of issues, which can range from the philosophical to the practical and mostly those identified by the parents themselves as being important. At an early meeting the parent representatives were asked to choose and order their priorities for young children at school. Discussions began with an emphasis on key academic skills such as reading and writing, but very quickly moved on to social, emotional and learning attitudes. Somewhat surprising themselves, their top choices became: 'building confidence and learning independence', 'a safe and friendly family environment' and 'being encouraged to interact with others in a group'.

More recently the value of the Parent Forum was clarified for us when sensitive questions about the social and racial mix of the school were raised. Opinions voiced suggest that there are small pockets of parents who feel under-represented and that more could be done for minority groups. We did not know this. There had previously been no real opportunity for anyone to say it.

Sharing our philosophy

At the beginning of the school year we now hold a curriculum meeting for parents entitled 'What does my child do at school all day?' Sharing our latest initiatives with the parents sets the context for the whole evening (such as the vision jigsaw [see page 60], the learning opportunities jigsaw [see page 150], wizard walls and the promise tree). This is followed up with information on how this is translated into practice in the children's learning and how families can become involved in school and at home. The meeting affords us the opportunity to stress the importance of developing a genuine partnership with parents. Some parents are gradually beginning to understand through this that they can support their children's learning more effectively at home by building a model with them than by sitting them down in front of endless workbooks. Feedback from parents demonstrates that sharing our vision with them in this way helps them to have a better understanding of how existing practice and new school initiatives fit into the bigger picture.

> Mustafa was a very high achieving, articulate child with excellent maths and literacy skills. However, when being confronted with a more open-ended task, such as designing and building a model, he lost all confidence, panicked and developed stomach pains: the physical symptoms of stress. Dialogue with his parents helped them to acknowledge his difficulties and adopt a broader view of learning. They supported the school in opening out his learning activities outside school to mirror what we were providing in school with the result that his confidence and enthusiasm blossomed. He began to relish design technology projects in particular but also to enjoy more open challenges generally, no longer clinging to the closed, the safe and the predictable.

However, for some it is more effective to show them our vision in practice, particularly for those parents who will come into school to support their own child but will not attend meetings. While educational research has not proved that parents volunteering and participating in schools has a direct result on children's attainment, we believe that it will undoubtedly promote the trust that we are aiming to develop and encourage more effective learning activities at home (Desforges with Abouchaar, 2003).

A key aspect of our curriculum planning involves the children in communicating outcomes of a project with an audience, who can be other children in the class or across the school, families or visitors to the school. Often sharing learning with parents takes the form of an assembly or performance but more adventurous models are being tried such as a tea party for families, designed for and catered by the children to encapsulate their learning around 'changing materials'. Recently one year group exhibited their learning in the form of a museum with artefacts made by the children. This involved a quiz for the parents to complete to increase their engagement in the experience. Parents' evaluations were overwhelmingly positive and the feedback from them made the children positively glow! These occasions strengthen the dialogue between children and parents about their learning and often lead to parents extending the learning through research and outings at home. Feedback from informal conversations, parental questionnaires and our curriculum evenings suggests that many parents increasingly share our vision of a learning community that develops the whole child, where school learning is a much wider opportunity than skill acquisition.

We see our task as to continue to welcome those groups on the 'outside' of our school community to spend time with us in school, through an increasing range of unthreatening opportunities, in the hope that, little by little, more and more of them come 'inside' and gain increasingly positive impressions of an alternative, more adventurous, learning environment. This is an ongoing process – not everyone will be convinced straight away but the door will remain open.

Valuing diversity

For their sense of identity, self-esteem and belonging, it needs to be clear that everyone's home and culture is valued in school. A parent or grandparent from a minority culture coming in to share a childhood toy or a religious ritual or tradition in a family show-and-tell session demonstrates to all the children that everyone is valued in our school. Despite our location in a busy, multicultural city, some of our children have had little experience in their early years of cultures beyond that of their own extended family and their first few weeks at school must often seem very strange.

Often our children and families are real experts in areas the other children and staff know little about and we want them to feel proud of sharing this expertise in school.

> Anjali brought tremendous knowledge of her family's Indian heritage into school, volunteering to read a Hindi poem in assembly and encouraging the whole class to give the parents a demonstration of Indian dancing. She shares her knowledge and experience with the other children with pride. When talking with her parents about this, they were quite clear that as first-generation immigrants in London 20 or 30 years ago they would have kept quiet about their roots and not have been encouraged, nor had the confidence, to see them as an asset.

We are very clear that we perceive our role and responsibility as articulating and realising the value we place on our community through:

- understanding the world as a global community;
- understanding and acknowledging the influence of different cultures and ideas;
- developing skills of communication to express respect, tolerance and empathy;
- recognising that conflict exists and identifying different ways to resolve it; and
- valuing our community.

A committed and supportive Parent Staff Association has worked conscientiously over many years to harness the richness of our community. In the past we have felt that the incredible diversity in our school is not always fully represented at meetings but this has improved recently, although there are still many families to bring on board. Similarly, the composition of our staff team and governing body has begun to change to better reflect our ethnic mix. We know that our responsibility in school is a big one: we need to challenge community barriers that exist and wherever possible reduce them.

However, it is not always easy. Families from minority ethnic backgrounds can sometimes be hard to reach. There may be language barriers and a lack of confidence in communicating on both sides, with staff as well as parents not sure of cultural traditions. Similarly, some families are used to a much more formal relationship with teachers and are shy to air their own views. Others do not share our ethical or cultural values, asking for their children to be withdrawn from certain curriculum activities, such as music or assemblies, on religious grounds. In the past we have respected their wishes but, more recently, are becoming more explicit about our expectation that all our children should have full access to the whole curriculum.

We undoubtedly have more work to do on understanding the perspective of all our families and in bringing different groups together. Developing strong positive attitudes towards difference is a high priority in our work with the children. On the whole we have been more successful to date in airing and exploring diversity issues with the children than with the wider community.

> Hari (Year 2) recently said to a student teacher: 'I really like England. It's the only place we can all live together. You see I'm Sikh and you're Muslim and he's Christian and everyone lives together'. Talking about his cousin's school, Hari said: 'It's not fair for everyone who wants to go there if they only let in Indian children.'
>
> Charlie said: 'Some children really struggle with their work and get cross with themselves but we still help them, and that's a good thing. It would be cruel and mean not to let them [children with behavioural difficulties] come to our school because they really want to come because we can teach them how to be good.'
>
> Leo said: 'People are born in different ways. I was born with autism.'

To support and develop these attitudes the school is increasingly proactive in designing the curriculum to value the community and its diversity. Teachers drew on the rich heritage of our community during a family history project in Year 2. Opportunities were created for the children to present a questionnaire to their parents posing a range of questions to facilitate fascinating discussion opportunities in class. This process was very revealing in that it demonstrated to everyone the significant journeys and experiences the parents had made. Some parents and grandparents came into the class to share their stories. The whole class was able to celebrate and respect each other's cultural roots.

Participation and contribution

We have increasingly found that the most effective approach for involving families, as with young children, is not so much talking as doing. And the most effective types of activity to draw the families in are those involving both parents and children together. We have always held social events, including a well-attended 'International Evening', Christmas parties and summer barbecues, but are increasingly encouraging all parents to take part in learning activities with the children such as 'Orchard Days', 'Family Learning Days' and themed week activities. Parents who would be reluctant to attend a party will often support groups of children alongside other adults on a challenge activity and it only takes one successful event to make someone feel part of the school community.

Parental involvement in reception classes has been an area we have been looking to develop for some time and staff confidence in the opportunities 'Grand Finales' provide has built up gradually. 'Grand Finales' are events organised to mark the end of a project. A vivid example of this was the 'Number Carnival' held recently by our reception classes where the children designed and manned a variety of fairground stalls involving counting, adding and using coins – stalls such as hoopla, beanbag toss and those selling popcorn and number biscuits. The parents were all invited and the children carefully explained the rules to them and supervised their activities. There was a wonderful atmosphere with children and parents enthused and involved, but the most encouraging aspect was that out of 30 children, 29 had family members present, despite the fact that it was held at 9.30 a.m. on a working day.

Arts Week has been running for over 14 years but has grown organically over that period to involve more and more family participation. In recent years over 100 parents have actively joined in with the children in practical projects throughout the school. The number of adults supporting the children means that we can attempt much more ambitious artwork than would normally be possible and give the children the opportunity to try out new and exciting media such as working with photography, metal and wire, welding and ICT.

A recent theme was 'Splash!', which linked to learning about sustainability and water conservation at home and in the wider world. The hands-on nature of Arts Week offers an unthreatening introduction to school involvement for many parents who lack confidence, particularly those for whom English is a second language. Some of these parents go on to support in classes generally, join the Parent Staff Association or take up other opportunities for involvement. Our annual Book Week is now involving more and more families as well, with a recent theme being 'Adventures in the Outdoors'. These weeks offer parents the opportunity to see that often the best learning may take place outside the classroom and involve no paper and pencils at all!

Another new development is the introduction of 'Family Learning Days'. The first event of this kind was a day when family members were invited to join in the 'Grand Finale' of a science project on forces. Parents and children were given the task of building a machine to move a ball over a distance and worked in groups to construct a wonderful variety of inventive solutions to the problem. Several parents who had never joined in anything before took part and the day was really useful in communicating to parents the possibilities of hands-on investigative learning. The evaluations from parents clearly expressed that they would definitely like more events of this kind. The children mostly loved having their parents in school to join in, though one or two felt the parents were enjoying it so much they didn't always let the children get a look in!

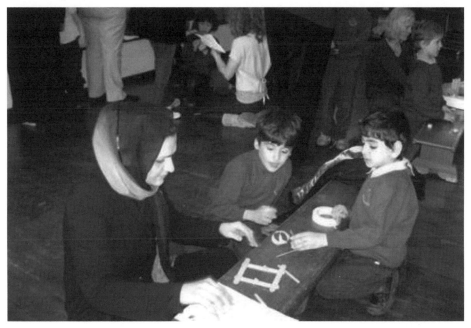

A thriving element of our school community is the group of staff and parents who maintain our orchard. Some years ago they totally redeveloped an overgrown and underused wooded corner of our grounds and redesigned it as a magical place to inspire the community with a love of nature. Each year, a few children who may not particularly shine in the classroom can be seen to be in their element in there, totally absorbed in the natural world. Parents were recently instrumental in saving our orchard from development by a local housing association. The parents continue to sustain this with enthusiastic attendance at weekly Orchard Clubs and Orchard Open/Clearance Days where families and children share the enjoyment of collaborating together to enhance this very special and beautiful place in the heart of the busy city. These occasions are almost an encapsulation of our vision in practice, with everyone nurturing and respecting the beauty and potential of the natural world together. Often these parents are those you hardly ever see in school, particularly some of the dads, and through these opportunities they gain a connection with the school they would not otherwise have. This project has enabled some parents not only to go on to attend meetings and participate in classroom activities but even to embark on furthering their own learning and training by signing up for National Vocational Qualification (NVQ) courses.

An exciting new development for the school, at the request of parents, has been the setting up of after-school provision in a brand new, purpose-built, timber pavilion, 'The Lodge'. This provision has been set up as a result of direct consultation with and feedback from working parents.

Next steps

We are currently developing our school learning website (Managed Learning Environment) using the learning platform 'Fronter' as a framework. This was introduced into the Early Years last year and is being extended up into Key Stage 1 this year. The idea is that families can access a range of classroom learning news, exhibitions of children's work, games and resources online at home that will encourage learning and learning conversations that link directly to what is going on in classrooms.

Another recent development has focused on nursery and reception class parents being invited into school on a regular basis to read and share their child's 'learning journey' with their child and the class teacher. This opportunity has proved to be very valuable in promoting a shared and enhanced understanding of the child's learning. Many of these initiatives are quite new and experimental but hopefully a beginning of another aspect of our adventure. What we would like to see over the next few years is a school where parents work with groups alongside and independently of teachers, leading and supporting a range of exciting projects that extend our curriculum and take our young adventurers down new paths and on new journeys. Equally, we want to see our children taking their learning attitudes home with them and taking their own initiatives to develop and extend what they have enjoyed and been inspired by in school.

Our first challenge is to ensure everyone develops the confidence to maintain and expand on these beginnings so that community involvement becomes an integral part of everything we do. Some staff feel more confident working alongside parents than others and there has been a degree of inconsistent practice, though gradually confidence and enthusiasm are growing and more confident staff are supporting their colleagues to experiment with a variety of models. Ideally we would like parents to come to us with ideas of their own for learning projects in school in view of the huge range of expertise that exists within our community.

Our new building, The Lodge, will also generate opportunities in the future for family workshops, parenting groups and community meetings. Opportunities for how this provision can be extended and shaped by the emerging needs of the community will continue to be a discussion point.

It needs to be acknowledged, though, that many families have full active learning lives already and may not need or have time to have their horizons expanded. Equally, parents of lower socio-economic groups or with fewer qualifications have sometimes also told us that they feel intimidated by some of our more 'successful' parents, so projects need to be designed for the less confident to become involved without being expected to take on more responsibility than they can manage. Ideally, in time, the creative planning of teachers will be augmented by innovative ideas from the community.

We have come a long way towards including our families and have our sights now firmly set on working more collaboratively with the wider community. We hope to forge closer links with community and faith groups in the surrounding area, though this has already begun with visits to local places of worship and from the local Muslim primary school, Church of England vicar and Hare Krishna Temple.

Conclusion

Our involvement with families and our community has been evolving with time to develop a sense of adventure and discovery for all. Each new initiative involves investment in time, commitment and resources, but gradually each one becomes embedded in school practice. As a result we continue to build up our stamina, confidence and expertise for future projects. Similarly, each project on its own will only shift a number of people. But collectively, over time, a positive transformation begins to take place. The rewards of effective partnership are huge. It is on the occasions when the partnership is working at its best that we see our vision becoming a reality and our children really thriving.

Chapter 7

Understanding and growing our place: St Vigor and St John Primary School

And as we let our own light shine, we unconsciously give other people permission to do the same. As we are liberated from our own fear, our presence automatically liberates others.

(Williamson 1992: 190)

Introduction

In this chapter we describe a number of the distinctive features of our community and how the curriculum we provide makes a direct response to them. We discuss the role the school plays in leading and responding to the adventure of learning within our community and relate this to aspects of recent work on community cohesion. We outline challenges for us in the relationship of our school to its community and the need for real, purposeful dialogues between every member so that the potential for generating social value can be realised.

St Vigor and St John Church of England Primary School is one of many church schools situated in the rural county of Somerset. It is set in a village context serving Chilcompton and the neighbouring community of Stratton-on-the-Fosse, which no longer has its own school. This was as a result of an amalgamation of three smaller schools. This change in school provision deeply challenged the identities of the two village communities, especially as one continued to lose its other amenities (for example the local shop) and the other continued to grow and develop.

The majority of the children are white and pupil mobility is low; 24 per cent of our children are identified as having special educational needs. The school is south of the cities of Bath and Bristol in the former Somerset coalfield that closed in the 1970s and remains an economically challenged area. Historically, agriculture has played a major role in the area and there are three large Duchy farms in the two villages. Present employment is diverse with a number of families leaving the village to work, some travelling long distances. Somerset has a considerable number of low-paid workers at and below the national minimum wage. A significant number of families have lived in the villages for a number of generations and are now challenged by the more recent property price rises which prevent the next generation from buying and staying in the village.

We have been making sense of what community cohesion might mean for us as a school. Community cohesion can be described as:

> working towards a society in which there is a common vision and sense of belonging by all communities; a society in which the diversity of people's backgrounds and circumstances is appreciated and valued; a society in which similar life opportunities are available to all; and a society in which strong and positive relationships exist and continue to be developed in the workplace, in schools and in the wider community.
>
> (Johnson, 2006)

This view might be perceived as more applicable to urban settings, but issues of equality, opportunity, relationships and engagement are just as challenging in rural areas such as ours. Indeed, issues such as racial intolerance are sometimes more hidden. There is a clear need for the curriculum developed by rural schools to respond to their local, rural community and the characteristics, needs, desires and aspirations associated with it. Leadbeater and Mongon (2008) identify that a route to delivering better outcomes is one where educational settings seek to develop an interactive community approach to generate wider public and social value. They describe how some of this value has to 'escape' or be shared with the local community. Schools in this way develop an 'outward-looking' stance as active participants within their community and locality.

As a school we aim to provide this kind of value and as rural schools are a key 'institution' or amenity within a relatively small community they play an important role. Schools can act as leaders or guides on the adventure of learning in its widest sense. They can form active communities that model or enable new initiatives, ideas and behaviours. For example, in our community where many residents are interested in environmental issues, our school's use of solar power has demonstrated the use of new technologies in a practical sense to both pupils and the community at large. We have secured funding that enables the children to promote energy-saving devices to a community audience.

Strengths and challenges of our school community: Their impact on our curriculum

Under the overall umbrella of our work on community cohesion we have identified a number of the key distinctive features of our community. We needed to do this to become clear about how our curriculum design could most appropriately develop the strengths and address the challenges of our context. Initially we identified seven areas that informed the community aspect of our vision statement and our resulting curriculum design.

Being rural

Our school lies in the north-west corner of Somerset with the fields and hills of the Mendips going towards Wells in one direction and the more densely populated areas of Midsomer Norton and Radstock in the other. We are immediately surrounded by agricultural land and, although fairly near a number of towns, are in a predominantly rural area. We teased out what we thought 'rural' meant for us and considered the many positives of our setting. The natural environment predominates with Duchy farms, Downside woods and the Mendip hills giving a strong sense of seasonal activities. Workers in the community have access to rural work, for example farming, cider making, cheese production, quarrying and rural crafts. There are opportunities for rural pursuits, such as horse riding and walking, and for peace and space and safer places to play outdoors.

> Our children hardly blinked when accompanied on a walk-to-school venture by a small lamb wearing a pink diamanté collar, who could not stay at home because she would miss her surrogate mother. The press thought differently and the resulting photograph made a suitable 'ahhhh' moment for the local community.

But there are also challenges. Services, advice, expertise and help are often a long way away. Family and friends can be scattered, leading to isolation. Staff of the school can live some distance away. The distance from cultural centres, entertainment and sports facilities can make access an issue: Bath is 15 miles away. Community members often have to travel to work, shop and for recreation. This takes time, money and energy.

We celebrate our 'ruralness' by deliberately choosing and incorporating knowledge and understanding of features and events that are characteristic of our place. We visit our local farms throughout the seasons of the year, drawing out the distinctiveness of Somerset apples, cheese and strawberries in focused learning weeks and making visits to explore issues of environmental sustainability at our local quarries. Children are able to see how quarrying disrupts the landscape and how the 'levy' funds are used to instigate conservation projects in the wider community.

We aim to provide a curriculum that enables children to explore, acknowledge and understand the outdoors as a learning environment. All our children are entitled to Forest School activities. Our global gardens project enabled children to experience the pleasure and challenges of growing their own food while acknowledging and learning more about the difficulties that some global communities have in doing the same. We also use the potential of our local woods as a stimulus for storytelling and developing the children's identity through adventurous pursuits such as den creation. We make links to artists, performers and cultural organisations who visit us to share and stimulate ideas, model skills and attitudes, and broaden our community's experience of the wider world. We ensure that each class reaches out to new opportunities by making three relevant external visits per year that go beyond the village boundaries.

Being a monoculture

End-of-year questionnaires would suggest that our parents think our community is ethnically and religiously similar and monolingual, that it is generally distinct and unchanging and they can clearly identify and know members within it. Parents believe the school is inclusive with shared values. Our own observations and analysis also endorse their views. The older generation is respected and important and there is a strong sense of the indigenous culture (i.e. what it is like to live in our particular Somerset villages). However, we notice a lack of awareness of other cultures, their strengths and contribution, and we have fewer opportunities to learn more by working and playing alongside them. At times there is stereotyping which relates to gender, race and culture. Members of racial minorities in the area can feel isolated.

We spend a considerable amount of time celebrating who we are in our place and in our time and the importance of diversity. Within a project on special places we sent cameras home to enable children to make a record of a place and time in the community that was important to each family. The diversity and significance of the resulting exhibition enabled us all to understand more about what was important. We have successfully used the extended family to stimulate and support our children's understanding about life in the village. We invite grandparents to tell stories of mining in our village and how life has changed since the mines have closed. The children become researchers and strong intergenerational bonds are formed.

We have found inspiration and helpful vocabulary within the recommendations on the eight dimensions of the Global Citizenship Curriculum (DfES, 2005). We have used a number of these dimensions for focused learning over a period of three years. The ideas were developed initially through focus weeks that were well planned and carefully carried out. A week on democracy included the setting up of a pupil parliament with full elections of children's chosen parties that included party political broadcasts! A week on sustainability unpacked the eight doorways to a sustainable world (DCSF, 2006). Both initiatives live on and are continually developed in the work of our school council and as part of our sustainable school status.

Our curriculum includes specific modules on bullying, racism and also specific foci on aspects of local diversity, inviting representatives from a range of different cultural backgrounds to aid our enquiries. We make deliberate efforts to invite experts from other cultures into school and we are fortunate to have strong international school links through the British Council with Ghana, India and France. We have a part-time French assistant who is stimulating and challenging us to speak French with the right accent and we have exchange visits from Ghanaian teachers that are deeply enriching. Nothing is more moving than being part of a harvest festival service where a Ghanaian music teacher plays the organ for us (we have no piano player) and his companion teaches us 'call and response' and how to move – all done with the biggest grin you could imagine!

Being Somerset

Many people may think that living in Somerset is equivalent to a rural idyll and indeed it is a very beautiful place to be. There is peace and tranquillity and a strong sense of heritage and distinctiveness, but if you scratch under the surface of this idyll there are other images to be found. The concept of a 'country yokel' is a negative one, and rural poverty and isolation can be more sinister and entrenched than the urban equivalent because it is hidden and taboo. Somerset is a county that people travel through, it is not a centre of industry, it has no university and there is little mobility. We do, however, host the Glastonbury Festival! There is a perception, together with a reality in some of the statistics, that achievement and aspiration are lower than you might expect. Although this cannot be cited as a generalisation, there appears to be difficulty for some people in breaking away from a predetermined life path, and gender roles in particular can seem fixed.

Therefore, central to the school's learning vision is our aim to develop an 'I can …' culture where children are enabled to develop adventurous thinking and where all learning is couched in positive terms. We specifically target underachievement, for example 'invisible children', mathematics for girls, and boys' writing have become particular priorities for us. In order to develop an understanding of the wide range of life opportunities that are open to our children, we make real contact with the world of work and its possibilities. For example, some classes made links with the bag manufacturer Mulberry, which has a factory in the village. The children designed a range of handbags, gave presentations to the company directors, and a chosen design was produced in the factory. The children had real opportunities to engage purposefully with aspects of enterprise. We put emphasis on spotting and developing children's 'talents' and provide opportunities for these talents to be fostered and expanded.

> During a focus on storytelling, we held a cinema evening at school with parents and children sharing film clips which promoted storytelling. During one of the silent movies we just asked one of our pupils if they were able to provide an impromptu piano accompaniment. With no hesitation, he walked towards the piano and played with confidence and aplomb … much to everyone's delight.

We are able to provide opportunities for parents to act as lead learners. Several share their expertise in clubs and many directly support learning in class in open sessions or in a regular weekly slot. Two parents from a very nervous starting base completed training and successfully enabled our older children to become cycling proficient.

Having a local legacy

Fostering a sense of connectedness for children and their families to their place and their history is important to us. Our area has a rich history that we draw on and use in our learning enquiries.

In our community we have mining, farming and quarrying that are industries from the past. There is also new industry: the Mulberry factory with its leather goods, the Massey Wilcox distribution centre, and small-scale businesses such as the Ellie-Poo exotic paper company. The Co-op is the only shop in Chilcompton and is a centre for collecting and distributing all information in the village. We make links to the shop's ethical stance on organisation and food distribution. There are also farms and a railway that is now closed but converted into a footpath. The churches, both Anglican and Roman Catholic, play an important part in village life. Nearby is Downside public school and Abbey from where senior pupils have played a significant role in our 'learning to lead' programme. We revel in our archaeological interests, using opportunities to explore Roman remains that relate to the nearby Fosse Way. We also love the 'dump' that is full of Victorian treasure and much mud!

We work hard to make sure that our children have a strong sense of local identity by ensuring that the content of our curriculum includes links to local people as well as places. These include connections to local individuals and groups such as the Chilcompton Society, the Art Group, Gardening Club and Mothers' Union and particular individuals who have a long legacy of life in the villages and know so much about the past. We have been treated to so many local stories about mining, ghosts and even Queen Victoria's visit to Shell House.

As a school, we make clear opportunities for parents and other members of the community to become learning partners with us. We hold parent partnership meetings when parents can contribute to discussions about the children's learning and well-being. In this way, expertise, knowledge, experience and values can be shared and a sense of legacy developed. We try to find opportunities where there is genuine partnership input to achieve a learning outcome.

As part of a project on healthy packed lunches, we invited parents and children to bring in and share their own recipe ideas that they had rehearsed, developed and made at home. We held a giant packed-lunch party where everybody shared the results of their expertise. Every family went home with the ingredients to make one recipe developed by our children in their 'Let's get cooking' club.

Being sustainable

As we outlined in Chapter 4 our belief in the promotion of sustainability within our community uses three simple elements: the power of love for ourselves, love for each other and love for our world and beyond. We are a sustainable school, influencing and being influenced by the wider community and concerned about what happens beyond the school gate. One aspect of our adventure involves us in building a caring, self-reliant and collaborative community that supports the development of local resilience along with the ability to change in response to circumstances. At the same time our work on sustainability promotes local pride and we encourage children to feel involved in their place and take responsibility for its future, learning about important environmental issues in the process.

'I wish that people would look after the environment; some people don't care. My wish is out there so everyone can see it.'

Amber, Year 3

This is Amber's response to the reading of *The Tale of the Heaven Tree* by Mary Joslin, which was part of the stimulus materials for a whole-school focus on sustainability. Each class adopted a tree in the school grounds and created their own 'heaven tree' that was filled with wishes for our world.

We promoted community involvement in a 'garden quest' that explored the significance of gardens in our place. It involved visiting and celebrating gardens in our village and bringing those gardeners back into school to enable us to build a garden we could be proud of. One local resident came into school the following week with a very sad expression, complaining that he had been left out and asking us when we would be going to his house. Obviously we subsequently did involve him in our visits!

We have installed a large array of solar panels with the technology that enables a rich data source that enhances the children's understanding and control of energy. For example they use a wireless data logger that reads real-time electricity consumption. It can be walked around the school as a monitoring device so that the impact of switching off lights and computers can be directly observed and appreciated.

We work alongside Somerset Waste Partnership to explore aspects of the citizenship, science and geography curricula which link to 'green' agendas. Recently we have worked with the group to build a greenhouse entirely constructed out of recycled materials.

'With Somerset Waste Partnership we are making a greenhouse out of two-litre recycled plastic bottles put on garden canes so it is really eco-friendly – it's all recycled. We're making it so everyone can grow some new vegetables. It is a normal greenhouse but more friendly. It's all recycled and less expensive. I hope that lots of plants will grow, especially tomatoes because it's warmer in there. I'll probably make a drink out of them or even a pizza! We can grow our tomatoes in the greenhouse and cook them next door in the pizza oven.'

Saul and Rosa, Year 5

It is important for us that we consider our school as a 'model' of possibilities – modelling what 'might be' for our community. Obviously we also need to be open to the learning opportunities provided by others – in terms of what 'might be possible' for us'.

Being 'on the edge'

As described above, our community lies 'on the edge' of a number of different areas. We are on the edge of the county and the edge of the Mendips and the divide between the large urban conurbations of Bath and Bristol and open countryside. There can be a feeling that nobody notices you in Chilcompton as we are not prestigious Bath! This can potentially have a strong effect on feelings of belonging and sense of place as well as provision of opportunity and access. There is also some division among community members in terms of 'where they look to' outside the village. Some of this is affected by where people work, where they live, where relatives live, where they have lived before and the availability of transport. Inevitably this leads to potential issues concerning belonging. The school is a long way from County Hall in Taunton and its services. Everybody moans about how far it is when they come to see us.

Our curriculum has to be strong in the way it allows for development of children's identity – a sense of place, history, relationship and therefore belonging. We aim for our children to develop a strong sense of pride in their place as well as seeking to discover the opportunities that lie slightly further away. A six-week whole-school local study on differing aspects of our two village communities offered pupils an opportunity to explore some of these issues more deeply. Our Year 5 class researched 'How green is our village?' The reception class enquired 'Would tourists like to come here?' And Year 1 asked 'How do stories help us to understand more about our village?'. Again, these opportunities promoted greater understanding for the school and wider community about the worth of their own place.

Being twenty-first century

In partnership with parents and the community, we have a clear role and responsibility to look ahead to the challenges and opportunities that the future brings to all our learners. It is increasingly important that we see ourselves not just as local citizens but also as global citizens and that we equip our children to share this vision now and as they grow older. Together we need to develop more understanding of the issues and challenges that face us, so that we can decide how we want to make a difference to our future and manage our lives accordingly. Our curriculum strives to support our community by declaring a strong, shared vision for the future; we want to equip learners with the tools they need to cope with this change. For example, we promote the ability to be a creative thinker, self-manager, to understand learning processes, to be globally aware and information technology (IT) literate. Central to all learning in our school is the importance of learning having a purpose. Exploring and articulating the purposes of learning with all our learners is central to what we do so that our learners are able to articulate purpose for themselves. This is fundamental to being an effective 'lead learner'. We foster learning cultures that enable children to develop and extend their ideas through play and exploration, strong provocation, questioning and enquiry. A stimulated, creative mind helps learners imagine what is possible and how things could be. For us, all of this is a prerequisite in the development of an individual's capacity to make well-formed, purposeful contributions in a changing world.

Next steps

Is what we think, see and understand about our community truly a reality? Are we actually guilty of presumption and stereotyping? What is the true community perception of us? In a village context, the status of a school is enhanced because it is one of the important places to meet other people and connect with village events. It is a significant employer and a hub for other services and recreational facilities. Where do we as staff fit into a community picture when most of us don't actually live here? How important are we as individuals? Does what we do make a difference? Are we seen simply as just a 'place' for the majority of residents who have no direct connection with the school through children? How broad should our concept of a community of learners practically be?

The 'community cohesion' section of the 2011 Ofsted self-evaluation form asked us to consider a number of key strands. These include inclusion and equal access so all can succeed, celebrating diversity and challenging stereotypes, and working to make meaningful connections and relationships with the community that will enhance learning for all. They remain implicit, and important, in the new frameworks.

In order for us to move forward we have to become more aware of the need for the community to express for itself its own understanding of the significance of the school and whether it *can* have a transformational role in people's lives. Effective transformations can only be done together. How clearly is the school on the community 'map'? Recent work on the official Village Plan has given us a new and very public way to do this. Our Children's Centre with its extensive outreach work again makes broader connections and opportunities for dialogue. Nevertheless we do need to be very sure that our analyses of our community are triangulated with the community's perception of itself and are not just the school's opinion.

Conclusion

When reflecting on the design of our curriculum we have found that it is extremely helpful to consider and respond to our community characteristics. In doing this we aim to embrace and enhance our children's connectedness to the place in which they live and to make learning relative, personal and grounded. We have always wanted children and their families to celebrate and be proud of their community as well as confronting together the challenges that concern them. There is obviously a balance to be struck between the focus on local, national and global perspectives in a school's curriculum. Central to this must be a discussion about the needs and identity of families in the school's community; needs that reflect their position as citizens of their village, county, country and the world.

Although our school is obviously only one part of our locality and its amenities, we hope that we can become a place where ideas and behaviours can be realised, shared and examined. In this way we can act as a 'light' that illuminates pathways; not that what we do is always the *only* way to do things or that we are always *right* in what we do. We can at least model possibilities for our children and community to consider and experience and possibly offer some direction and purpose. What is vital to this is that we enable our community to have real contact with these possibilities that are relevant to them.

Questions for discussion

- What are the main social, economic and environmental issues facing your community at the moment?
- To what extent do the needs of your community influence the setting of priorities for your school?
- Could a community perspective be more prominent in your curriculum?
- How is the community and locality a site for learning for your school?

Part 3

CURRICULUM

Reflections on the curriculum chapters

What would happen if we took a completely fresh look at the way we organize the interconnected phenomena affecting our lives and then used this as a basis for curriculum design?

(Whitaker, 1997: 156)

Our next enquiry invited us to look at how the vision of the schools and the pattern of their relationship to their community are brought to life in the curriculum. As one of us commented wryly during our enquiry, if getting to the Nile was an attainment target you could 'visit' it on the computer and not have an experience of anything that was real at all!

Wrigley (2003: 91) notes 'how strangely silent' the school improvement literature is about the curriculum and adds: 'The collegiality it invites does not, apparently, extend to jointly discussing what should be taught and why.'

In our enquiry we concluded that for an adventurous school the curriculum is a way of structuring, enacting and realising the learning adventure. It serves both purpose and pedagogy and is the engine and structure for the power that enables effective learning. Also, it is the way that the five elements of adventurous learning (purpose, creativity, contribution, place and celebration) are brought to life and achieved in practice.

Visions determine direction and purpose, and communities and the wider world provide the location, the rationale and resources for the adventure (including people and co-adventurers). These are only brought to life in the activities, opportunities and initiatives that each school creates for and with learners. The curriculum is an overall design for learning, a way to

,ganise time and space and maximise opportunity so that the vision and principles become part of each school's everyday way of life. David Perkins (2009: 217) identifies this kind of learning as playing 'the whole game':

> Learning by wholes aims squarely at learning from the lively now. Its goal is to build learning out of endeavours experienced as immediately meaningful and worthwhile. Its commitment is to leverage features of good naturalistic learning ... its credo says that good learning is learning from a richly experienced today with tomorrow in view.

The curriculum stands in a direct and interdependent relationship with the values and beliefs of each school. These inform the content and learning opportunities that each setting provides. At the same time the choice of activities and the way in which children learn help promote and vitalise these values and principles. Children, their participation and learning are central. Curriculum design can also engage and empower communities, contributing to the growth of social capital, community cohesion and public value. The schools in this project have witnessed how communities grow in self-belief as they and their children begin to achieve shared success. Planned curriculum initiatives have provided opportunities for the community members across generations and ethnic divides to contribute, learn and grow together. The curriculum is personal to each school, designed to celebrate and embody the needs of their community. The schools in this project place the child firmly at the centre when designing learning, but are consistently aware that each child is a child of their family, community and their world.

As a result of this project the schools involved have come to an understanding that truly empowering children to become twenty-first century, global citizens means that learning happens everywhere. They have shared ways in which they have extended learning beyond the classroom and school day, welcomed different ways and time frames of learning, and embraced the value of private, personal and collaborative learning rather than just the publicly valued elements of attainment. Through each school curriculum, they aim to enable true learning for life – learning for each child's current life, learning for their future life and learning for all life in our world, now and in the future – the learning for life outlined in Chapter 1.

An understanding emerged in our enquiry that the adventure for twenty-first century education is to create, as we outlined in Chapter 1, organic, holistic, integrated learning and a curriculum to serve it. What has previously been termed the 'hidden curriculum' is taken out of hiding and made visible. Contexts or 'topics' for learning are chosen not just based on the criteria of relevance and interest to children but more importantly on their worth, their contribution to the development of a whole person, their engagement with each other and the world, and their sense of social and ecological responsibility. This includes values, ethics and mindsets. The curriculum can deliberately provide opportunities that are designed to enable children to reflect on and develop their attitudes and sense of purpose.

McMahon and Portelli (2004) note that in popular educational discourse the curriculum is predominantly seen as official documents and subject matter or content and plans. They identify a definition of curriculum that reflects a 'curriculum of life' that is a dynamic relationship between students, teachers, knowledge and contexts.

A curriculum design in an adventurous school is holistic (taking account of all aspects of what it means to be human), active and integrated. It takes place in clear, meaningful, big-picture contexts, which culminate in a finale of creating, performing and sharing. Children learn by embarking on 'junior versions' (Perkins, 2009) by doing real things. They deliberate over real problems and real issues. They have adventures rather than just researching or watching or hearing about someone else's adventures. Nothing is kept secret about learning, so children can more easily connect to it because they are shown the big picture. They drive and co-create their learning, and thus can see how it fits together both in their learning and in their life. Portelli and Vibert (2002: 38) note the characteristics of this view of curriculum:

> Grounded in the immediate daily world of students as well as in the larger social and political contexts of their lives, curriculum of life breaks down the walls between the school and the world. It is an approach that presupposes genuine respect for children's minds and experience – without romanticizing either.

This form of curriculum design requires a shift in the traditional locus of control, as outlined in Chapter 1. Opportunities and systems are actively created to empower children to take responsibility for their own and others' learning. It builds on the self-direction, creativity and personal responsibility of the Foundation Stage principles. Learning is designed around open enquiries, quests and challenges. It involves seeking and getting inside ideas rather than being presented with them. Children's ideas, knowledge and questions determine the direction and methodology of their learning. The curriculum is generative; as children learn they co-create the next steps. They construct their own learning adventure rather than following a predetermined path. Outcomes are planned for in a broad sense but children expand and interpret and take charge of these through their learning.

The adventurous curriculum is alive and constantly evolving. If we are to pass through the 'bottleneck' identified in Chapter 1, as Perkins (2009: 224) suggests, the adventure of learning needs to be able to feel and respond to the unknown: 'We should think of the multiple fronts of learning that invite or may soon invite attention in terms not just of educating for the known but of educating for the unknown.'

In the following three chapters the schools in this project present the journey they have been on in their curriculum thinking. They describe the methodology and rationale behind their quest to find a curriculum design that is fit for purpose. The purpose keeps evolving so this is a snapshot of their curriculum at this moment in time.

Chapter 8

A design for broad, deep, active participation in learning for life: Limeside Primary School

It is our choices, Harry, that show what we truly are, far more than our abilities.

(Rowling, 1992: 333)

Our curriculum stands in a reciprocal relationship with our values and vision. It is shaped by our beliefs and wishes for our children, our community and ultimately our world. At the same time it gives form to our pedagogies and deepens our principles. The opportunities we provide enable children to explore and create their own views and philosophy. In this chapter we explore how our values and vision, together with the needs of our specific Limeside community context, help shape our curriculum. We examine how we have tried to build on the pedagogies of the Foundation Stage so that our curriculum acknowledges the wholeness of children and attends to multiple dimensions of learning.

The model shown in Figure 8.1 depicts our view of the curriculum at Limeside Primary School. Creating our curriculum is a two-way process. The school and community's values and vision, their needs, interests and priorities feed into and influence the learning opportunities we provide. At the same time the curriculum brings the values, vision and pedagogy we have for our children and community to life. Just as the heart pumps life into different organs of the body enabling them to function, so the learning opportunities we design vitalise the wishes we have for our children and community. The curriculum is more than a set of schemes for learning and scheduled opportunities. It is a beating, throbbing, generative powerhouse. Like a living organ, it is also constantly renewing itself, adapting and changing.

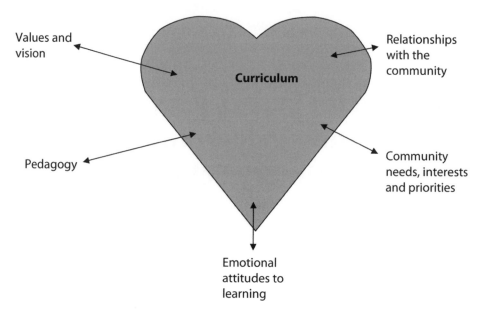

Values and vision

Relationships with the community

Curriculum

Pedagogy

Community needs, interests and priorities

Emotional attitudes to learning

Figure 8.1: The Limeside view of the curriculum: A design for broad, deep, active participation in learning for life

There is a second reason for our seeing the curriculum in this way. This revolves around the traditional view that relationships develop in the heart. Learning is relational. Our vision of flying involves learning with and from community members. We want the curriculum to help learners learn together at all levels of the community. The curriculum takes place in the community at the school level, the local level and increasingly the global level. However, more than this, the curriculum is for the Limeside community and should reflect its needs and interests. It is a shared adventure.

The third reason for our seeing the curriculum as a heart is that learning is emotional and emotions are associated with the heart. Children's feelings about what they are learning – their passions, fears, and concerns – influence the learning opportunities we provide. Our curriculum needs to create time for children to follow up these interests. Learning can also be difficult and complex. While we want all learners to ultimately love learning, we also need to build in opportunities to help them cope with difficult situations, to have courage and determination to continue when faced with a challenge. After all, these are the characteristics that equip them to face not only the learning adventure but also the adventure of life. These are the building blocks of our vision, the attitudes and faculties that will empower them to actively create their own and ultimately the world's future.

Building from Foundation Stage pedagogies upwards

Our journey to create a curriculum that was relevant and personal to the needs of Limeside's children and community, and consistent with our values, has taken several years and is still evolving. A wall display of artwork epitomises what was wrong with the learning opportunities we were providing and why we needed to change. Children had been taught to rip tissue and layer it to create pictures with perspective. They had enjoyed the activity but it seemed that there was something sterile and disconnected about the task. It was a one-off activity, which didn't relate to anything else the children were learning. It had few opportunities for creativity or learning from mistakes. There was a clearly defined lesson space in which to produce a picture and then it was time to move on, back to the conveyer belt of subjects. The skills learnt were not built on or used in any other context. There was little scope for individuality or co-operation. We were trying to develop a culture of independent, active, collaborative learning but the curriculum activities we were planning were hindering this.

As mentioned in Chapter 2, it was a comment from an Ofsted inspector that endorsed a need to change. She helped us recognise that we needed to trust the children and give them more scope and responsibility. We needed to let them fly. Our aim had been to encourage children to become increasingly active in their own learning. They were now ready to take on this responsibility but the curriculum we were providing was clipping their wings.

However, children in the Foundation Stage were driving their own learning and taking responsibility. They were closer to realising the images in our vision. We needed to build on this curriculum philosophy and develop it in our pedagogy as the children moved up through the school. A staff enquiry revealed the following points to be the most pertinent pedagogical principles of the Foundation Stage:

- An emphasis on talk.
- An integrated thematic approach to curriculum design, organisation and assessment.
- A broad view of skills.
- Children learning together.
- Children having a say, an element of control and independence in learning (there is a balance between adult-led and child-initiated experiences).
- Flexible groupings.
- The outside classroom and first-hand experiences.
- The process of learning being as important as the outcome.
- The importance of play.
- Children feeling happy, safe and good about themselves.

As Stephanie Pace Marshall (1995: 11) states: 'Adding wings to caterpillars does not make butterflies, it creates awkward dysfunctional caterpillars. Butterflies are created through transformation.'

These principles look very different in practice as children grow older but we feel that it is important to plan opportunities to develop them into our curriculum design. Our curriculum aims to develop the whole child. Tweaking our existing provision and adding in extra elements was not enough. It needed a complete metamorphosis. This was going to be a bold step but, inspired by our vision, we realised that we needed a complete curriculum restructure. What could we learn about building our curriculum from those Foundation Stage principles?

The Foundation Stage curriculum is centred on developing the whole child and all aspects of their learning simultaneously. Although practitioners plan primarily to address specific areas of learning, they are aware that they are simultaneously developing other aspects of the child. Learning is seen as holistic and multidimensional. We came to the understanding that the whole school should also embrace this multidimensional attitude to curriculum planning. Our curriculum needed to be more than subject opportunities but should actively seek to develop different aspects of each child. The dimensions all work concurrently and are interrelated. Trying to isolate them is difficult but for the purposes of this case study it seems helpful to examine them under the four pillars of learning proposed in the United Nations Educational, Scientific and Cultural Organization's (UNESCO) *Learning: The treasure within* (Delores, 1998).

- ♥ learning to know;
- ♥ learning to do;
- ♥ learning to be; and
- ♥ learning to live together.

We have gone on to create contexts for learning that, although loosely planned around subject opportunities, embrace all these dimensions. For us this is the true meaning of cross-curricular provision.

Learning to know

Zander and Zander (2000: 55) tell the tale of a young girl picking up starfish and throwing them back into the sea after the tide had left hundreds stranded on the sand. When asked by her grandmother why she bothered when she couldn't save them all, the girl replied that at least it made a difference to the one in her hand.

Our ultimate aim is for children to grow up caring enough about the world they live in to do their part to make it a better place. We want them to make a difference, no matter how small. We want them to make an active contribution. To do this they need many chances to find out about the world as it is now and has been in the past. We therefore view the subject areas which enable children to investigate, know about and understand the world, as the heart of our curriculum design. Traditionally they would fall under the banner of humanities and science. They provide opportunities for children to learn about the human and natural world and the interconnections, both positive and negative, between these spheres. These subjects provide the stimulus for our contexts for learning. They focus on human endeavour, error and achievement on the one side of the coin, and on nature and our planet on the other side.

Viewing these traditional subjects as a way of understanding the world also changes the emphasis that we give to different aspects within them. Our curriculum time is limited and precious. For example learning about human motivation and understanding the consequences of different actions in history becomes far more important than recall of historical facts and dates. When deciding on the content, we need to bear in mind the role and impact any specific focus will have in promoting children's understanding of their world, and in developing their sense of values about the people and features of the world.

We see the other subjects as tools to enable this to happen. They are a means to enable children to be active and contribute in their world. Art, for example, is primarily a means to communicate a message about an aspect of the world. Through looking at a piece of art, children try to understand the message about the world an artist was trying to convey, or what it makes them think or feel. In creating their own work, children use art to communicate their own ideas and understanding about an aspect of the world, whether it be their current situation or an imaginary realm. Maths is ultimately a way to better understand a scientific phenomenon, or to inform others about a phenomenon using data to aid the message. Problem solving and investigations seek to throw light on patterns and systems that help shape our world.

Seeing them in this way gives these subjects a purpose and reality, other than merely being a subject on a timetable. Viewing them as tools does not denigrate them in any way. Artists spend much of their time sharpening their tools and developing their skills in using them. Children practise skills but are not always aware of why they are doing so. However, developing them in the context of learning about the world gives them additional relevance and promotes multi-subject planning. In *Making Learning Whole*, David Perkins (2009) uses the analogy of learning to play baseball to describe effective learning. He advocates junior versions of whole games to give learning a purpose. Knowledge and understanding of the world lie at the heart of our curriculum, and the other subjects are tools to facilitate this (Figure 8.2). This grounds them in real life and gives them relevance.

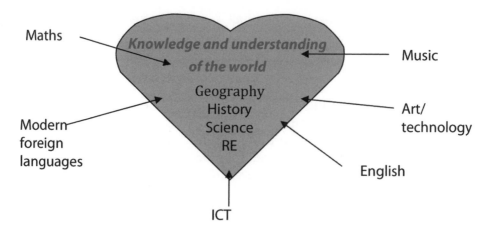

Figure 8.2: Knowledge and understanding of the world lie at the heart of our curriculum. The other subjects are tools to facilitate this

While our curriculum planning meets National Curriculum requirements, we took the brave step to interpret it in our own way. Somewhere a myth seemed to have sprung up among the teaching fraternity that the National Curriculum actually contained far more prescription than was the case. Our approach was to work backwards. Instead of beginning with National Curriculum requirements we started by consulting with children, parents and the wider school community to ascertain the kind of things they would like to learn about or felt that we had a duty to study. Suggestions were wide ranging and showed an insightful awareness of the needs of the world. They included concerns about rainforests, local environmental issues, areas where different local ethnic communities originated, and natural disasters. It also included topics virtually guaranteed to engage children's interests such as dinosaurs and castles. Only once we had established a core of contexts did we work out how we could include National Curriculum edicts. This approach now seems fundamentally in line with the Rose Report (2009).

The knowledge available to our children grows greater each day. Accordingly, we are becoming increasingly aware that for a context for learning to earn its place in a time-bound curriculum, it must have an element of worthiness. It must reinforce the values which underpin our vision and help children learn about and explore them. Year 6 children were horrified when they researched the working hours and conditions of Victorian children. Their sense of outrage and shock grew when, as part of a philosophical enquiry, they were confronted with a picture of a manufacturer of training shoes in the Third World using child labour. The parallels the children drew between the two scenarios deeply reinforced their values of justice and exploitation. Their understanding and empathy for historical figures helped them appreciate an element of the modern world and reinforce a value, which may, we hope, enable them to play a part in making a more equitable world in the future. Looking at contexts for learning from the point of view of worthiness helps determine what elements to focus on. In a study of Florence Nightingale, her courage to do something different and subsequent feelings are equally, if not more, important than the conditions she worked in and the equipment she used.

All of our planning is skills based. Schemes for learning are based around developing subject-specific skills. A significant step for us was to change short-term planning so that there was no allocated space for detailing activities but greater emphasis was given to establishing what skills and knowledge would be developed and how success in these would be demonstrated. Skills from all subject areas are mapped into different contexts for learning. Plans for ensuring continuity and progression in traditional subject skills are tight. On the other hand, plans for content are very loose, allowing teachers to respond to children's interests or current local or national events. For example a recent local carnival led to a whole-school investigation into Limeside through the ages. Children made banners to present their findings and learnt dances from different historical periods. They gathered on a Sunday morning to parade their banners through the streets along with community groups and residents. The dances were performed for the community as part of a show in a marquee in the local park.

While contexts for learning are mapped onto a two-year cycle, teachers and classes are free to interpret and engage with what they see as the most relevant aspects of such contexts. The two-year cycle allows classes to work flexibly as needed and provides opportunities for children to assume the mantle of expert or wizard learner and teach others. As Zander and Zander (2000: 68) state: 'The conductor gets his power from his ability to make others powerful.'

It is hard to be adventuresome if you have little say in the direction or challenges you are going to face. We want the children to take as much control of their learning adventure as possible. To facilitate this we have devised a number of tools. Each class contains a wizard wall. This displays the main skills children will be developing in contexts for learning so that they can plot their progress and needs. Also, wizard walls contain a few key enquiry or umbrella questions. Under the umbrella of these enquiry prompts, children ask their own questions to promote ownership and motivation. These questions may form the basis of group or class investigations. They reflect the interests of different classes and individuals and vary with each year. The teacher's task is to marry the development of skills to the questions the children want to investigate. As they pursue these enquiries the class co-constructs their knowledge. Although planning and wizard walls provide a series of stages children will need to pass during their adventure, the route, the timings and indeed to some extent the destination of each context is determined collectively.

As mentioned above, we acknowledge the need for children to develop subject-specific skills. Alongside wizard walls, classes also use jigsaws to plot the steps the children will need to take to master a specific skill in maths or English. At the start of a context for learning each teacher turns the six main skills the children will need to develop in maths and English into a jigsaw piece. These are displayed on the wizard wall. As they learn the children are able to decide when they feel confident enough in the use of each skill to add that piece into the jigsaw. Teachers and children can visually track their progress towards mastering a new concept. When jigsaws are complete, children apply the whole caboodle of skills from the jigsaw in a mastery challenge and evaluate their achievements. Thus the learning journey is made entirely visible. From the outset of each context for learning the children know exactly what they are aiming for and how they will evaluate their progress. Mastery challenges are recorded in a special book that children keep with them throughout school. They become a record of achievement and a means for teacher and child to look back and build on previous learning.

Learning to do

'I have learnt that when I am a group leader I mustn't be bossy. I should let everyone in my group get on with their jobs and trust them. Then I can do my jobs instead of trying to do everything all at once. Next time I will encourage more but not take over. I want to say thank you to all my team for doing very well.'

This is Sarah (Year 4), aged 9, reflecting on her role as team leader in a TASC challenge (discussed below) to make an information book about Ancient Egypt.

Bronowski (1973: 360) states: 'It is important that students bring a certain ragamuffin, barefoot irreverence to their studies. They are not here to worship what is known but to question it.' Knowledge on its own is not enough. Children need to be able to use it, apply it, and almost 'bash it around' in order to test it out and make it theirs individually and collectively. As a staff we frequently used to complain about lack of retention among our children. Aspects that staff clearly remembered teaching previously were met with blank stares in subsequent years. Our curriculum needed to plan for providing children with opportunities to use their knowledge in relevant contexts. Not only should this help retention, but we believe knowing why they were learning something would also increase motivation and create a greater sense of purpose.

To this end, Belle Wallace's TASC (Thinking Actively in a Social Context) wheel (2000) has become a key element in our curriculum design. Each context for learning incorporates a TASC challenge, which draws on many elements of the learning within that context. These TASCs form the grand finales of each context for learning. They are open-ended, collaborative and encourage children to be creative and to take control of and build on their own ideas. As children move through school, TASCs become one of the major opportunities for play, which we recognised as a fundamental principle in the Foundation Stage. They are also becoming a vehicle for children to apply and embed the enterprise elements of our curriculum.

The TASC wheel serves as a tool to take children through a collaborative process of gathering ideas, identifying success criteria, planning, doing and evaluating a project. However, it goes beyond some more traditional plan/do/evaluate models because it also incorporates two final stages: one which encourages children to share their learning by teaching others; and second, and most importantly, a meta-reflection stage whereby children identify how they have learnt from experience. Having completed the challenge, children reflect on the process. They consider the skills they have used, and identify how they are going to take these forward into their future learning. Once used to the process, children have shown great honesty and insight into their own behaviours and team dynamics. They have also shown sensitivity to others and a willingness to accept constructive criticism.

Personal, learning and thinking skills

'I'm coming into school by myself today because I am a good self-manager. I can organise myself and be independent.'

'I put my idea together with Thomas's idea and we got a really big idea of how to make it. That's what happens when you are a creative thinker and you have ideas and then you change them.'

These are comments from Dan and David, both aged 5, two weeks into starting Year 1.

The TASC wheel provides opportunities for children to reflect on, apply and evaluate their skills in an extended challenge. We recognise that this is important at all times. Our curriculum provides opportunities for children to reflect at a meta-level about their learning behaviours. To do this we make such behaviours highly visible and audible so that children can develop a vocabulary and understanding around such often taken-for-granted behaviours.

Initially we built in opportunities for this by putting a strong emphasis on learning to learn. Key learning skills were displayed in all classrooms. Children were constantly asked to reflect on how they had learnt, on the specific skills they had used, and on how they could build on these. The wizard became the embodiment of learning expertise and a central motif of our school. Our children became experts in meta-learning.

More recently we have extended this by trialling Personal, Learning and Thinking Skills (PLTS) for QCA. Younger children have PLTS hats for specific skills. Older children have learning journals in which they reflect on the behaviours and skills they have used during an activity, noting their strengths and how they could make it better. Children were asked to find examples of independent enquirers, self-managers, creative thinkers and effective participants during the annual learning treasure hunt. Displays are labelled with the major learning skills children drew on during that specific context for learning. Commendation certificates in Celebration Assembly relate to PLTS behaviours. Our stage has six PLTS hats on it and children identify the hat that best celebrates the behaviour they have demonstrated. Staff have spent time understanding collectively what each PLTS would look, feel and sound like in their classes and have begun their own learning journals. Teachers' planning deliberately emphasises key behaviour skills in a column that lists the key skills to be developed alongside each learning objective. By giving these key skills such a high priority in planning, we have learnt to tweak activities to give them a wider skill focus.

We also aim to create a special extended 'doing' entitlement for each year group. For instance Year 6 now annually undertake a major community enterprise project, which culminates in a project planning certificate. Year 5 children write, direct and produce their own films. Their finished films are premiered at a regional film festival, held in a Manchester cinema with invitations to parents and friends. Other extended 'doing' projects include a garden show and a fashion show. We hope that these are regarded as rites of passage that children anticipate as they enter each year group.

Learning to be

'It doesn't matter whether famous people think they are important or not. We are all famous to the people who matter like our families and friends. It's what we do that make us important and how we act not what other people think of us. It is more important that we like ourselves and are proud of ourselves and that the people we know like us and are proud of us than it is to be famous.'

These are Sally's (Year 5) last words in a philosophical enquiry with community and school members that considered the question: 'Why do famous people think they are important?'

The learning adventure is not just about developing new skills and knowledge. We are becoming increasingly aware that it must also involve an exploration, a discovery into minds, attitudes and emotions.

Scharmer's (2009) *Theory U* work with the German health system inspired us to create our own iceberg model for education (Figure 8.3). The vast majority of recent public attention focuses on the visible aspects of the education iceberg. It centres on attainment (largely in the form of test performance) and endless debates about the knowledge children should be expected to have at various stages of their education. Less attention is paid to the kind of behaviours children should develop. However, we are becoming increasingly aware that for us the key factors in creating lifelong, active, passionate learners and doers, who care about the world, lie under the surface of popular scrutiny and are harder to see and to develop. They centre around the attitudes, beliefs and values that children have about themselves, others and their world. It is these sometimes hard-to-unearth attributes that will act as catalysts for children to become lifelong adventurers.

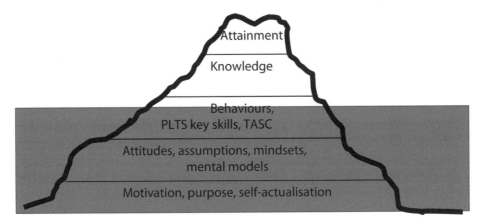

Figure 8.3: Our iceberg model for understanding learning

One of the Foundation Stage principles we identified to build on through school involved children feeling happy, safe and good about themselves. For this to happen, we believe that our curriculum needs to provide opportunities for children to learn to know themselves and to form beliefs and values. Our curriculum is designed to reflect and create the values we recognise in our vision. As stated above, we are realising that a context of learning needs to have an element of worthiness to earn its place in the curriculum. In *Making Learning Whole*, David Perkins (2009) asserts that learning should centre on threshold experiences to make it worthwhile. For us threshold experiences enable you to see the world and your place in it in a new light. They shift understanding and concern. They focus on attitudes and ways of thinking. Our curriculum needs to be planned around providing such opportunities.

Examining actively the values and mindsets that underpin ideas is part of the adventure of coming to know yourself and what matters to you. To facilitate this we need to provide opportunities for children to express, discuss and challenge ideas. Philosophy throughout school has become a key pin in facilitating this. Class groups regularly initiate questions and discuss them. In planning contexts for learning we look for areas that would be good as starting points for enquiries.

Another key factor has been in slowing the curriculum down to allow space and time away from what can easily become a conveyor belt of activity.

A major element for us in providing opportunities to help children create a personal identity and value system has been trying to build in times for them to be still. We now offer yoga as a goal-den activity (see below) and are gradually introducing breathing and relaxation techniques throughout the school. A personal well-being and motivational coach works with our Year 6 children, teaching them to visualise and to use and understand aspects of neuro-linguistic programming such as using aspirations and motivational language. Our team of children stole the show when they were invited to talk about how the school promotes well-being at a multi-agency conference. They prepared and presented a PowerPoint presentation to leading professionals from health, education and social welfare organisations, before singing the school song. Aspects such as these don't fit easily into traditional curriculum subject categories but we believe they are essential in creating self-aware children, who are ultimately able to find a role for themselves in the world and to grow into it.

Goal-dens are the Limeside twist on golden time. Children opt for a Friday afternoon den, which reflects their personal interests and the interests of the staff. Currently they can choose from activities such as singing, movie making, ICT, sewing, sports and salsa dancing. Dens run across the school so children from Year 1 to Year 6 learn together and from each other. They allow children to venture into different areas of the school and to appreciate people whom they would not normally mix with. Perhaps more importantly, goal-dens allow children to pursue their personal interests and passions. A core part of learning to be is discovering, acknowledging and honouring your own strengths and passions as an individual while accepting and valuing the differences between others.

'It's like Disney Miss. I didn't know that it was really like this. I thought it was just in films. Everything is so tiny.'

A Year 4 girl comments on the view from the top of a hill overlooking the Saddleworth Moors and a village in the distance, during a day trip to an outdoor centre.

'Where's my beans? I peeled loads and they were all pink and black spotty. I can't see them, only white' Kevin, aged 4, enquires as he peers into his soup during the harvest supper.

This year, instead of collecting tins for charity, we went back to the historical, rural roots of harvest. The children harvested, cleaned and prepared vegetables grown in our new polytunnel, and helped the cook make soup for the school and invited community members. Photos of all stages of the process, taken by our school photographer, aged 10, appeared in the local press alongside the professional journalist's pictures.

Closely linked to the need to respect themselves as individuals is the need for our curriculum to provide opportunities to develop children's sense of spirituality, including their awareness of themselves as part of a wider world. Our children and community spend most of their time in an urban environment.

We have to try to bring a sense of a different realm to our children, particularly in terms of the natural world. Trips are planned into curriculum contexts. We have re-branded assemblies as times for Awe, Wonder and Worship. We have acquired a large polytunnel where numerous vegetables are grown and we have started planting up raised beds as allotments. Our ultimate aim is to spread this into a community growing project.

Learning to live together

The final dimension of our curriculum builds on the emotional intelligence needed for children to know, respect and honour themselves and others. It involves providing opportunities for children to learn to find out about other people. We want them to recognise commonality while valuing diversity. Through our curriculum contexts we aim to develop a sense in the children of themselves as individuals, as part of the community, and as part of the wider world.

For Limeside, as a virtually all-white community in a town with very segregated ethnic communities, finding out about different cultures within Oldham is vital. To this end, we have established close links with a partner school serving a mainly Pakistani community. Children from this school have taken their partner class to visit their mosque. Classes have worked on extended projects such as the *Dragons' Den* project detailed in Chapter 5 and philosophical enquiry. In planning our contexts for learning we have included investigations into local areas, which enquire into what it must have been like for these residents when they first came to Oldham.

Our next focus under the umbrella of learning to live together needs to be an emphasis on intergenerational learning. It is hoped that the Limeside Garden Show will provide an ideal opportunity for bringing different age groups together and people from different occupations as a starting point for developing this next element of the curriculum.

Next steps

At the time of writing we are currently restructuring our curriculum in the light of our new understanding about values. While the structures outlined above will continue to serve us well, the big issue seems to be an imperative to move from a largely skills-orientated curriculum to a values-led curriculum. Although we have taken the first steps in this adventure, our next path will be identifying the values that we wish to develop through specific contexts for learning. Our vision and the work we are starting to do on developing values personae will play a significant role in helping us to determine these. As a start, we have selected six themes that will guide our selection of contexts. We believe these will allow children to explore worthy enquiries into aspects of our world, including sustainability and community cohesion. They are: adventure; heritage and identity; growth; cultures; logic, patterns and symbols; and our world and beyond. All classes in school will work on themes within these starting points, giving unity and buzz to the school and allowing assemblies and whole-school celebrations to reinforce learning. Plus, we are hoping that a whole-school focus will generate greater inter-age learning and teaching.

Our growing understanding of our local community and work on enterprise projects has also led us to conclude that enterprise must be a key feature for our future and thus needs to be prominent in our curriculum design. Currently we are collaborating to create an enterprise continuum, encompassing personal and interdependent skills and understanding that will be incorporated into our curriculum. Each context for learning will detail opportunities for enterprise and each class will have a major enterprise venture at some point in the year.

Challenges

Our children, staff and families have adapted to this way of working. The children want to understand and steer the direction of their learning and yet there are times such as Standard Assessment Tests (SATs) when they have to work within given structures to tight systems. In a sense they have outgrown such systems and find it difficult to understand why they should complete a piece of writing in three-quarters of an hour, why they can't use resources to assist them. This presents us with a challenge. We still feel the pressure to perform in such tests and conform to the system. Also, the children are more likely to question the purpose of activities that they are asked to do and this can present challenges to new or temporary staff.

Conclusion

To invent an airplane is nothing

To build one is something

To fly is everything
(Otto Lilienthal, aviation pioneer, 1848-1896)

During the process of writing this book, it has become increasingly clear that each school needs to personalise its curriculum to meet the needs and values of the school and its local context. It takes courage to do this but the rewards are great. However, needs and priorities change. Our curriculum must also be flexible and dynamic enough to respond to currrent issues and concerns. Our values and vision help us build a framework of entitlement within which there is space to follow children's and teachers' interests and respond to community initiatives. Within this we are constantly reviewing our provision as our understanding of our vision deepens. Perhaps the key note to hold on to is that our curriculum is a design for active participation in learning for life in its broadest sense, but life in a future which we can only guess at.

Therefore we believe that if our curriculum gives children experiences and skills to develop their IQ (intellectual quotient in its widest sense), their EQ (emotional and empathy quotient) and their SQ (spiritual quotient, understanding and respecting their values), it will release their aspirations and potential (Figure 8.4). This in turn will lead to true learning and achievement, a sense of self-efficacy and the abiility and will to create the future world. This is flying in its widest sense. What greater adventure can there be for individuals and a school?

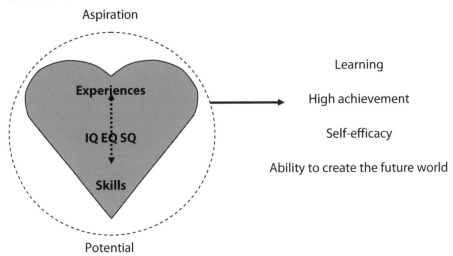

Figure 8.4: A curriculum model for true learning for life

Chapter 9

Learning to inspire and inspiring to learn: Malorees Infant School

Learning and teaching should not stand on opposite banks and just watch the river flow by; instead they should embark together on a journey down the water.

(Edwards *et al.*, 1993)

This chapter describes how we drew on our vision and values to determine the type of curriculum we would need to achieve our aims. It tracks how we developed contexts for learning within a value system to inspire our children with a love of learning. We outline how we created a 'learning opportunities jigsaw' that synchronises with our vision jigsaw and defines the experiences we offer to the children. We then explore and exemplify the elements within it. Finally we map out how the more adventurous rationale and model of learning at Malorees Infant School differs from the more traditional version.

Learning at its best is like an octopus deciding to use its natural agility to streamline its body and swim through a pipe of its own accord. Teaching at its worst feels like trying to stuff the octopus through the pipe. One of the keys to learning in the adventurous school must surely be the children's whole-hearted engagement and curiosity. The learning octopus wants to explore the other end of the tube and enjoys the challenge of wriggling through (even when nobody is watching and congratulating it).

The heart of our philosophy at Malorees Infant School resonates with the rest of this book. Learning for life, developing confident learning attitudes and an enthusiasm for learning are first and foremost. This is what we know enables the children to THRIVE. Of course we all want our children to read avidly, write beautifully and calculate effortlessly but working away at flashcards as soon as you can walk isn't necessarily the best way forward. Working towards standard benchmarks and acquiring skills and knowledge, motivated by extrinsic rewards is, as we noted in Chapter 3, like taking part in a competitive race rather than embarking on an adventure. We want the children's school experience to feel more like growing or exploring than being driven or herded.

Developing our curriculum

The drive for curriculum change at Malorees was two-fold. First, we wanted to enliven the content of the curriculum. Second, we wanted to reconstruct the way it was structured and delivered to encourage the development of key life skills. For some time we had been moving away from the QCA schemes of work as a blueprint for curriculum content, believing that knowledge is not hierarchical; castles are as valid an area to study as homes, volcanoes as valid as islands. This gave us the whole world to explore. We had also become much more led by the children; we were no longer happy with children working away at discrete tasks, with no sense of direction, connection, purpose or ownership. If we were going to give them opportunities to be in the driving seat they would need to know where they were going.

The changes we made independently have turned out to have been very much in line with the recommendations of the Rose Report on the primary curriculum (2009): grouping and overlapping subject areas, increasing the emphasis on speaking, listening and thinking skills and weaving personal, emotional and social skills through everything we do.

To support the shift towards becoming more of a learning school we used our vision jigsaw to map out a curriculum or 'learning opportunities jigsaw'. At a whole-school professional learning day we agreed that 'inspiring' (another theme in this book) summed up for us the way we wanted adults and children to feel about the curriculum. We mapped out on this jigsaw our design principles for a curriculum we felt would support our vision, mapping the elements of our vision onto opportunities we could engage the children in to enable them to experience a more adventurous version of learning.

We then set about redesigning the way we present the curriculum to make it more purposeful and inspiring. The model we decided on revolves around 'contexts for learning'. Typically a context is built around one or two specific learning intentions, taken broadly from the National Curriculum. These objectives can link any combination of subject areas but usually arise out of one of the six areas. We mapped the National Curriculum skills and knowledge onto whole-school grids for each subject to ensure varied coverage and progression. A context can then be designed for the particular cohort, to reflect their interests and enthusiasms. For instance a science-based context 'Minibeasts', which traditionally involves investigating animals in the local environment, was transformed one year into an exciting project on sea creatures, which was much more inspiring for a large group of boys who really liked studying sharks.

A 'Grand Finale' is planned from the very beginning of the project, giving the children a clear idea of the intended direction for their learning. If children know they are going to be building a Christmas-tree decoration that will light up, they appreciate why it is essential for them to understand how to build a circuit with a switch. The Grand Finale is designed to communicate and present to an audience, it could be artefacts or models, an exhibition, a performance, a book, a celebration. The achievement of this Grand Finale will also draw together learning from a range of curriculum areas.

Increasingly, an adapted TASC wheel is used to plot out the course of the context for the children. This enables children to develop an understanding of the type of learning they are undertaking: planning, research, making decisions, communicating, evaluating or reflecting. A 'Big Bang', an exciting launch activity, is starting to be used to generate excitement at the beginning. Within this structure we are trying to include as many opportunities as possible for the children to steer the direction of their own learning, encouraging questions to pursue from the start and choices throughout. At the same time social and life skills are promoted through collaborative and problem-solving activities.

An example of a context: 'Cooking Up a Treat'

This was a Year 2 context, based around the usual 'changing materials' science objectives. We started with the children experimenting with making chocolate crispie cakes without a recipe. From the resulting chocolate soup they learnt a lot about solids, liquids and the unpredictability of materials. Following more experimentation with heating, cooling and combining, they designed a menu and catered for a tea party for the parents, with a presentation of the learning they had achieved in preparing for the party. In some ways as much learning was done in preparing the presentation, reflecting on the experiments and investigations, as had happened during the activities themselves.

Through these sorts of events we are working to communicate our vision to the parents. At the same time we are trying to broaden the scope of 'home learning', away from workbooks and spelling practice. A half-term task for Year 2 recently, as part of a context on 'Intrepid Explorers', was to go exploring with an adult, collect interesting finds, take photos and make maps, with the child very much in the driving seat making the decisions. Feedback was very positive and since then the children have been enthusiastically exploring at playtimes, weekends and on the way to and from school and bringing in specimens (mostly dead creatures!).

This 'exploring' version of learning is what we are aiming for. However, it is undoubtedly a vision we are working towards rather than one that we have achieved. Due to the constraints of educational policy, including the National Curriculum and assessment, inspections, class sizes and the physical constraints of the school environment, a fair amount of 'herding' is still going on, particularly in literacy and maths. We recognise that developing the self-confidence of staff is crucial and bringing them all on board with the changes has been a gradual process that is not yet complete. However, over the past few years we have put many things in place to shift the balance, as outlined in the commentary on the learning opportunities jigsaw in Figure 9.1.

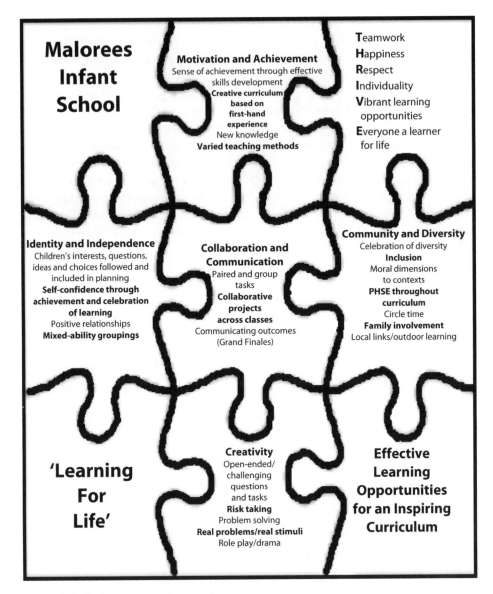

Figure 9.1: The learning opportunities jigsaw

Motivation and achievement

- A creative curriculum based on first-hand experience
- Varied teaching methods to cater for all learning styles
- Fostering curiosity through finding out about new things
- A sense of achievement through effective skills development

Motivation and achievement are very closely linked. Nothing motivates so much as achievement and nothing stimulates achievement so much as motivation to learn – these two are in a reciprocal relationship that we are aware of in our thinking and planning.

Children who are feeling shy or reluctant can be invited and encouraged into learning through novelty, fun and excitement. Creating opportunities for the children to experience something really new for themselves, first hand, is a core curriculum design principle for us. Each year in Arts Week we employ professional and amateur artists and craftspeople to extend our repertoire and throughout the year we invite performers and experts to visit the school.

Perhaps more important than these special learning events is a climate of experimentation within everyday learning opportunities in the classroom. Varied activities that include drama, role play, outdoor learning, paired and group learning, games and challenges, and stimulating resources create the interest and enthusiasm to engage children in their learning. Those who don't like drawing because they feel they aren't any good at it, and who in the everyday situation of illustrating a story would produce lacklustre figures, can produce the most beautiful artwork faced with a real fish from the fishmonger's to look at and represent during a 'Splash' Arts Week.

Motivating children is sometimes as simple as teaching them something interesting! Younger children are not necessarily going to be interested that olives come from the Mediterranean while bananas come from Africa and the Caribbean. On the other hand they can be fascinated by the right sort of factual information, presented effectively: the story of Scott of the Antarctic, how snow forms, volcanoes, the scary creatures that live at the bottom of the ocean. They don't need to be restricted to a nursery diet of myself, my family, toys and the school environment. There is nothing more rewarding than a class fired up with enthusiasm about something, asking questions and really wanting to know and find out. As Walt Streightiff states: 'There are no seven wonders of the world in the eyes of a child. There are seven million.'

Through developing a sense of achievement children become more ready to focus on the acquisition of necessary but perhaps less exciting skills, such as perseverance, concentration, spelling and handwriting. We recognise that developing skills continues to be essential and if children see their skills grow that will in turn hopefully foster their motivation to learn. It is a continuing challenge for us to balance our creative curriculum with systematic skills teaching, and our unimpressive attainment in spelling suggests we may not yet have got the balance quite right, but we continually evaluate and readjust to make improvements.

Creativity

- Open-ended, challenging questions and tasks
- Risk taking
- Problem solving
- Real problems and stimuli – making links with their known world
- Role play and drama

An adventure is all about making choices, meeting forks in the road or going off the path, coming across the unexpected, feeling a little bit unsure but pressing on regardless. An education system that guides children through small, safe, set tasks doesn't offer these opportunities. At Malorees we have been trying to introduce genuine chances for children to use their creativity, not limiting it to the arts but in the broader sense encouraging children to come up with a range of ideas themselves to solve a problem or set about a task. These types of tasks lend themselves particularly to scientific investigations, such as: 'How could you test the strength of a magnet?', 'How could you use forces to move a ball from one table to another?' and 'How can we set up a sustaining home for a woodlouse?'

A Year 1 class were working on the story of the 'Three Little Pigs'. Instead of asking what the pigs made their houses from, the teacher asked what materials the children might choose if they were trying to build a safe house. The responses were many and varied and demonstrated good thinking skills, particularly the suggestion that wolf bones would be the most effective in intimidating the wolf!

One of the advantages of our context-based curriculum planning is that while coverage of key knowledge and skills is planned for, there is the flexibility in each context to follow teachers' or children's ideas as they crop up part way through. If a class is particularly inspired by the amazing ability of spiders to build webs, we will have a go ourselves, using whatever materials we can find. When den building in the orchard, reception children are encouraged to work out their own ways of making a structure that will create shelter from the rain.

We have found that role play by teachers has been a very powerful way to stimulate the imaginations of the children. When learning about Mary Kingsley (an extraordinary, but slightly inaccessible Victorian explorer), we decided that the best thing would be to invite her to the school to answer questions, and while it was of course a teacher dressed up and acting in role, you would never have known it from the respectful questioning by the children. Staff, as well as children, need to take risks in an adventurous school and innovation needs to be welcomed. Not everything will work – our first 'Family Learning Day' could have been a complete disaster – but if the children are to take risks they need to see risk taking modelled by adults.

As part of our work with an artist from the Creative Partnerships[1] recently, our 60 reception children were each given a large cardboard box. The task was open, giving the children the opportunity to develop their own responses. Some worked alone, others joined together, some decorated their box, and others spent quite long periods just sitting in their box. They all loved it.

Recently a group of Year 2 children worked with a group of severely disabled children from a local special school to design and build musical instruments adapted to their limited abilities. This was a real problem to solve and resulted in creative and imaginative solutions such as a jangly ball that could be rolled along by a wheelchair.

Identity and independence

- Positive relationships
- Self-confidence through achievement and the celebration of learning
- Children's interests, questions, ideas and choices being followed and included in planning
- Mixed-ability groupings

Within large busy classes, ensuring that each child's voice is heard is crucial – stronger, more vigorous plants can choke a tender shoot. At Malorees listening to children is of primary importance because we know that being heard will help a child to build a strong identity. One of the saddest things we hear from some of our troubled children is that it is only at school that they feel listened to.

Listening and positive relationships are crucial in everything we do. Children who are struggling with creativity are never going to spread their wings if their first unusual idea is greeted with any kind of scorn. We may have overdone it at Malorees: whenever a wrong answer is given nowadays it tends to be greeted by a chorus of children's voices saying, 'Don't worry, we can learn from that mistake!' For the same reason we have moved away from ability grouping. What identity as a learner will a child develop if they always sit at the 'bottom' table? What attitude will a child from the 'top' table develop towards their peers from the 'lower' tables? The pecking order may be impossible to eradicate entirely but we don't need to encourage it.

> Rima, a little girl who rarely shone, positively floated after an assembly where she read her best story ever. Ibrahim moved from being a serious worry in maths to being one of the higher achievers, largely through being repeatedly noticed and rewarded as a wizard learner for his growing learning attitudes.

Equally important is to have structures in place to celebrate achievement and learning. In the Early Years, children work together to perform stories they have made up and dictated to an adult as their story is read out and enjoyed by the whole class (the 'helicopter' technique). The Grand Finales play a crucial role in celebrating children's achievements with an audience and making them aware of how much they have learnt. One of our most recent Grand Finales (which was the culmination of quite a knowledge-based context around invertebrates) was a quiz the children organised for the parents in our orchard. The children devised particularly tricky questions that left many of the parents stumped (but impressed) and the children were very proud of their superior knowledge.

Collaboration and communication

- Paired and group tasks
- Collaborative projects across classes
- Communicating outcomes through Grand Finales

Learning at its best is a social activity, with learners bouncing ideas off each other, amending, improving and probing, with everyone participating. Increasingly at Malorees, children are working in pairs and small groups to brainstorm and extend ideas, investigate possibilities, edit and improve their work. Young children are sometimes perceived not to be able to give feedback, but we recently undertook some research into children's reactions to feedback on their writing in literacy, and the results were fascinating. What transpired was that at our school children preferred critical, but kind, feedback from their peers so that they could improve their writing and then present it to their teachers for praise! As a result we endeavour to provide opportunities for children to collaborate in a group and to draw on peer assessment and support.

Adults in schools cannot support all the children all the time. Collaborative projects where children support each other not only free up adults but can often be more effective than adult teaching. The supporting children often explain things in language the learner understands more readily, while deepening their own understanding in the process of teaching another. At the same time the children are developing their emotional literacy through practising being kind, patient and empathetic.

In September we traditionally twin Year 2 and reception classes and run a 'buddy' system for the new intake, with a Year 2 child taking care of a new entrant at key points in the day – the time when the new entrant needs to leave their carer, playtime and lunchtime. Parents have given us a huge amount of positive feedback on this project, not only reception parents, but also Year 2 parents who have reported how much their children have talked about their 'buddies' and how seriously they take their responsibility.

Just as teaching a peer can deepen understanding, so too can communicating what has been learnt. Many classes have used a learning log, where pupils dictate things they have learnt into a class record, ranging from simple skills to extraordinary facts, or to the implications of anti-social behaviours. The Grand Finale involves sharing the learning from a context with an audience in some way – reading individual homemade books to another class, performing an assembly, creating an exhibition or display. A recent Year 1 context based around the science of plants culminated in the vegetables they had grown being cooked and served for lunch, with the children involved proudly explaining the cultivating processes to anyone who would listen!

Community and diversity

- Celebration of diversity
- Inclusion
- The moral dimensions of our learning contexts
- PSHE throughout the curriculum
- Circle time
- Family involvement
- Local links and outdoor learning

Of the five jigsaw pieces, this one in particular informs the content of the curriculum while the others concentrate on shaping the delivery. Our curriculum, though now our own, has historically been determined by the National Curriculum and the National Strategies and Frameworks. The National Curriculum is helpfully broad, leaving plenty of scope for individual and school choice. For example in history children should learn to 'identify differences between ways of life at different times'. Most of our choices now are informed by our vision and the learning opportunities we think the children will be inspired or excited by, informed by our conversations with them, or by opportunities for inspiring stimuli that arise from an exhibition or a local event.

At Malorees we try to put a particular emphasis on curriculum content that promotes racial and cultural diversity, and increasingly disability too. Luckily, with our intake, we have a wonderful resource in the classroom, with support from families from all over the globe. We take advantage of this, quite unashamedly, encouraging family members into the classroom to tell their stories, explain their cultures and bring in artefacts. Projects of this nature have included a family history project in Year 2 and family show-and-tell events in Year 1. We also incorporate specific anti-racist teaching into our curriculum, either through PSHE/circle time or through contexts such as 'Heroes from History' that included the story of Martin Luther King and Rosa Parks.

There is no fixed model for the way in which curriculum content is chosen, but we are beginning to feel the need to ensure coverage of various 'big ideas' in the way that we try to include our celebration of diversity. An example of this is the importance of giving young children an idea of the huge importance of sustainability for the future of the planet and an understanding of how each individual has a responsibility and an effect. A recent UNICEF (United Nations Children's Fund) fundraising project included learning about how we can reduce water waste, with children building a 'fountain of promises' with droplets of pledges: that they would turn off the tap while brushing their teeth, wash the car by hand, and take showers rather than baths.

We are now looking to build community involvement into our curriculum plans, so that the children can play a bigger part and forge links with others around us. Hopefully we will soon be sharing our Grand Finales with a wider audience, performing at homes for the elderly, designing games for playgroups, or promoting ecological projects in the neighbourhood.

Another curriculum emphasis at Malorees is on developing our outdoor learning opportunities. We are lucky to have beautiful grounds and a wonderful orchard area, which we described in Chapter 6. We try to design our curriculum to gain maximum benefit from these advantages, to give the children a respect and love of all things growing (setting up gardening projects, raising chickens from eggs, studying minibeasts at first hand) and to involve the children wherever possible in designing any changes and improvements. Our work in this area was recognised when we were awarded first prize in the London Schools Environment Awards.

Our curriculum – a summary

Table 9.1 summarises the way we think about the curriculum. Our curriculum content beyond the bare bones of the National Curriculum is harder to pin down and it is one of our key principles that individual teachers and teaching teams should be empowered and trusted to make their own choices about curriculum content and learning opportunities. At Malorees we rarely try to run the same context twice, or if we do, it never turns out the same way. Designing a lesson, a sequence of lessons, a context for learning, is for us a professional art that requires knowledge of the pupils and their own ideas and input, alongside the use of creativity. Teachers have the freedom to design their own short-, medium- or even long-term planning. 'A bit risky?' you ask. Not really, we trust our teachers and it is much more fun this way.

Table 9.1 Comparison of traditional learning with adventurous learning at Malorees Infant School

Curriculum outcomes	Adventurous learning	Traditional learning	The adventurous model at Malorees
Motivation	Children are motivated by curiosity and an enjoyment of learning.	Children are motivated by extrinsic measures of success and/ or a fear of failure.	First-hand experience and stimuli (e.g. outdoor learning, 'Big Bangs', outings, visitors, themed weeks, quality resources, varied teaching methods). Children encouraged to carry out their own research, stemming from their own interests. Children introduced to new and exciting knowledge.
Achievement	Children achieve across a whole range of areas, social and emotional as well as academic.	Achievement is measured in terms of success at a narrow range of academic tasks.	Wizard wall rewards for learning attitudes. Certificates of achievement given for social and emotional targets. Emphasis on personal progress. Formative assessment given priority over summative.
Identity	Children's self-confidence is high and they have a clear sense of identity.	Children's self-esteem relies on others' opinions. May be competitive.	Diversity valued and strongly promoted. Skills developed effectively, including intervention for children with special educational needs within mixed-ability teaching. No regular table groupings based on attainment levels. Positive relationships of respect fostered within the school community, including no 'put downs' either by other children or staff. Children's voice respected and listened to. Children given responsibility (e.g. playground leaders). Learning valued and shared (e.g. helicopter stories). Children's questions, ideas and choices incorporated into planning contexts.
Independence	Children are actively engaged in their learning/ have ownership of their own learning.	Children passively develop skills and absorb knowledge.	Structure of contexts for learning using 'Grand Finales' and TASC wheel gives children understanding of the 'bigger picture'. Formative assessment techniques help children to understand how to improve.

Creativity	Children enjoy a challenge and use it as an opportunity to think creatively (i.e. they engage in finding solutions to problems, take risks and learn from mistakes).	Children are given excessive guidance, discouraged from taking risks and making mistakes. They prefer known tasks and safe options.	Learning attitudes promoted through use of the wizard wall (especially learning from mistakes). Tasks (especially in maths) are differentiated through optional challenges. Varied teaching and learning activities, including use of creativity exercises (e.g. Diamond Nine,[a] problem-solving activities). P4C – posing questions. Drama/role play. Open questioning/higher order questioning.
Community and diversity	Children are proud of their community and cultural heritage. All children are valued.	Learning in school may not acknowledge community or cultural viewpoints.	Learning linked, where possible, to the children's life outside school. Contexts for learning often have a moral dimension or encapsulate a 'big idea' (e.g. sustainability, cultural identity, the wonder of nature). Parent involvement in learning encouraged and promoted.
Collaboration and communication	Children develop an understanding of the value of true collaboration. They learn to genuinely support each other.	Children see the teacher as the guide. They do not develop their own roles to support each other's learning.	Frequent paired and collaborative group learning activities within class. Collaborative projects across different year groups (e.g. reception 'buddy' project, junior reading partners, secondary-school partnership project).

[a]   Diamond Nine is a well-known classroom activity to prioritise ideas into a diamond shape and promote decision making.

Next steps

While literacy skills frequently form a major part of our learning contexts, as yet we have only managed to include maths in a more limited way. We currently teach maths in discrete lessons, albeit with an increasing emphasis on problem solving, investigations and challenges along with plenty of practical activities. However, the problems tend to be artificial ones and it would be good to find a way to reconcile our young children's necessarily fairly basic skills with more real problem solving in meaningful and purposeful contexts.

We would also like to extend some of the successful learning practices that are in place in the Early Years to support transition into Key Stage 1, particularly with regard to outdoor learning. We feel there is a lot of potential to inspire our learners by using resources more creatively to encourage their own investigations and learning constructs. Generally we are working towards children taking more ownership of the direction of their learning, with children being more involved in the planning and choice of contexts for learning and specific projects.

As mentioned previously, we would also like to extend our involvement in the local community and design more contexts to address real problems – offering the children more experiences of contributing to others and making a difference, experiences which hopefully would develop lifelong attitudes of good citizenship.

Conclusion

If the children's time at school is the adventure, then the curriculum provides the learning they engage in along the way. At Malorees Infant School we are trying to adapt the activities to the terrain we come to, be creative about opportunities that arise, take advantage of things that spark our adventurers' interest, and go out of our way to find those moments of awe and wonder.

We recognise that an inspiring curriculum involves additional time and effort and we need to have a realistic expectation of how quickly staff can collectively set out on the adventure, but the rewards are clear. Like everyone else, we experience periods of dip and drift, when the pressures of improving narrower indicators of attainment shift our focus, and it is an ongoing challenge to re-energise and engineer the 'WOW!' moments. When they do occur, however, the children's engagement, energy and enthusiasm are visible and infectious. This in turn creates a dynamic and motivating climate for staff, which keeps up the momentum and drives the adventure forwards.

Note

1.   The Creative Partnerships programme brings creative workers into schools to work with teachers to inspire and help young people learn.

Chapter 10

Building a sustainable community of adventurous lead learners: St Vigor and St John Primary School

We rise or fall by the choice we make

It all depends on the road we take

And the choice and the road depend

On the light that we have, the light we bend,

On the light we use

Or refuse

(Okri, 1999: 15)

Introduction

In this chapter we examine the relationship between our vision, community and curriculum. We outline the key ideas that shape our curriculum and give examples of the curriculum in practice. We describe how the four key areas of questing, ethics, connectedness and relationships outlined in our vision chapter (Chapter 4) are implemented and how their development promotes good learning. Finally we describe how our curriculum may develop in the future and how it might connect to existing and new developments in learning.

It is so important to make a clear connection between our vision statement and our curriculum; the curriculum makes the vision possible and real. Building community is central to our vision, one that is sustainable, adventurous and composed of lead learners; a community that is related strongly to its place and working to develop and enhance it. If we behave in particular ways we hope that we will be successful in making our vision real.

In the vision chapter we identified four important behaviours or characteristics that centre on relationships, questing, ethics and connectedness in our setting. The curriculum we provide celebrates and enables these behaviours to develop. Questful, ethical, connected learners with strong, meaningful relationships are essential to the growth of our sustainable, adventurous community of lead learners. All of these need to be viewed through a community 'lens' or perspective, in order to keep the context relevant, the relationships involved in the learning firmly in view, and to develop a connection to our place.

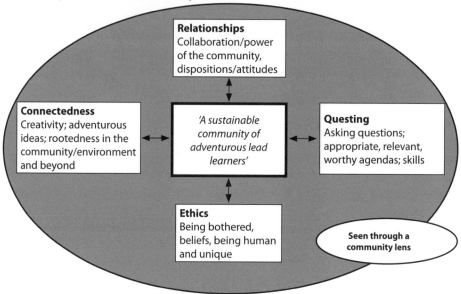

Figure 10.1: Key curriculum behaviours derived from our vision statement

It is useful for us to view these behaviours and the linkage of vision, curriculum and community in the schematic forms shown in Figures 10.1 and 10.2. Figure 10.2 describes the cycle of the relationship between vision, curriculum and the characteristics/behaviours of learners in the community. Our vision grows from an understanding of, and response to, the nature of our learning community. Our curriculum needs to respond in turn to this vision and further key behaviours. As we then evaluate and deepen our understanding of these behaviours as they grow, the characteristics of the learning community mature.

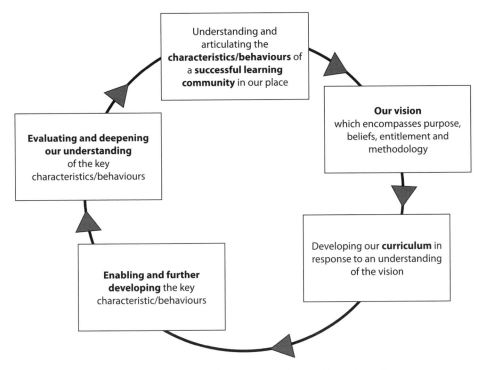

Figure 10.2: The cycle and relationship of vision, curriculum and behaviours in our learning community

We will now examine how these concepts and related behaviours are enabled and how their development promotes good learning and a sense of adventure.

Questing

We think of this first behaviour in three ways:

- the content – the 'what' and 'worthiness' of questing;
- the skills – the 'how' of questing; and
- the attitudes and dispositions – the 'why we do it' of questing.

The 'what' and 'worthiness' of questing

To support the development of adventurous learning we organise the majority of our curriculum content using a questing approach. Each class undertakes six different quests in a year and each one enables different aspects of our four cornerstones of effective learning (identity, problem solving, communication and creativity). So, for example in Year 2, a quest that develops a strong sense of *identity* would be 'How can I tell other people about myself by making a portrait gallery?' (Figure 10.3). It explores the things that make us what we are and ultimately this is shared through a community exhibition. Core subjects are fully integrated into the quest. For example the literacy strand has two connecting aspects. First, by writing a well-developed set of instructions that enable visitors to have an effective exhibition visit. And second, by writing poems that relate to self-portraits and express 'who I am'.

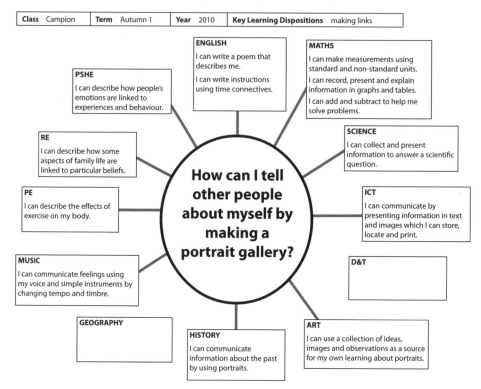

| Class Campion | Term Autumn 1 | Year 2010 | Key Learning Dispositions making links |

ENGLISH
I can write a poem that describes me.
I can write instructions using time connectives.

MATHS
I can make measurements using standard and non-standard units.
I can record, present and explain information in graphs and tables.
I can add and subtract to help me solve problems.

PSHE
I can describe how people's emotions are linked to experiences and behaviour.

RE
I can describe how some aspects of family life are linked to particular beliefs.

SCIENCE
I can collect and present information to answer a scientific question.

PE
I can describe the effects of exercise on my body.

ICT
I can communicate by presenting information in text and images which I can store, locate and print.

MUSIC
I can communicate feelings using my voice and simple instruments by changing tempo and timbre.

D&T

GEOGRAPHY

HISTORY
I can communicate information about the past by using portraits.

ART
I can use a collection of ideas, images and observations as a source for my own learning about portraits.

How can I tell other people about myself by making a portrait gallery?

Figure 10.3: A Year 2 overview plan for a termly quest

Another Year 2 quest focuses on the cornerstone of creativity. It particularly emphasises the development of ideas through a quest called 'How can I be a good storyteller?'. This particular quest starts with a strong provocation to stimulate children's imaginative ideas and leads them into adventures of mind, body and spirit. They undertake a visit to a local forest with a splendid tall tower where, rumour has it, a giant lives. An old woman who is very familiar with the giant happens to meet the children in the forest – wonderful ideas abound and are the foundations of what follows. Children walk into unknown forests, find strange objects in the undergrowth and meet and invent characters, as they become adventurous storytellers. The adventure invites children to imagine possibilities and be brave in their decision making. The stories that result are jointly edited with a Year 5 class who use their coaching skills to question and heighten the quality of the storytelling.

'We walked on a really slippy path and it led to a big tower. Behind the tower was a woman with a key on her neck. She told us a story about a giant living in the castle with a little boy. The forest was spooky and sometimes scary because I didn't think we'd find our way back! Somewhere in the middle of the wood I saw this huge bale of hay with something inside it – I think it was the iron giant.'

Nicola, Year 2

One particular Year 6 quest centres on river investigations as identified in the National Curriculum and develops strong *communication* skills at Levels 4 and 5. The quest, 'How can I produce a report to communicate with pupils in Ghana the contrasting features of the river Severn and the river Volta?', focuses on the wider world. The important feature of this quest is our strong relationship with the Army Basic School in Kumasi, the visits and paper communications we have between our two communities, and the opportunity to interview our Ghanaian teachers when they visit us. The children have a visit to the river Severn, working with the Rivers Authority on physical and environmental features. The quality of the communication in the report that goes to the Ghanaian school is the important focus.

There are a number of influences on the content and worthiness of our quests as described below.

(a) National Curriculum balance and linkage

We include statutory subject content from the National Curriculum and use skills progressions that we have developed in our school as the basis for planning. We always aim to emphasise quality rather than coverage.

(b) Pupil and staff interests

When staff are personally interested in a particular quest, it is more likely that there will be inspirational and enthusiastic teaching and learning. For example our Year 5 teacher is passionate about dogs, environmental issues and chocolate! These themes are successfully used as vehicles in her curriculum planning.

In response to the quest 'How can I be a good storyteller?', the children help to form the methodology and materials through which the exploration takes place by sharing their interests. Much of the children's influence within the research is in *what* they want to *do* in order to respond to the question. Figure 10.4 shows the children's responses to the research question in terms of what the class could explore. They have been categorised by the teacher.

Collecting ideas
meet a storyteller
go on a trip to see a story in a cinema or theatre
read and listen to stories
watch films of stories
use the computer to find stories

Growing ideas
make and play with a 'story town'
make a story museum
read and make books
make story boxes
practise handwriting
make a library
practise telling stories well
tell stories with puppets
make a film

Sharing ideas
use drama to tell a story
read and tell stories to people
record stories on a tape
invite people to our 'story museum'
let people read our books
show a film
share story boxes

Figure 10.4: Notes made on a class whiteboard; collecting ideas from children about what could be learnt within a Year 2 quest

(c) Community connections both near and far

As we discussed in our community chapter (Chapter 7), our quests draw on the characteristics of our place and the people who live and work there to make local connections. We connect to the wider community of the Mendips and the cities of Bath, Bristol and London, again through the people and characteristics of the place. Our global connections are also embedded and important. Some quests relate to our links with communities in Ghana; some deal with specific issues such as sustainability, fair trade, freedom and slavery.

(d) Worthiness

There are two aspects to this theme: first, *how* the quest will be (e.g. it will be of high quality, inclusive and enable pupils to contribute and have a voice); and second, the *worth* of the content of the quest. This becomes an ethical dilemma in its own right – who decides what is worthy in order that you can have a fulfilled life? Having shared beliefs helps in deciding what is important here. For example we are passionate about sustainability and therefore have a focus on learning in the outdoors in a number of our class quests.

(e) School improvement priorities

Part of the school self-evaluation process is to identify key areas of improvement. These could relate to key aspects of the strategies, such as speaking and listening, or social and emotional issues that are barriers to learning. Each year our school concentrates on three targets: the first is to advance an aspect of our vision for learning, the second to address key standards issues in core subjects, and the third to improve the organisational strategies which serve the above. Quests are part of the process for addressing these targets as they can be used to focus learning on key elements that need improvement.

(f) Unexpected opportunities

Heavy snowfalls in the winters of 2009 and 2010 gave everyone the opportunity to observe and enjoy child-initiated learning and instigate quests into the properties of snow! It is important to take advantage of such opportunities when they confront us.

Often visitors to the school offer unplanned opportunities for learning. Our whole-school quest to understand the nature of adventurousness has benefited from visitors from the community who have shared their personal perspectives of what adventure means to them. Parents often visit to talk to children about how they have been adventurous in their lives. This invitation into school is ongoing rather than planned and focused around a particular event or theme.

One of our parents came to talk to us all about his childhood dream to see the pyramids of Egypt for himself. He went on to tell us that when he was 18, with little preparation, he climbed on his bike to cycle from Somerset to the pyramids. He told us of the high points and the challenges of his adventure, the dangers he encountered, but most of all how, through many obstacles, he reached his destination and it was everything that he had ever dreamt it would be.

(g) Working in partnership to enhance innovative learning

Our involvement with external partners who are making similar quests has enabled us to take steps that would have been harder to do alone. Working in partnership offers us the opportunity to expand our ideas, to experience other viewpoints, to access places, people and events, to deepen our learning experiences. It provides us with stimulation and excitement. For example membership of the action research organisation '5×5×5=creativity' provides us with links to research networks both near and far and helps us form conversations with colleagues whom we join in our adventures in learning. Specific project grants that we have bid for have greatly supported thinking and innovation in relation to our curriculum. Research projects with Creative Partnerships have encouraged us to develop links with scientists, artists and film makers in order to explore aspects of creativity and identity.

(h) Focus weeks, theme days, theme weeks

In order to advance *whole-school* improvement we have developed a range of focus days and weeks where we can all concentrate on one key aspect of learning. For example a focus week on the theme of 'Adventure' enabled the whole-school community to explore the attitudes, skills and values associated with being adventurous in mind, body and spirit.

All our classes learnt alongside an artist, who had constructed an installation in the form of a horse stable that filled most of the school hall! The children were inspired to explore the inside of the stable, which was filled with clothes, models and a live-link video camera. Their play, exploration and adventures were self-initiated and supported with only small provocation from Niki, the artist.

'I loved doing the camera the most so people could see us performing outside. It was an adventure to them. It might have been to me because it was a bit like James Bond going through a movie. It was really fun. I never did something like this before. I loved playing cowboys. We did a cowboy dance – we could choose what to do – we just told Niki that we were going to do it.'

Will and Charlie, aged 8

'An adventurous person is someone who makes the most of every opportunity. With faith in others and a resilient attitude they are able to achieve their best.'

Megan, aged 11

Skills – the 'how' of questing

The planning of our curriculum is underpinned by an understanding of the appropriate skills, both generic and subject specific, which enable both whole-school and class quests to be successful. We think it is important that skill acquisition is not left to chance. Therefore we use the following methodologies to ensure all our children have a range of appropriate skills. By 'teaching' we mean telling, modelling, inspiring, coaching, mentoring or enabling.

- We teach specific subject skills by making reference to a well-thought-through skills progression 'ladder' in each subject area.
- We teach critical thinking skills.
- We teach problem-solving skills, sometimes using Belle Wallace's TASC wheel (Wallace, 2000).
- As we have already mentioned we teach 'learning to learn' skills using Guy Claxton's (2002) approach – 'Building Learning Power'. We have been more successful in teaching these by focusing on one key learning disposition each half term and therefore developing a deeper understanding of each one while not neglecting previous learning about other dispositions. A whole-school approach to the skill of planning (involving Building Learning Power) was launched in an assembly where the head teacher presented each class with a £10 note. The children were challenged to plan and design an

innovative activity for the summer fayre, which would make a profit on the original £10. The head and deputy modelled *their* approach to the challenge!

- We link our current approach to 'learning to learn' to the PLTS (Personal, Learning and Thinking Skills) which formed part of the National Curriculum reforms of 2009. We have linked clusters of learning dispositions to each of the six key roles identified within the PLTS (e.g. the dispositions of questioning, imagining and link making are linked to being a creative thinker, while the dispositions of meta-learning, distilling and reasoning are linked to being a reflective learner).

In everything we do, we promote and enable the belief that everyone has the capacity to be a 'lead learner' and the development of skills that underlies this capacity. This is central to our vision. Lead learners are capable learners who are always willing to share their capabilities and to be receptive to the learning of others. Becoming a lead learner is not a game of chance. Learners all need quality information, direction, support and involvement in order to be successful. It is easy to see that you need to take your learning 'armoury' with you on a quest. It makes you far more effective, especially when the learning becomes challenging and adventurous. It is also important that effective learning skills can be modelled and shared with others who come on a quest with you. Learning is a collaborative activity.

Attitudes and dispositions – the 'why' of questing

The desire to learn, to participate in learning, is the key to success. One of the biggest challenges of questing is not just knowing *what* the quest is or even knowing you have the appropriate skills to undertake it, but it is knowing whether you wish to, whether you are motivated to, whether you are enthusiastic to, or whether you are even bothered to set off on the journey. So how do we enable children to join us on adventures and quest with us? We think the following are important:

- Co-ownership of the quest, making it personalised and inclusive.
- Being inspirational – creating a 'WOW!' effect.
- Quests that are real and relevant.
- Quests that invite adventure and that are exciting.
- Children having a strong sense of well-being and confidence; they are well cared for, loved and healthy and therefore not distracted by other agendas.
- Everyone being enabled to have an 'I can' attitude.
- Being celebratory.
- Attainable goals with a frisson of challenge.

Relationships

The power of individuals to rise to community challenges, and the resulting action, come from the quality of the relationships. This is also very true of a school. In our definition of sustainability, mentioned previously, we suggest that the relationship between individuals, each other and their place, both near and far, is based on love and care – probably the most important of our stated school values. Sustainable communities know, respect and develop the importance of the individual in the context of the group. Day to day, the quality of our relationships is lived out in the way that we interact with, talk to, respond to and care for each other. All adults and children model behaviours and therefore have an ongoing responsibility to promote good relationships in all that they do at school. Codes of conduct, safeguarding policies and professional protocols are important but are no substitute for real, high-quality relationships that need time, understanding and commitment.

These are some of the key aspects that enable us to go on adventures together. Spending time teasing out the behaviours that make a difference helps our understanding of what a quality relationship is. We have outlined in our vision that our school places the teaching of values, which we closely link to the Social and Emotional Aspects of Learning (SEAL) curriculum, at the centre of what we think is important. We have developed a programme of themes of SEAL linked to values for relationships that can be easily exemplified through that theme. For example at the beginning of the school year we follow the theme of 'new beginnings' from the SEAL materials that we link to the two values of hope and unity.

> 'It's better together, more fun. If someone doesn't know how, we help them. I learnt that you can't get anything done in a team if you don't talk to them properly.'
>
> Emily, Year 1
>
> 'It's better to all work together than all fall out.'
>
> Archie, Year 4
>
> 'We help people in trouble; we don't just walk on by. We make sure that everyone feels valued by making sure that everyone is involved.'
>
> Albert, Year 4

There is also a link to learning the skills of being a good team learner (PLTS). The messages of these units are communicated through school and class assemblies and discrete PSHE sessions using circle time. For example we have recently explored the tension between the 'I' as well as the 'we'. How are we part of a new class team, united in our approaches to learning through team rules, and also a unique child with our own interests, desires and adventures?

'We are united when we work together in teams to reach our goals. Yet I am unique because I have my own feelings and opinions.'

Connie, Year 6

'We are united because we are all one class and one school that works together.'

Jack, Year 6

'We all work together and not one of us is leaving all the work to anyone else.'

Michael, Year 5

In addition, we develop termly research quests that provide opportunities for exploring relationships in deeper ways. Many have strong elements of personal identity within them. Schools have a responsibility to choose worthy agendas and themes that enable the deeper understanding of what good relationships are, as well as opportunities to live them out. Even the choice of books and the spaces we use for learning can impact on the opportunities for learning about relationships.

Ethics

The ethical stance we take in our school is guided by our value system. As stated in our vision chapter (Chapter 4), we have worked hard to try to describe our value system by listing those values that we consider to be most important and relevant to our context. We have identified 24. We know there are more but they serve the purpose of clarifying what we mean by a value system. There are no surprises, as our values link to our vision statement. They all connect back to sustainability, being a lead learner, an active member of a learning community and connected to our local place. Our list includes values such as respect, love, freedom, peace, hope and simplicity. As mentioned in our section on relationships, the teaching of ethics is both implicit and explicit. They are taken into consideration in the way we develop partnerships with the community, even down to how we run the summer fayre. For example we always run one stall that is fair trade and we give 10 per cent of our proceeds to a chosen charity. Ethics would also include how we welcome visitors to our school, how we dispose of our rubbish and how we grow, harvest and distribute our organic vegetables.

Our Lent project this year posed the question: 'How can we make the world a brighter and happier place?'. The only rules of the project (apart from happiness) were that the number 40 must be included and that the decision-making process must be corporate. Each class was truly innovative and projects included the presentation of 40 trees to community members (advertised at the Co-op), a 40 smiles tombola, 40 Easter cards sent to people who needed love, and 40 ways of reusing a plastic bottle in a useful or interesting way. A total of £1,000 was raised for the International Red Cross.

Our work in ethics cannot be separated from our work on questing, relationships and connectedness. We know whether or not we are making a good or bad curriculum decision by examining our ethical stance to that particular choice. Our guiding star is value laden.

Connectedness

As we said in our community chapter (Chapter 7), the concept of 'being connected' for us is about being rooted and grounded in our own place through the security that that affords us. The notion of place can be described in many ways. First, it can be described by its environmental features (i.e. its physicality), which relates closely to our senses and gives huge security and belonging through the familiar. Second, place can be described in its connections to the people who live in your place and know you and accept you – again that important feeling of worth and stability. Third, through the power of generational links, there are also connections through time – the wisdom of the ancestors – which give us an understanding of who we are.

> A Year 1 quest on discovering the origins of an old teddy bear gave children opportunities to connect with other generations. The class held a coffee morning where children interviewed their grandparents about a special old toy they brought in. This, in one simple activity, gave a sense of time and connection because both generations talked about toys that are of equal importance to them – one in reality, one in memory. The established family relationship helped enormously.

Connectedness is essentially to do with the sense of the spiritual. It is a deeper understanding of self and a desire to reach out and connect to others, to understand and create our place in the wider world and to actively create a sustainable future. In our curriculum we link firmly to our place by ensuring that a number of the quests we pursue relate to our local area and particularly celebrate our rural roots. As we described in our community chapter we are fortunate to have good practical links to the local farms, businesses and shops and also to individuals in the community who are so willing to share their talents and experiences. We find that a deeper experience is achieved by linking to the people as much as to the physicality of the place.

A Year 3 quest on being healthy links closely to the work of the health centre as the children create brochures designed for children that will be displayed at the centre.

> 'Our leaflets went to the doctors' and dentist and Daphne's mum so that when children go to have a check-up they could look at them. They could find out about how to be healthy, what you should eat and what exercise you should do. It went to the surgery because otherwise no one would know about our ideas if they just stayed here in school.'
>
> Lavinia, Year 3

We are increasingly placing an emphasis on learning out of the classroom. This includes our immediate outdoor space at school that offers developing opportunities for learning. We also extend the outdoors to visits within the villages and to our local towns and cities. This enables the children to connect and make useful comparisons to their rural location. Times away on 'residentials' also form a key part of our outdoor learning. They give good opportunities to know yourself and others better and really help a class to become cohesive. There are three opportunities for residential experience in our children's primary school life. We choose locations that are ethical in their organisation – two are organic farms and offer a further exploration of our environment. All three are adventure orientated.

> Year 3 pupils spent two days at the Magdalen Project near Chard in Somerset.
>
> 'We were learning about the environment and how people affect it. We went to the Magdalen centre because they do loads of outdoor things that are environmentally friendly. We made dens and we all slid down a mud slide on a hill. Sophie and Tim discovered it and everyone joined in. We had to climb up trees to find marshmallows. That was really adventurous. We explored the forest, fed animals and had to watch out for the pig's sharp teeth. If you weren't adventurous you'd just be normal and boring. You wouldn't have as much fun!'
>
> Lily and Amber, Year 3

It is important for us to reach out further afield to partnership schools in London, France and Ghana. We exchange staff and in some instances children, so that we have opportunities to explore the concepts of diversity and global citizenship. Our International School status has given us the opportunities to set up parallel curriculum experiences across two cultures and to share outcomes. A good example would be our linked project with our Army Basic School in Ghana where we both worked on creating a global garden.

> Children in Kumasi, Ghana, and Chilcompton, Somerset, exchanged and grew the same types of seeds. We established a keyhole garden and they cleared a huge area of banana plantation to grow the most amazing lettuces and other seeds in more conventional beds. We exchanged ideas about the growing cycle, the use of our harvests and the collaborative work needed in order to be successful.

Taking responsibility for our place, or at least an aspect of it, helps us to be more connected to it. We are now working on a project called 'Learning to Lead', which involves all classes actively developing and becoming responsible for a particular aspect of school and community life. For example one class may become responsible for the well-being of our chickens, another may develop opportunities for imaginative play on the playground at break times or oversee the setting up and co-ordination of lunchtime musical events that will be open to our community. These activities are negotiated with the children so that each class has a strong sense of ownership of the project. The whole school has a designated afternoon for 'Learning to Lead' activities so that all pupils are engaged at the same time. We are supported by a number of sixth-form students from a neighbouring school.

> 'We are organising a soup kitchen with our mums to raise money to buy the materials to make a bird hide in Lilly's Wood. We have been collecting all the scraps from school to feed the birds but we want to watch them now.'
>
> Jonti, Year 4
>
> Year 6 pupils wrote to the head teacher as part of their project to keep chickens at school:
>
> 'We are writing to ensure you agree that we can take on the responsibility to look after chickens extremely well. We are sure that you will agree. We have been trying our best and have been researching all we need to know.'
>
> Lucy and James, Year 6

If the curriculum makes no connections of worth – is it irrelevant? We feel it often is. Often the challenging areas of curriculum are the ones that are hard to connect to: improper fractions spring to mind, rivers if you have never played by or in one, Islam if you know no members of that faith, butterflies if you have never kept a caterpillar and seen a butterfly emerge.

Next steps

Having made a conscious decision, after much discussion and debate, to develop our curriculum and embed these four behaviours of questing, relationships, ethics and connectedness, we have to keep asking ourselves the question: 'How do we use existing structures and develop new structures to ensure that the behaviours are both implicit, explicit and continually evolving in our curriculum?'. We think deeply about our existing quests and are carefully considering new aspects as we plan our next. Some of these aspects are discussed below.

The worth of an individual quest

This gives real opportunities to consider ethics, values and interest. Even the title of the quest itself is of paramount importance when setting the tone and expectations for learning.

PLTS targets

We were impressed by the Key Stage 3 work on PLTS developed by QCA in 2008. We found them to be extremely useful in categorising groups of learning skills that we had already developed through 'Building Learning Power'. The descriptors provided useful nomenclature for the different skills you need to be an effective learner. There are six descriptors: creative thinker, team player, effective participator, self-manager, independent enquirer and reflective learner. We are developing a whole-school plan that enables us to focus on each of the descriptors through an academic year. They are beginning to form the basis for some learning assessments and we therefore need to develop a clearer understanding of progression within each of them.

Key values

These are published for children and parents and a two-yearly programme describes how we ensure each value is given due consideration in whole-school assemblies and throughout the curriculum. We need to continue to seek new opportunities to bring values to life in tangible and real ways, explicitly and implicitly. A good example of this would be our involvement in a two-year project on the Olympic values that aims to engage our children in researching where these values are demonstrated both within everyday life and through stories that are told and created. This will culminate in a shared communication piece between ourselves and a partner school in London as part of the Cultural Olympiad.

How quests acknowledge the key dimensions that are embedded within the National Curriculum revision

Although this particular curriculum was abandoned in 2010, it contains useful and relevant ideas that link to our vision. These include sustainability, identity and cultural diversity, healthy lifestyles, community involvement/participation, enterprise, a global dimension, technology and communication, creativity and critical thinking. A new, slimmed-down curriculum will give opportunity for each setting to include learning that is essential to their particular learners. We know we would want to continue to include these aspects in future plans.

How our quests enable children to connect with people, communities and places

These are places and people both near and far, now and in the past. Such connections help make quests more purposeful and personal and provide opportunities to explore personal, social and ethical issues in a variety of contexts. We need to continue to research new connections, working in partnership with our community near and far.

How quests provide opportunities for out-of-the-classroom learning (including outdoor learning)

This includes consideration of the context for learning beyond the classroom. It demands decisions on where and how learning can take place and can help make learning more real, connected and purposeful. Out-of-the-classroom learning is demanding on any organisation in terms of resourcing and expertise but can provide a new way of thinking about learning.

How quests enthuse, stimulate, inspire and 'wow!' children

This considers the real adventure of learning and how learners become self-motivated and engaged at a personal level. It considers how children 'own' their learning and develop a desire for learning. This is the aspect in which teachers let go of control and learn to broaden and deepen their role as facilitators of learning.

Using the new elements as a checklist, we are beginning to monitor our curriculum closely for breadth, balance and purpose. Most of all, we continually need to ask questions about how relevant, personal and worthwhile our provision is. If we keep asking the questions it is more likely that, at least some of the time, we will achieve our goal.

Conclusion

The relationships between the component parts of our curriculum are complex and have developed many layers over time. This makes it hard to describe clearly. As we wrestled with this, two parts of our thinking are critical. First, we know that all learners can become lead learners when supported in their learning within a loving community. This is the essence of our vision statement. Second, you become a successful lead learner when you have the opportunity to quest, to connect, to develop strong relationships and most of all to take an ethical stance on all you learn, balancing carefully what is of worth. You will recognise these as our four key behaviours, the building blocks of our curriculum structure.

Interestingly, it is only through writing this chapter that we have been able to articulate, at least to ourselves, what is important to us in our place and at this time. We have never been more aware of how fast our own conceptual thinking has moved on and that is not taking into account the external pressures and political changes which can influence thinking as well. What we are proud of is how we have a greater clarity of what is *essential* for effective learning. We feel we can sustain this clarity regardless of the changing demands of curriculum content and the coming and going of new initiatives, which we know from experience can easily steer you away from what you believe is important.

We want to conclude by restating how essential it is to think about what is of *worth* when considering the curriculum. This notion of 'worth' is the area we debate more than any other. What is truly of worth and relevance to be included in a curriculum? How does a curriculum structure reflect this? Who decides what is of worth? We need to think about *what* we do, *how* we do it and *why* we do it at all times. If we do, we believe it is possible to provide the best curricular opportunities to develop and sustain a successful community of adventurous lead learners. This is with the realistic knowledge that high ideals are possible – but hard to realise every day of the week!

Questions for discussion

- How does your curriculum currently relate to the vision you have for your school?
- What opportunities are there for children to steer and contribute to the curriculum?
- How does the curriculum reflect the priorities of your community?
- How does the curriculum encourage real learning for life?

Part 4

LEADING THE ADVENTUROUS SCHOOL

Chapter 11

Leadership as if the future really matters

Leaders in the next decade will not just be leading organisations they will be leading life.

(Johansen, 2010: 12)

The stories in this book have been about the renewal of primary education in action. They have described the practical activity, openness and optimism that are among the ingredients of an adventurous school. The schools' stories have outlined the journey towards vision, community engagement and curriculum that are creating outcomes with which to build a better future with our young people. The adventures contain an innovative approach to school improvement for social and environmental change. A recent National Endowment for Science, Technology and the Arts (NESTA) report (Mulgan, 2007b) describes innovation as new ideas, products, services and models developed to fulfil unmet needs. They identify this kind of innovation as deficient because, they say in their report, too much attention in the public sector in England is being paid to performance and target setting.

Colleagues have been sharing as well as learning more about their leadership practice in the process of writing the book. This process has itself been an adventure. They have at times felt isolated by their workload and commitments. It has been important to them to step outside their immediate workplace in this project and be with other leaders to compare and discuss what they do. The adventure of the project has been important to them partly because of the self- and collective discovery they have been engaged in, together with a chance to reflect. In the process they have come to know themselves, their schools and communities better. They have realised they are learning to act from a place where the future they are trying to create can be evoked through their leadership.

The primary focus of an adventurous school is adventurous learning: learning that releases potential and leads to children's participation in their life journey and the lives of others. At the heart of the adventure is the contribution primary children make to their community, the planet and the future they want to create.

'Implementation means doing it!' exclaims Sam. He and five mates from Year 5 are sitting in the school conference room explaining their most recent project. They are about to put the insect hotels they have just finished making in the school garden. They outline the process they have used every week for ten weeks with the Oldham enterprise team and a group of mentors from Year 9 in the local secondary school. 'It's DPIE,' says Jo, 'design, plan, implement and evaluate. We knew what two of those meant but didn't know about implement and evaluate before.' Kylie explains, 'We started by learning about all the invertebrates and thinking what a hotel might look like for them. We did two, a big one and then we each made a small one.' The 'hotels' are small wooden boxes with a roof and each of the children's names written on them. Inside are two kinds of materials: bamboo on the bottom and straw, 'to keep them warm', on the top.

The group laugh loudly when they discuss what they had expected the hotel design to be. 'We thought a hotel would have king-size beds, keys and room service!' says Hannah. 'So when I got on the Internet and saw what an insect hotel really looked like then I said to myself oh RIGHT! It doesn't have any escalators!' chuckles Danielle. She opens her diary of the project where she has written about her learning. It includes 'I learnt change can be fun' and 'I learnt to work as part of a team'.

It's a soggy, cool, grey June morning as the children walk across the large urban playground of Limeside Primary School that has recently been filled with willow arches, a pirate ship and planters. At the entrance to the garden they excitedly point out the pile of six pallets that make up the big insect hotel. 'We worked in three groups,' explains Andrew. The decomposers put their pallets on the bottom with soil, acorns and leaves, then the predators put their two pallets on next with damp materials, wood and twigs. 'My friend put her apple core in,' says Danielle. Then the pollinators put their two pallets in next with the plants in pots to attract the bees and wasps. Holly adds, 'There won't be many insects in the hotel yet, they have to get used to it first.'

Twenty-first century children need a sense of adventure because, as we have suggested in this book, they are the ones who will take us through the 'bottleneck' we face as a global community as described by James Martin (2006). The future is increasingly unpredictable and challenging and our learners need to be resilient and adaptable to deal with what is up ahead for them. The combination of too much technology and safeguarding can both lead to children being overprotected and much of their adventure lived inside and virtually.

The adventurous school can have influence beyond the boundaries of its traditional role. These include renewing existing models of purpose, power and pedagogy that are founded on values of care and passion for children, their communities and the planet. The global community is in need of positive images of successful venturing rather than prescribed and reactive solutions. Care and passion are not optional, they are vital nutrients in the educational diet to nourish and catalyse everyone's learning so they can embark together on the task of creating a world where each person can contribute and make a difference.

The stories in this book have not been explicitly about the leaders or their leadership; they have been about the community, and particularly the children, learning in ways that create a new sense of what life is for. They are stories of learning that deliberately aim to exert positive control over the future.

It is not easy to distinguish what leadership is and isn't in an adventurous school because it is everyone's responsibility; leadership is a set of skills and processes available to all. As Knapp *et al.* (2010: 7) write: '"Leadership" we define as the shared work and commitments that shape the direction of a school or district and their learning improvement agendas, and that engage effort and energy in pursuit of those agendas.'

It is a task of leadership to model and encourage the change in mindsets, culture and forms of activity needed for the shift we are describing in this book. In this sense leadership, improvement and transformation are part of each other and work closely together. There is still, however, a crucial role for those with the overall responsibility for the school to promote these collaborative forms of leadership in their school communities and to structure and create an environment where it can happen. Leaders in adventurous schools have a specific sense of purpose: they are inviting people to participate in the creation of the future, not just to deal with the now. Leaders of adventurous schools have to draw on and develop new forms of power and pedagogy to fuel this purpose. Our enquiry has shown that adventurous leaders are designers, gardeners and inventors who don't just accept, comply and deliver policy and external expectations.

Scharmer (2009) distinguishes between reacting, re-designing and re-framing in organisational change. He makes the connection between these three responses and single-, double- and triple-loop learning. In this book we have described how these schools see their purpose as a call to adventure. This is more than just the re-engineering of traditional school improvement or Scharmer's first three levels of learning and change. The leaders are co-creating the purpose of their schools and then steering the enterprise in the direction they see is required for the future. This is akin to Scharmer's fourth level of learning and change and Senge *et al.*'s notion of dual awareness (2010) that they both term 'presencing', learning from the future, as it emerges based on a deep understanding of the present.

The schools in this book have described a process of being constantly under construction, in a process of semi-permanent review and development. Their attention to the power of dual awareness means their dreams are constantly taking them in new directions and working with new influences. Leadbeater and Mongon (2008) use the image of navigators who secure vision, set direction and promote change. The leadership at the same time knows its purpose and keeps its vision open to change.

Sergiovanni (2005) suggests that effective leaders have working theories about their leadership and we identified four theories at work in the leadership of an adventurous school. These are theories of action, public value, comfort and safety, and holism. These ways of thinking and constructing the task of leading provide ways of being and doing that nurture and clarify the purpose and create the power and pedagogy that will bring it about.

Action

The leadership of an adventurous school is working with a particular theory of action; senior leaders don't spend very much time in their offices. It is a theory that is based on a belief that they can make a difference, they know that what they do and how they behave has consequences and that they can affect outcomes. This view of action inspires collective efficacy (we can do this together, it's down to all of us) rather than ego (I am doing this by myself and it's down to me). This doesn't mean, however, the achievements of individuals go unnoticed and in many ways they are celebrated more. Action is a mixture of the carefully planned as well as the spontaneous.

In his writing on power, Johnstone (2010) notes how 'static thinking' is a barrier to change. It tends to produce mindsets of resignation to the way things are. The type of leadership discussed in this book knows how to influence action for the change that is required and to bring it about in a successful way. It is generative and inclusive of everyone.

Public value

The leadership of an adventurous school is working with a theory of public value. Leaders of the adventurous school have an enlarged sense of purpose and work on a playing field that has wider boundaries than the traditional school. Leadbeater and Mongon (2008) suggest that schools are more likely to be effective if they:

- draw their community into the work;
- reach out to work in their immediate social networks;
- work with their wider community to create social capital and cohesion; and
- provide services with no immediate feedback to themselves.

Public value is an expression of altruism and provides a richer and wider sense of educational accountability. It also serves a longer-term view of what the schools are about, which in this story is the contribution their children can make. 'Public' refers to the whole global community and 'value' refers to the way children engage in and draw on their education to make a difference.

Comfort and safety

The leadership of an adventurous school is working with a theory of comfort and safety that is different to the traditional one. They know that in order for the community to learn and change, everyone – parents, staff and children – needs to come out of their comfort zone and engage with the new and different, to come together in new ways. They engage with, rather than retreat from, their fear. Adventurous leaders are continually pushing the boundaries of what is known and encourage their community to live with uncertainty and be in contact with what is not known. They have an inner compass and sense of purpose that is strong enough to overcome the fear that is part of the job. The passion and care they have for children, their lives and the future of the world help sustain them in the face of fear. The leadership's task is to communicate to people their worth and potential so clearly that they begin to believe it themselves. For example at Limeside Primary School they tell parents continually that they have wonderful children and the children are told that they have wonderful parents. Outside the comfort zone, leaders are questing and questioning. There is restlessness in being an adventurous leader – they are always on the move.

Holism

Leaders of adventurous schools work with a theory of holism. They know that learning and leadership don't take place in the mind alone. They lead from the spirit, the heart, and the hand as well as the head, knowing these are in living interconnection and support each other. They value instinct and intuition as well as more rational approaches; they celebrate different ways of knowing. Their holistic understanding doesn't just stop, however, at the school gate; as Johansen (2010) says, they know they are in transition to a model of leadership that includes the larger systems of which we are all a part, that we live in an interdependent world in which their school is a living hub and their task is to ensure that the children recognise and find their place in the whole. They are continually learning how to see the larger systems of which they are a part (Senge *et al.*, 2010).The beginning of the twenty-first century is a time of many new forms of awareness which impel us to new forms of action and new ethics based on interconnectivity (Olds, 1992).

The leadership of the adventurous school is *adaptive and creative*. The leaders are constantly involved in designing and testing new forms of engagement that do not only reflect an existing vision and purpose but also help it to evolve. They are prepared to let go of old identities and intentions and allow the new to emerge on behalf of the future. In the process they are highly innovative and while they draw on others' ideas they are confident in producing their own.

Conclusion

1. There is a 'call to adventure' for each school that the leaders make real for everyone. This inspires the team, builds efficacy and optimism, and helps to militate against fear and despondency in the face of challenges. They avoid the three most powerful sources of organisational resistance: fear, judgement and cynicism (Scharmer, 2009).
2. There is a real belief in the ability of the whole community to use that inspiration to shape their own destiny and gain personal but non-egotistical value from the adventure.
3. There is flexibility to enable the community to help choose paths that might meander, the climate is neither rigid nor prescriptive and there are opportunities for everyone to be involved in decision making.
4. The leaders provide and enact a range of roles to create the adventure and provide challenge and support: guide, priest, negotiator, parent and sibling.

The leadership is also reflected in the characteristics of adventure we came up with early in the book:

- creating and inventing your path rather than looking for one that's already there;
- the capacity to imagine what might be and seize opportunities;
- developing a confident spirit and hardy disposition;
- having a map to help you plan the route and a compass to guide you but not being static about the journey, and being prepared to face the unknown;
- evolving, moving on, taking risks;
- lively and living exploration;
- questing, questioning, enquiring, not knowing all the answers;
- travelling with others, knowing guides and mentors you can trust; and
- non-conformity and having faith in your beliefs.

In *Theory U* Scharmer (2009) reflects that it takes an organisation to pass through the eye of a needle to prevent regression and giving up on efforts to be innovative. 'Although many of us know various positive transformation episodes, often transformed institutions and groups eventually fall back into their old behaviours because the larger institutional ecology in which they operate puts too many constraining demands on them' (Scharmer, 2009: 331).

The leaders who have been writing in this book are not naïve; they know that passing through the eye of the needle is not a one-off experience. To take their school into a new field of activity and to move it on daily is the adventure. As Sergiovanni (2005: 143) points out: 'Leaders continuously struggle to develop a binding and solid agreement that represents a value system for living together and forms the basis for decisions and actions.'

In addition to working with theories of action, public value, comfort and safety, and holism, these leaders have particular qualities that they are cultivating not just in themselves but in their communities that help to build the value system which creates healthy, living, resilient schools. These qualities are developed so that they can be shared and be given away and this may be the heart of what is really meant by 'distributive leadership'. The qualities are used to build trust, honesty and respect and create authentic learning and living environments. These leadership qualities are similar to the ones identified by Whitaker (1997).

The leaders of these three schools are coming first from a position of deep and genuine appreciation (Whitney *et al.*, 2010), they value what happens now, who is in their community and what happens to everyone; but as in appreciative enquiry they don't stop there. They know that they must build on the best of what they have already to create greater outcomes, but they also know this is possible and that moving forward through challenge, bureaucracy and all forms of negativity is the adventure they are called to. They take no one and nothing for granted. They always live on the edge of the unexpected.

Appreciation that is authentic leads to trust and care. It is the stuff and fuel of good relationships of which the adventurous leader knows they cannot be without. So these leaders are also very affiliative, with a respectful concern and care for their community, they know they rely and depend on people to get things done. In their work Bryk and Schneider (2002) refer to this as 'relational trust'.

In return they communicate the type of confidence and inclusion that Moss Kanter (2004) describes. They espouse confidence in others, they embody it and they exemplify it. This leads to a sense of belonging that is so needed in a volatile, uncertain world. It provides a vital sense of safety for the children. As Franke-Gricksch points out:

> School as a new life component, and learning per se can make children feel insecure, and this insecurity is easier for them to deal with when they receive acknowledgment in everything that they bring with them to the classroom.
>
> (Franke-Gricksch, 2003: 16)

Authenticity, appreciation and affiliation are qualities that work together and interact to help create the fourth quality that is altruism. These leaders, while having healthy self-esteem and respect, are motivated from a primary altruism that is worthy in itself but is also an essential feature of an adventurous school. It is altruism that takes the focus away from the ego of the leader. It helps to prevent the isolation that many leaders encounter because it is the living connector of one to another that builds genuine community. The leader's anxiety and sense of success and failure, while always present, are not limiting the evolution of the school. While they know they are ultimately responsible, they do not try to exert control that stifles and weakens initiative or creates inertia. These are servant leaders (Greenleaf and Spears, 2011), in service to goals that go far beyond surface appearance and success.

The fifth quality is animation: what they are leading is alive. As Johansen (2010) says in the introductory quote to this chapter, these leaders are leading life, and the lives of others, including the next generation, they are not just leading an organisation. Their schools are a living, growing, moving enterprise, not an inert or mechanical one. So this in itself causes them to behave in particular ways. They give priority to what Sergiovanni (2005) calls the 'lifeworld' of a school rather than the 'systemsworld'. The lifeworld consists of the bigger questions about purpose, beliefs and response and Sergiovanni observes: 'The lifeworld of a school is its heartbeat. This heartbeat is weakened whenever the systemsworld determines the lifeworld – whenever our means determine our ends rather than the other way round.'

We can begin to see the leadership of the adventurous school portrayed as shown in Figure 11.1.

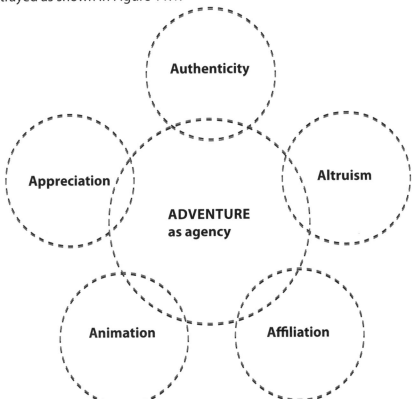

Figure 11.1: The leadership qualities that support the creation of the adventurous school

The combination of authenticity, affiliation, appreciation, animation and altruism each help to resource and nourish the adventure and the models of learning that are a part of it. These are qualities of the leaders, of the shared leadership and are ultimately being developed in the whole school community. However, without each of these creating the most important outcome of agency, there could be a well-intended, authentic, adventurous, spirit abroad in a school but nothing of any real significance happening. Agency is the power of the purpose, people and place all coming together to know that they can act, that it is theirs to do so and that they can make a difference. They do this with renewed models of power and pedagogy.

'Leadership exists when people are no longer victims of circumstances but participate in creating new circumstances' (Jaworski, 1996: 3). The adventurous school is one that is leading the way in creating the shift of paradigm that we described in *The Intelligent School*, one that is based on interconnection, participation and learning. This is a move from the more traditional view of schooling that is based on narrow views of what it means to be academic – it is a model based on an outward orientation that has the whole person and their engagement in their life as its focus. It has the possibility to renew the models of scholarship that we dream of for our young people.

> *What are the dreams of our educational systems? Are we dreaming old dreams, tired dreams, dreams that you must lose if I am to win? Can we change the way education dreams? Can we dream the kind of dream that Shrif Abdullah dreams when he writes of creating a world that works for everyone?*
>
> (Fox, 2006: 27)

Questions for discussion

- How does leadership promote adventurous learning in your school?
- What qualities do you believe are important if leaders are to create adventurous learning?
- How does leadership nurture and feed the purpose, power and pedagogy in your school?
- How does leadership in your school understand and create public value?

Chapter 12

Conclusion

The Wright brothers were hoping that their flying machine would turn out to be useful and make them lots of money, but what kept them working day and night on their hare-brained scheme despite constant failures and frustrations was the challenge of a fascinating goal.

(Csikszentmihalyi, 1993: 255)

What else have we learnt about adventure?

We held the final enquiry of our project on a grey London day in early February. We gathered in our now familiar meeting place in a retreat house in Stepney, a place that has inspired and supported us to bring this book to fruition, in a room lined with adventurous paintings and where we have been meeting over the past five years. We set about a process of capturing the essence of what we have described in these pages and hovering above it in order to see the extent of the adventure we had been on and if there was anything to add.

First, we clarified that, although none of us would claim to have arrived fully at this point, the core of the adventure is to enable children to seize the reins of their lives and their collective future. The school designs the environment and the structures for this to happen. Creative, adventurous learning, we reasserted, is the pathway: it's a living process which creates the future as it goes. It happens when uncertainty and not knowing can become an exciting place to be.

In this quest for adventure the culture, outcomes and operating processes of the traditional school begin to change. We agree with Fielding (2007) that this approach to education values both people and community building and the relationship between them:

[This is] a person-centred approach in which the purposes of educational organisations are accomplished, not by abandoning their distinctively educational aspirations, but rather by transforming

> *their organisational forms and capacities into the vibrancy and creativity of inclusive educational communities.*
>
> (Fielding, 2007: 405)

Attention to new ways of seeing the purpose, pedagogy and power of a school facilitates the opening up of the pathways that, step by step, lead a school to be more adventurous and in the process become adaptive to its environment and able to look the future fully in the face.

Thresholds, pathways and new tools for school improvement

We then identified six tools and processes that can be used for school improvement and help to clear the pathways. They can be used very literally to clear the ground that the adventure can take place on. They each speak for themselves and are described in different parts of the book:

- acting on behalf of the whole;
- confronting and changing traditional assumptions;
- coming from explicit values and beliefs;
- creating reciprocity and co-creation;
- sharing power; and
- building resilience, responsibility and shared endeavour.

As we noted in the Introduction, we also identified that true adventure involves crossing a threshold: a time when you realise, looking back, that you have changed, grown, or come to see life or the purpose of your work differently. Perkins (2009) describes a threshold as an experience that takes you from a state of disorientation to a sharper sense of what action needs taking. In discussing the nature of a threshold, as we understand it in this group, we described it as having any combination of the following:

> *A flashpoint, a crystallisation, a sudden moment of realisation; not just having a good idea, but it's about the right action, it becomes clear what you need to do, you can see what tools you need, the pathway becomes clear even if there are still obstacles to overcome.*

A threshold 'falls out', it exists in some way already but you haven't seen it before.

Colleagues at Malorees Infant School said that:

> *For us it was involvement in the learning project with The London Borough of Brent and the IOE, and connecting to what we really believed about learning and realising we could lead from our deepest beliefs and turn them into reality.*

For St Vigor and St John Primary School:

It was when we first discussed the concept of our 'four cornerstones' and had time and space in the process to really clarify why the children and ourselves come to school. Another time was when we really understood that everyone is able to lead learning. It was a turning point and exhilarating for us.

For Limeside Primary School:

It was when we realised that we had been holding onto the children too tightly and we were going to let the children fly and that we had been holding their reins, also when we heard Benjamin Zander say everything is invented so we thought, well we might as well join in and invent our own future as well.

A key insight in this discussion was that following your beliefs and testing and refining them in the context of leadership in action is a continual process. It enables leaders to have foresight, to see what the direction is even if the way isn't that clear. It resources and strengthens them. 'But,' asked Jane, 'how do you come to see what you see?' The group replied:

Well, you see something, you step outside your day-to-day habits, you start doing something, you see if it is beneficial, you think some more and then you do some more and see the benefits. You also put yourself in the enquiry.

This, we realised, was an example of real learning in action and with all the characteristics we have come to attribute to adventure.

The image of being on board a ship suddenly emerged in our discussion. One of the group said:

Leaders need to believe the adventure is possible, that it's going somewhere and it's going somewhere worth going. It would be a very miserable journey, in fact you might not want to get on board in the first place if the captain thought it wasn't likely that you could reach your destination or if everyone on board thought they were going somewhere different to where the captain was actually taking them.

Next we reflected on what helps to create the 'shift' to new ways of doing things. Colleagues were clear that it involves seeing the territory differently. Malorees said that for them it's when you realise that you have escaped the 'shackles of authority'. They described what they meant by this. The shackles tie you down and give power to 'they that know better than oneself'. Limeside said, 'Yes we are here to serve our principles rather than someone else.' 'What we do is respond to a call,' agreed St Vigor and St John, 'It's not a job we do. The moment you think it's a job, you've lost it.' They added that reflecting is really important in the process of leading in this way. Malorees said, 'It's all about trusting and having faith in our decisions and having the confidence to believe we are on track.'

These are just some examples of how these leaders are constantly interrogating their beliefs and testing them out in action. The process of aligning beliefs and actions is what helps to create authenticity and credibility and enables them to take charge of the long-term destiny of their schools. This in turn creates the affiliation of others and a culture of appreciation. Coming from our own beliefs, the group agreed, gives intrinsic and natural authority. Taking charge of our own direction then provides greater satisfaction and fulfilment and releases potential; it affects our relationships with the community who we can see do this too, and with the curriculum where designing for threshold experiences is critical. Colleagues said that what they had to avoid was the impeding of critical threshold experiences.

What helps you across a threshold?

In his work on *Theory U*, Scharmer (2009) asks: why is the journey to the deeper levels of the 'U' always the road less travelled? He talks about something similar to crossing a threshold, which was noted in the leadership chapter (Chapter 11) as the need to go through the eye of the needle, a process akin to going through the bottleneck, which requires that three main voices of resistance are noted and overcome. These are the voices of cynicism, fear and judgement – each of which blocks the pathway of adventure. It was an important breakthrough to bring the route through the bottleneck that James Martin (2006) describes and the passage through the eye of a needle from Scharmer's work alongside each other. But we also asked: how do leaders keep those three voices at bay?

One colleague began the conversation by speaking about her head teacher, 'being positive is catchable and it breeds trust'. Another colleague observed that what helps is to encourage solutions rather than problems and that professional learning itself, if well set up, can keep those voices at bay. 'If you enable colleagues to really feel they can be competent and that you believe in them then they will be more happy with a shift of focus into the unknown.' Listening and allowing mistakes also helps, along with an expectation that back-up is there, along with support for the fearful. Helping everyone in the community to see the impact they can have and allowing them to build on and develop a sense of achievement is also important.

Another colleague said this is very patient work, in that sometimes there is a long time between a threshold appearing and actually going through it. Getting under the surface of problems, starting to do something, also helps.

Flying, growing and illuminating: Are there any further insights?

Flying

> *'You are not telling me you did fly here?' said Hermione.*
>
> (Rowling, 1998: 66)

Being able to take control of the destiny of a school and be able to go beyond normal limits, to be able to rise above, to take off and to see things in new ways is essential in the adventurous school. Flying for the group was active, optimistic, free and fun! Using your imagination could take you into a place you have never seen before. When you are flying, one colleague observed, you see below in a different way and the frustrations either disappear or look quite different. All the restrictions and regulations take on a different perspective. You go a distance far and fast and you don't have to land if you don't want to! The capacity of individuals varies when they are flying, they need refuelling in different ways. Aerodynamically the bee can't fly, but it can actually. When you are flying you are more likely to trust that things will work out. It implies a capacity to work on multiple levels. As the songwriter Mary Chapin Carpenter and the children of Limeside Primary School sing 'Why walk when you can fly?'

Growing

> *Schools that adopt a growing community concept can completely change how they interpret, understand, relate to and use their public spaces.*
>
> (Clarke, 2011a)

Our reflections about the image and use of 'growth' as a metaphor linked to the importance of tending and nurturing. The adventurous school has a compassionate and caring heart and nurturing its people and encouraging them to see the value of doing that for each other is food for the adventure. You really can't go venturing without it. Also, as a leader you need to know what to look for in your garden and know it is healthy and thriving. The adventure can't happen without identifying what's growing in the soil that might be in the way. The weeds and brambles need to be cut from the path and the ground dug and enriched.

'The over testing of children', said one colleague, 'is tantamount to continually digging up the plants in our garden to assess the functioning of their root system and then expecting them to keep growing as normal.' Colleagues also agreed that leaders are grown not born and that everyone can be one. Noticing buds starting to shoot in our communities is part of our work, but as one colleague remarked, 'The tadpole doesn't need the same as the frog.'

Illuminating

> Happiness can be found, even in the darkest of times, if one only remembers to turn on the light.
>
> (Rowling, 2004)

In the adventure clarity is a necessary tool. Even if you are in unknown territory, until there is sufficient clarity you don't know what to do. As one colleague remarked, when you shed light on something you see it differently. Reflection is a way to shed light on something and show a way forward; light is warm, it's connected to a human process. We also agreed that we had been shedding a great deal of light on what each school did, believed and wanted and that that 'light' had had a rigour about it in our enquiries. Not many stones had been left unturned; the light had been shone on many cracks and crevices in our thinking and actions.

The main aspects of an adventurous school

Finally we drew our thinking from across the book together by getting in our metaphorical helicopter and hovering above what we had been doing. We could see a picture emerging that we hadn't quite expected. Up to that point we were only aware of the parts, not the whole.

We decided that the three themes that the schools had written about – vision, community and curriculum – were the visible known level of the adventurous school and the focus of our main enquiry. In the process of enquiring into them they showed us something else. They were connected to a less-noticed contextual level that had to be given as much attention in the creation of adventure. This was the level of purpose, power and pedagogy, which we could now discern had been the level at which the excesses of prescription and traditional thinking had taken hold and been suffocating the innovative power of a school. These in turn were nurtured by the leadership characteristics of appreciation, authenticity, altruism, animation, affiliation and agency. Together these three sets of processes can work together to produce the overall outcomes we most wanted for the children. These we identified in the Introduction as purpose, creativity, celebration, place and contribution.

We have portrayed our overview in Figure 12.1.

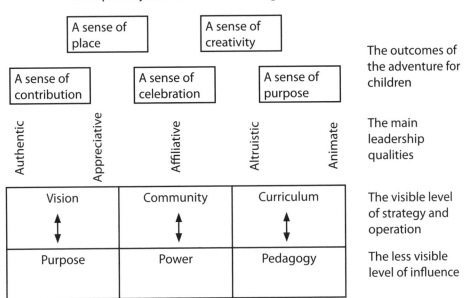

| A sense of place | | A sense of creativity | | The outcomes of the adventure for children |
| A sense of contribution | A sense of celebration | A sense of purpose | | |

Authentic | Appreciative | Affiliative | Altruistic | Animate — The main leadership qualities

| Vision | Community | Curriculum | The visible level of strategy and operation |
| Purpose | Power | Pedagogy | The less visible level of influence |

Figure 12.1: The main aspects of an adventurous school

Final Reflections

> *We are functioning below our potential for love, justice and creating a good world.*
>
> (Okri, 1999: 42)

In the Introduction we described the main purpose of an adventurous school as we have come to understand it. The adventurous school is a place where we all learn to take the reins of our lives and support others to do that too. We do so by learning about who we are, and our relationship to the world, so we ensure we bring about the best future possible for ourselves, our communities and those who will come after us.

One of the essential features of these three schools is that children are learning to be agents in their own learning and development. But that is not the end of the story. The development of children's agency and leadership brings a wind of optimism, energy and openness to all the adults around them. Children who have purpose in their learning are doing well and are feeling fulfilled, misbehave less, achieve more and enjoy coming to school. Adventurous learning creates a setting that is in service to the lives of their families as well as the children, and in which their school is not separate from its community.

The schools have as their primary task the provision of education. But the education provided, as these pages have shown, is so much more than mere provision. It is carefully designed and orchestrated with particular goals to achieve. The contributors to this book have come to see more clearly that success, well-being and learning as goals are all as important as each other. Learning and well-being are not servants of success – they are equal partners. A much more grounded and natural approach to outcomes is achieved when this more holistic approach is used. This understanding provides a rich and nourishing environment for everyone to feel that they can participate, that they have a place, and that – to draw on the schools' metaphors – they can fly, grow and become enlightened.

But this is not yet the end of the story. The call to adventure goes out to all the stakeholders. Each community sets out on their own adventure in partnership with the children, but what they have in common is a desire to set out together from what is comfortable, known and usual and be prepared to act together differently. They do this because they share a concern about the world they live in; they believe they can evolve, create and move into a future that will allow them to continue to flourish and free their potential despite all the obstacles and barriers in their way. They know that 'the way things are' is neither fixed nor pre-determined, and that there is always an opportunity for another adventure.

> *We are a young species who, uncertain of our niche, has very recently – in a virtual second of life's day on earth – expanded to fill the world. In a sense we are like teenagers, full of enthusiasm and energy, and more than a bit confused. And, like every teenager must, we are about to discover that we are not the center of the universe – not even the center of life on this planet. We are but one of millions, and our merit depends not on our ego but our contribution.*
>
> (Senge *et al.*, 2010: 380)

References

Ai WeiWei (2010) Sunflower Seeds interpretation texts. Tate Modern, London, October 2010.

Alexander, R. (ed.) (2010) *Children, Their World, Their Education: Final report and recommendations of the Cambridge Primary Review*. Routledge, London.

Barnardo's (2011) Online. <http://tinyurl.com/7nk7efk> (accessed 11 February 2011).

Barth, R. (1990) *Improving Schools from Within*. Jossey-Bass, San Francisco.

–– (2001) *Learning by Heart*. Jossey-Bass, San Francisco.

Bawden, R., Guijt, I. and Woodhill, J. (2007) 'The critical role of civil society in fostering societal learning for a sustainable world'. In A. Wals (ed.), *Social Learning Towards a Sustainable World*. Wageningen Academic Publishers, Wageningen.

Birney, A. and Reed, J. (2009) *Sustainability and Renewal: Findings from the Leading Sustainable Schools Research Project*. National College for School Leadership (NCSL), Nottingham.

Bowers, C.A. (2001) *Education for Eco-Justice and Community*. University of Georgia Press, Athens, Georgia, USA.

Bronowski, J. (1973) *The Ascent of Man*. BBC, London.

Brown, L. (2008) *Plan B 3.0*. W.W. Norton, New York.

Bryk, A.S. and Schneider, B. (2002) *Trust in Schools: A core resource for improvement*. Russell Sage Foundation, New York.

Buddha. Online. <http://thinkexist.com> (accessed 11 March 2011).

Campbell, J., Moyers, B. and Flowers, B.S. (1988) *The Power of Myth*. Doubleday, New York.

Capra, F. (2007) 'Foreword'. In A. Wals (ed.), *Social Learning Towards a Sustainable World*. Wageningen Academic Publishers, Wageningen.

Carnell, E. and Lodge, C. (2002) *Supporting Effective Learning*. Paul Chapman, London.

Clarke, P. (2011a) *Education for Sustainability: Becoming naturally smart (the new critical idiom)*. Routledge UK, Abingdon, Oxon.

–– (2011b) 'Cultivating a future: Sustainable schools and sustainable communities'. Paper presented to the International Congress for School Effectiveness and Improvement, Limassol, Cyprus, January 2011.

Claxton, G. (2002) *Building Learning Power*. The Learning Organisation, Bristol.

–– (2008) *What's the Point of School?* Oneworld, Oxford.

Clifton Diocese (2012) Online. <http://wwwcliftondiocese.com/assetts/files/pdf/2005/oct/oct2005newsletter.pdf> (accessed 5 January 2012).

Coelho, P. (2008) *Brida*. HarperCollins, London.

Contour Housing Group and Limeside Primary School (2007) *What If …?* Contour Housing Group, Oldham, Greater Manchester.

Cooke-Sather, A. (2002) 'Authorizing students' perspectives: Toward trust, dialogue, and change in education'. *Education Researcher*, 31(4), 3–14.

Csikszentmihalyi, M. (1993) *The Evolving Self*. HarperCollins, New York.

Delores, J. (1998) *Learning: The treasure within. Report to the United Nations Educational, Scientific and Cultural Organization (UNESCO) of the International Commission on Education for the Twenty-first Century*. UNESCO, Paris.

Department for Children, Schools and Families (DCSF) (2003) *Excellence and Enjoyment: Learning and teaching in the primary years*. DCSF, London.

–– (2006) *The National Framework for Sustainable Schools*. DCSF, London.

Department for Education and Skills (DfES) (2005) *Developing the Global Dimension in the School Curriculum*. DfES, London.

Desforges, C. with Abouchaar, A. (2003) *The Impact of Parental Involvement, Parental Support and Family Education on Pupil Achievements and Adjustment: A literature review*. Department for Education and Skills, London.

Douglas, J. (1964) *The Home and the School*. MacGibbon and Kee, London.

Dweck, C. (2006) *Mindset: The new psychology of success*. Ballantine Books, New York.

Eckert, P., Goldman, S. and Wenger, E. (1996) 'The school as a community of engaged learners'. *Wingspread Journal*, 9(3), 4–6.

Edwards, C., Gandini, L. and Forman, G. (eds) (1993) *The Hundred Languages of Children: The Reggio Emilia approach to early childhood education*. Ablex, Norwood, New Jersey, USA.

Fielding, M. (2007) 'The human cost and intellectual poverty of high performance schooling: Radical philosophy, John MacMurray and the remaking of person-centred education'. *Journal of Education Policy,* 22(4), July, 383–409.

Fink, D. (2005) *Leadership for Mortals.* Paul Chapman, London.

Fox, M. (2006) *A.W.E. Project.* CopperHouse, Kelowna, British Columbia, Canada.

Franke-Gricksch, M. (2003) *You're One of Us: Systemic insights and solutions for teachers, students and parents.* Carl-Auer-Systeme Verlag, Heidelberg, Germany.

Frost, D. (2008) 'Researching the connections, developing a methodology'. In J. MacBeath and N. Dempster (eds), *Connecting Leadership and Learning: Principles for practice.* Routledge, London.

Gershon, D. (2009) *Social Change 2.0: A blueprint for reinventing our world.* High Point, New York.

Greenleaf, R. and Spears, L. (2011) *Servant Leadership: A journey into the nature of legitimate power and greatness.* Paulist Press, Mahwah, New Jersey, USA.

Harbottle, T.B. (1897) *Dictionary of Quotations (Classical).* Swan and Sonnenschein, London.

Hargreaves, A. and Fink, D. (2006) *Sustainable Leadership.* Jossey-Bass, San Francisco.

Hick, D. and Holden, C. (1995) *Visions of the Future: Why We Need to Teach Tomorrow.* Trentham, Stoke-on-Trent.

James, S. (ed.) (2007) *Transforming Neighbourhoods.* The Young Foundation, London.

Jaworski, J. (1996) *Synchronicity.* Berrett-Koehler, San Francisco.

Johansen, B. (2010) *Leaders Make the Future.* Berrett-Koehler, San Francisco.

Johnson, A. (2006) Secretary of State for Education and Skills, speaking in Parliament on 2 November 2006 based on the Government and the Local Government Association's definition first published in *Guidance on Community Cohesion*, LGA, 2002 and resulting from the Cantle Report in 2001. In *Our Shared Future* (2007) Department for Education and Skills, London p.3.

Johnstone, C. (2010) *Find Your Power.* Permanent Publications, East Meon, Hampshire.

Jung, C. (1954) 'Psychic conflicts in a child'. In Carl Gustav Jung, *Collected Works*, Volume 17: *The Development of Personality*. Online. <http://www.brainyquote.com/quotes/quotes/c/carljung108028.html> (accessed 5 January 2012).

Kaser, L. and Halbert, J. (2009) *Leadership Mindsets.* Routledge, London.

Knapp, M., Copland, M., Honig, M., Plecki, M., Bradley, S. and Portin, B. (2010) *Learning-focused Leadership and Leadership Support: Meaning and practice in urban systems*. University of Washington Press, Seattle.

Leadbeater, C. and Mongon, D. (2008) *Leadership for Public Value*. National College for School Leadership (NCSL), Nottingham.

Lodge, C. (2008) *Student Voice and Learning-focused School Improvement*. Research Matters Series. Institute of Education, University of London, London.

Lodge, C. and Reed, J. (2003) 'Transforming school improvement now and for the future'. *Journal of Educational Change*, 4, 45–62.

Louv, R. (2005) *Last Child in the Woods*. Workman Publishing, New York.

Lowe, R. (2007) *The Death of Progressive Education: How teachers lost control of the classroom*. Psychology Press, Hove, Sussex.

MacGilchrist, B., Myers, K. and Reed, J. (2004) *The Intelligent School*. Paul Chapman, London.

Macy, J. (2005) Facing Climate Change and Other Great Adventures. Online. <http://old.coinet.org.uk/discussion/perspectives/macy> (accessed 27 March 2012).

Martin, J. (2006) *The Meaning of the 21st Century*. Transworld, London.

McMahon, B. and Portelli, J. (2004) 'Engagement for what? Beyond Popular Discourses of Student Engagement in Leadership and Policy in Schools', 3(1), 59–76.

Mitchell, C. and Sackney, L. (2000) *Profound Improvement*. Swets & Zeitlinger Publishers, Lisse, The Netherlands.

Mitchell, S. (1988) *Translation of the Tao Te Ching*. Harper and Row, New York.

Mongon, D. and Leadbeater, C. (2010) *Leadership for Public Value: Achieving valuable outcomes for children, families and communities*. Draft of final report by the National College for School Leadership (NCSL), Nottingham.

Morpurgo, M. (2011) 'Set our children free'. Richard Dimbleby Lecture, 15 February 2011. Online. <www.bbc.co.uk/programmes/b00ymf57> (accessed 16 February 2011).

Moss Kanter, R. (2004) *Confidence: How winning streaks and losing streaks begin and end*. Crown Business, New York.

Mulgan, G. (2007a) *Social Innovation*. Young Foundation, London.

–– (2007b) *Ready or Not? Taking innovation in the public sector seriously*. National Endowment for Science, Technology and the Arts (NESTA), London.

Murray, R., Caulier-Grice, J. and Mulgan, G. (2009) *Social Venturing*. National Endowment for Science, Technology and the Arts (NESTA)/The Young Foundation, London.

Nicholls, J. and Hazzard, S. (1993) *Education as Adventure*. Teachers College Press, New York.

Nietzsche, F. (1885) Online. <http://refspace.com/quotes/Thus_Spoke_Zarathustra> (accessed 19 May 2011).

Office for Standards in Education, Children's Services and Skills (Ofsted) (2004) Limeside Primary School Inspection Report. Ofsted, London.

Okri, B. (1999) *Mental Fight*. Phoenix House, London.

Olds, L. (1992) *Metaphors of Interrelatedness*. State University of New York Press, New York.

Olson, D. (2003) *Psychological Theory and Educational Reform*. Cambridge University Press, Cambridge, Massachusetts, USA.

Orr, D. (1992) *Ecological Literacy*. SUNY, New York.

–– (1994) *Earth in Mind*. Island Press, Washington DC.

O'Sullivan, E. (2001) *Transformative Learning*. Zed Books, London.

Pace Marshall, S. (1995) The Vision, Meaning, and Language of Educational Transformation: How chaos, complexity, theory, and flocking behavior can inform leadership in transition. Online. <www.stephaniepacemarshall.com/articles/SPM-Article8.pdf> (accessed 22 May 2011).

Palmer, G., MacInnes, T. and Kenway, P. (2007) *Monitoring Poverty and Social Exclusion*. Joseph Rowntree Foundation, York, UK.

Perkins, D. (2009) *Making Learning Whole*. Jossey-Bass, San Francisco.

Portelli, J.P. and Vibert, A.B. (2002) 'A curriculum of life'. *Education Canada,* 42, 36–9.

Reed, J. (2010) 'School improvement in transition: An emerging agenda for interesting times'. In F. Kagawa and D. Selby (eds), *Education and Climate Change*. Routledge, Abingdon, Oxon.

Reed, J. and Lodge, C. (2006) *Towards Learning-focused School Improvement*. Research Matters Series. Institute of Education, University of London, London.

Reed, J. and Stoll, L. (2000) 'Promoting organizational learning in schools: The role of feedback'. In Askew, S. (ed.) *Feedback for Learning*. Routledge, Abingdon, Oxon.

Rifkin, J. (2010) *The Empathic Civilisation*. Blackwell, Oxford.

Rose, J. (2009) *Independent Review of the Primary Curriculum*. Department for Children, Schools and Families, London.

Rosenholtz, S. (1989) *Teachers' Workplace*. Longman, New York.

Rowling, J.K. (1992) *Harry Potter and the Philosopher's Stone*. Bloomsbury, London.

–– (1998) *Harry Potter and the Chamber of Secrets*. Bloomsbury, London.

–– (2004) Online. <www.quotegarden.com/bk-hp.html> (accessed 4 July 2011).

Royal Society of Arts (RSA) (2011) *From Social Security to Social Productivity: A vision for 2020 public services. The final report of the Commission on 2020 Public Sector Services*. RSA, London.

Sackney, L. and Walker, K. (2006) 'Leadership for knowledge communities'. Paper presented to the Annual Conference of the Commonwealth Council for Educational Administration and Management, Nicosia, Cyprus, October 2006.

Saint-Exupéry, A. de (1950) Online. <http://www.goodreads.com/author/quotes/1020792> (accessed 4 February 2009).

Sarason, S. (2004) *What Do You Mean by Learning?* Heinemann, Portsmouth, New Hampshire.

Scharmer, C.O. (2009) *Theory U*. Berrett-Koehler, San Francisco.

Senge, P., Cambron-McCabe, N., Lucas, T., Smith, B., Dutton, J. and Kleiner, A. (2000) *Schools That Learn*. Nicholas Brealey, London.

Senge, P., Smith, B., Kruschwitz, N., Laur, J. and Schley, S. (2010) *The Necessary Revolution*. Nicholas Brearley, London.

Sergiovanni, T. (2005) *Strengthening the Heartbeat*. Jossey-Bass, San Francisco.

Starratt, R.J. (2004) *Ethical Leadership*. Jossey-Bass, San Francisco.

Sterling, S. (2001) *Sustainable Education Re-visioning Learning Change*. Green Books, Dartington, Devon.

Stoll, L. and Fink, D. (1996) *Changing Our Schools*. Open University Press, Buckingham.

Stoll, L., Fink, D. and Earl, L. (2003) *It's About Learning*. RoutledgeFalmer, London.

Streightiff, W. Online. <http://thinkexist.com/quotes/walt_streightiff> (accessed 26 June 2011).

Swarat, C.V. (1948) *Thoughts into Poetry*. Self-published. Online. <http://scdsb.on.ca/media/files/programs-and-services/specialeducation/Elementary-to-Secondary.pdf> (accessed 17 June 2011).

TASC wheel (2008) Online. <www.tascwheel.com> (accessed 5 March 2008).

UCAS and Forum for the Future (2007) *The Future Leaders Survey: 2006/07*. UCAS/Forum for the Future, London.

Udall, N. and Turner, N. (2008) The Way of Nowhere. HarperCollins, London.

United Nations (UN) (1989) Convention on the Rights of the Child. United Nations, Geneva.

Wallace, B. (2000) *Teaching the Very Able Child*. David Fulton Publishers, London.

Wals, A. (ed.) (2007) *Social Learning Towards a Sustainable World*. Wageningen Academic Publishers, Wageningen, The Netherlands.

Watkins, C. (2005) *Classrooms as Learning Communities*. Routledge, Abingdon, Oxon.

–– (2010) *Learning Performance and Improvement*. Research Matters Series. Institute of Education, University of London, London.

Watkins, C., Carnell, E. and Lodge, C. (2007) *Effective Learning in Classrooms*. Paul Chapman, London.

West-Burnham, J., Farrar, M. and Otero, G. (2007) *Schools and Communities Working Together to Transform Children's Lives*. Continuum, London.

Wheatley, M. and Kellner-Rogers, M. (1999) *A Simpler Way*. Berret-Koehler, San Francisco.

Whitaker, P. (1997) *Primary Schools and the Future*. Open University, Buckingham.

Whitmore, D. (2008) 'Working with at risk young people, empowerment rather than control'. Paper presented at The Bioneers Conference, Findhorn Foundation, Forres, Moray, Scotland, 30 October–2 November 2011.

Whitney, D., Trosten-Bloom, A. and Rader, K. (2010) *Appreciative Leadership*. McGraw-Hill, New York.

Williamson, M. (1992) *A Return to Love: Reflections on the principles of a course in miracles*. HarperCollins, New York.

Wrigley, T. (2003) *Schools of Hope*. Trentham, Stoke on Trent.

Zander, R. and Zander, B. (2000) *The Art of Possibility*. Harvard Business School Press, Boston, Massachusetts, USA.